DATE DUE

THE BOOK OF
JAZZ

OTHER BOOKS BY LEONARD FEATHER

INSIDE JAZZ
THE ENCYCLOPEDIA OF JAZZ
THE YEARBOOK OF JAZZ
THE NEW ENCYCLOPEDIA OF JAZZ
LAUGHTER FROM THE HIP

THE BOOK OF

JAZZ

FROM THEN TILL NOW

A GUIDE TO THE ENTIRE FIELD

BY

LEONARD FEATHER

HORIZON PRESS NEW YORK

ACKNOWLEDGMENTS

The musical illustrations in Chapter 22 were obtained from the following sources: *Trumpet Blues* (Roy Eldridge), *Bloomdido* (Charlie Parker), *Confab with Rab* (Johnny Hodges), *The Opener* (Lester Young), *Platinum Love* (Coleman Hawkins), *Blues in B Flat* (Art Tatum), *Blues for the Oldest Profession* (Teddy Wilson), and *Hallucinations* (Bud Powell) are all copyrights from the catalogue of JATAP Music Inc., and are reproduced by the arrangement of and through the invaluable coöperation of Norman Granz. *Jessica's Day* (John "Dizzy" Gillespie) is reproduced by the permission of Silhouette Music Inc. I am deeply indebted to Quincy Jones, who worked closely with me in selecting the material for the above illustrations, and through whom their documentation in this book was made possible.

Slipped Disc (Benny Goodman) was copyrighted in 1945 and is reproduced by permission of Regent Music Corp.

Muggles (Louis Armstrong) was copyrighted in 1930 and 1947 and is reproduced by permission of Leeds Music Corp.

Up on Teddy's Hill (Charlie Christian) is reproduced by permission of Thornwood Music Co.

Indiana Winter (Jay Jay Johnson), *Blue Funk* (Jack Teagarden), and *Monogram* (Buddy De Franco) are reproduced by permission of Modern Age Music Co.

Congeniality (Ornette Coleman) was copyrighted in 1960 and 1961 and is reproduced by permission of MJQ Music, Inc.

I am grateful to Gerald Siddons, a staff member of the Berklee School of Music in Boston, for his transcription of the John Coltrane solo of *Greensleeves*.

THIS BOOK IS FOR JANE AND SWEET LORRAINE

CONTENTS

FOREWORD

BY JOHN "DIZZY" GILLESPIE

Some time ago I pointed out in a magazine article that in spite of all the excitement about jazz and all the things that are happening with it in this country, there are still a lot of developments that have to take place before it will be as big, and mean as much over here as it does in some of the countries overseas where they call it our most important export.

As I said then, it seems to me that a big majority of the American people still think of jazz as music you hear through your feet, not your brains; lowbrow music that's not good enough to listen to and study and get kicks from, the way the serious fan does abroad.

I can't remember any experience in America that compares with what happened when my band played in Ankara and Istanbul, when the only way we could stop the show was by playing the Turkish national anthem and closing the curtains when the audience just wouldn't stop screaming for more. And I will always remember the fantastic scenes in Athens, where some of the students who were supposed to have been involved in anti-American demonstrations gave us the greatest reception of our lives.

I know that Benny Goodman in Thailand, Louis Armstrong in Scandinavia and Ghana, and Norman Granz' *Jazz at the Philharmonic* in Europe and Japan have had similar experiences. Even in Iceland and Java and Argentina they have their own publications and jazz clubs. It was in Europe that the first real books on American jazz were published; it was in Europe that the first critics started writing seriously about it 25 years ago when it was almost completely ignored in this country. It is certainly high time for us to build up our own monument to the jazz culture, in the form of a national jazz collection, maybe as part of the Library of Congress, with all the music as well as the books and magazines and records under one roof, and tape-recorded interviews with some of the great pioneers while they are still around to tell their stories. For the same reason, I believe this new book by Leonard Feather is a step in the right direction.

In *The Book of Jazz* he has a lot of information that has never been put together in this particular (and very useful) way. First there is the part about the backgrounds of jazz, which was always supposed to have originated in the bordellos of New Orleans. Personally, I never did go along with that theory. I figure jazz to be a parallel for what happened in, say, the different cultures of the Caribbean. For example, the musicians ·in Haiti may play their drums one way, and in Jamaica or Cuba another way, but no matter how different they are, there is a basic root for all their music. Maybe in one place they call it a rhumba, some place else it's a mambo, and in Trinidad they have the calypso, but essentially it all springs from the same thing.

In the same way all the different forms of jazz grew up separately. It's a long distance from Trinidad to Cuba, and a long distance from New Orleans to New York, and people didn't travel much in those days or have the communications we have now, but I'm quite sure that there were the same sort of guys up in the North who had the same influences—African influences—that they had down in the South. I can't see where it could have all originated in any one city.

This past summer, when I was teaching at the Music Inn School of Jazz in Lenox, Massachusetts, I was talking to Rex Stewart, the cornet player, who gave a lecture up there. It was very enlightening. He said that when Buddy Bolden and those guys were playing in New Orleans there were plenty of musicians up in the North and the East that were wailing them up some, too. This reminds me of when people walk up to me and try to start an argument by telling me, "Say, Dizzy, Charlie Parker said he invented bebop." And I'll tell them, "Well, yes, he did; *his* contribution is what *he* put into it, but I wouldn't say that Charlie Parker was the originator of my style, or Monk's style or Kenny Clarke's or any of the guys who were supposed to have had anything to do with inventing this music." In the same way I think Leonard Feather has pointed out some important misunderstandings about the origins of jazz.

I found a whole lot of knowledge, in fact many things I didn't know, in the instrumental chapters that show the progress and evolutions of the various instruments. I've never seen a book on jazz done this way before and it's a very useful approach to the subject.

As for the chapter on improvisation, I think this is a very, very wonderful idea. I know that when a musician plays a solo he does some things, some effects, that are so personal that if you write them out for someone who has never heard the original, they would have a tough time duplicating it from just looking at the music. If the solo is by some great individual artist like Charlie Parker or Cootie Williams or Johnny Hodges, it would be very difficult to get the same feeling again. However, when you are studying this music without trying to duplicate it, and particularly if you have the record to listen to along with looking at the music, it becomes very fascinating.

It's pretty strange to look at your own solos. When I looked at the solo from *Jessica's Day* that's reproduced in this book, my first reaction was "Wow! Did I play that?" But then I listened to the record and looked at the music again and I found out it was accurate. You can see and hear all the notes, and Leonard Feather explains all about the passing chords and everything, which is very important, because in jazz you are always using these chords to find a new route to travel. It's like walking into the future. The guy that has the perception to get there more smoothly than another guy, and to reach out in a new direction along this route, is the one who's creating something.

I have known Leonard Feather since my very, very early history. when I was on 52nd Street with Oscar Pettiford. In fact, it was Oscar who was responsible for bringing him in to hear me at the Onyx Club. He gave us a lot of write-ups in the early days and helped the new movement quite a bit. He was a very early booster of Charlie Parker and, in fact, all the modern cats. He has heard all the musicians and their records all the way back to the early days of Louis Armstrong and the other pioneers, and he knows their stories and their place in the scene. He has done an excellent job in *The Book of Jazz*, and I think it will be a very valuable addition to our literature on the subject. I hope it can be used as a searchlight along the route for that walk into the future.

PART ONE

THE SOURCES

CHAPTER 1

PERSPECTIVES AND OBJECTIVES

> "All music's gotta be 'folk' music: I ain't never heard no horse
> sing a song."   —Louis Armstrong

With the belated emergence of jazz from its long-suffered
role as the Cinderella of esthetics, and with its gradual acceptance in many previously closed areas, the definition of its
nature, always disputed among critics and to some extent among
musicians and the public, has become a near-impossibility.

Until recently, most of the literature on the subject approached
it from an academic viewpoint, usually that of a well-meaning,
factually informed historian with no inside knowledge of jazz.
A seemingly inevitable corollary was the insistence on recogniz-
ing jazz only as a folk art, one in which almost all the practitioners played in sporting houses—simple, unlettered folk whose
great spirit lifted their work out of the constrictions of squalid
surroundings.

A more realistic view of jazz shows that the conceptions of its
early creators were hampered more often than helped by such
material factors as the lack of social acceptance and musical
knowledge as well as the lack of good instruments and intonation; and that as far back as the early 1920s such pioneers as
Ellington and Henderson were becoming aware of the value of
musically educated control over natural artistry. If the definition
of jazz as folk music held true for almost 100% of what was
played before their time, it described perhaps 25 to 50% of what

3

was played up to 1940. It applies to barely 5% of what is being performed and generally accepted as jazz today.

To some this may mean that the incidence of valid, authentic jazz has diminished in direct proportion. Among the vast majority of professional musicians, however, the consensus is that while jazz of the folk or semi-folk variety has its place on the contemporary scene and will endure, the tremendous strides in harmony, melody and rhythm—and the increasing indications of a wedding, or at least a flirtation, with modern classical music—mark a logical and desirable outcome of the jazzman's attempt to achieve musical maturity.

These developments have been anathema to many writers who have made a lifelong study of their early heroes and condemned as charlatans those who attempt to rescue jazz from the musical strait-jacket to which it was confined in the early stages. One writer, denouncing the swing music of the mid-1930s as a bastardization of jazz, and summing up the genius of Charlie Parker and his colleagues with the conclusion that bop "appeals only to the analytical musical mind and evokes about the same amount of emotional pleasure as a Euclid theorem," described himself "as a purist and proud of it" and announced that jazz would remain jazz only if it remained "steeped in the virile tradition of New Orleans." In effect he was speaking for dozens of self-styled "purist" critics who have been trying to place roadblocks in the path of jazz evolution.

Most of the leading jazzmen today are products of a new tradition of musical literacy and restless ambition. But to the traditionalists, from the moment it began to strain at its folk roots, jazz was no longer entirely jazz. When it could no longer be restrained, they announced that it was now a different animal: one French critic has gone to ludicrous lengths in an attempt to prove that bop is not jazz. The more time goes by and young musicians dominate the scene with naturally more advanced ideas, the less traditional or "New Orleans revival" music there will be for the traditionalists to cling to; they will be forced gradually to the conclusion that jazz as they understand the term is dead.

The realists, on the other hand, are faced with a converse

problem. So much music in the name of jazz is being performed today that one wonders where a line may be drawn, or whether the use of the term jazz is advisable at all. Is the music of Gunther Schuller or the bossa nova of Joao Gilberto jazz? Is the latest LP by a singer of popular tunes who has been hailed in *Down Beat* as a "a promising new jazz voice" really jazz, or just an empty echo along Tin Pan Alley? Are the atonal, sometimes out-of-tempo explorations of such avant-gardists as Jimmy Giuffre, Cecil Taylor and Don Ellis jazz, wholly or partially or not at all? Are those critics right who claim that improvisation is all, that "written jazz" is a contradiction in terms?

My own feeling is that the jazz label is applied too frequently nowadays to experiments that have little or nothing in common with the essential nature of jazz; that some of the "new jazz voices" are minor talents whose work should not be so classified; that Frank Sinatra, though certainly the jazzmen's favorite singer, is not a jazz artist; and that the modernists are as guilty of over-indulgence in their broad use of the word jazz as are the traditionalists in the restrictions they place on it.

For the purpose of this book, it is my intention to place a liberal construction upon the term. Anything that has been accorded a wide degree of acceptance among musicians as jazz will be dealt with—whether it be the blues-shouting of a favorite rock-and-roll singer or the filigree arrangements of the Modern Jazz Quartet. It does not seem to me to be the main function of a critic to determine what is *not* jazz.

The attempts to define jazz have frequently reached an *ignotum per ignotius* dead end. The task of imbuing in the layman, with expositive words, a sensitive understanding of the dry, ascetic beauty of a Miles Davis improvisation is as hazardous an undertaking as an effort to explain English grammatical construction by playing a trumpet solo. Many have tried to explain jazz in words; all have failed. But the more persuasive writers and lecturers, impressing their audiences with the subject's validity as material for serious discussion, have drawn into the orbit of jazz appreciation a number of potential converts, willing to listen with a broader mind, a more receptive ear.

The artist complains that the role of the critic is parasitic;

pragmatically he observes that criticism is often hopelessly ineffective. Art Tatum and Bud Powell were the favorite pianists of critics in the '50s. In polls taken among critics and musicians, they surpassed all other contenders; scarcely any votes were registered for Dave Brubeck, who has been criticized almost continually by most jazz writers. Yet while Brubeck has won a long series of ballots conducted among the readers of music magazines, the combined influence of the critics could not bring the prestige of such recognition to Tatum or Powell.

But the jazz expert, if unable to mold public opinion through direct criticism, can fulfill many other valuable functions. The most important of all has been John Hammond, more a catalytic agent than a critic, responsible for the launching of the entire swing era (via Benny Goodman), of the boogie-woogie piano phenomenon, of such talents as Count Basie and Teddy Wilson and innumerable others for whom he secured jobs, agency contracts and record sessions. The major contribution of Dr. Marshall Stearns was his founding of the Institute of Jazz Studies, the unique jazz research center.

The objectives of the present book are twofold. In the early chapters I have attempted to put between covers for the first time some recollections of the early days of jazz. They may help to counterpoise, against the enormous documentation concerning New Orleans, a number of views that present other sides of the picture. Recollections of New Orleans have been presented extensively in a dozen books; no attempt has been made here to overlap into this well-covered ground. In the main this is a book about the present and future of jazz rather than its distant and endlessly chronicled past.

Its second and main objective has been to offer, in narrative form, a series of instrument-by-instrument histories enabling the reader to see each artist's role, period of impact and relative importance, and to correlate this information with the recommended phonograph records. These instrumental chapters will, I hope, be of value both to the young jazz fan who asked me the other day "Who is Frank Teschemacher?" and to the older aficionado who meekly inquired: "Who is Paul Horn?" There will be areas of information for the musicians themselves; once a noted west coast jazzman startled me by asking: "Who is Bessie Smith?" There are also several musical illustrations, with analyses, of solos by performers most of whom have never before been the subjects of this kind of scrutiny in a jazz book.

I have not attempted to present the personal stories of these artists, most of whom were represented in *Hear Me Talkin' To Ya*, edited by Nat Shapiro and Nat Hentoff; nor is there any extensive attention to the African backgrounds and other pre-jazz historic data, since this would merely duplicate the exhaustive documentation in Dr. Stearns' *The Story Of Jazz.*°

The main intent of these chapters is to focus attention on the comparatively small number of artists who are key figures in their respective categories. There is a secondary group in each chapter whose contributions, though of no major significance to jazz history, have given considerable pleasure to fellow-musicians and jazz lovers. Though every artist in the leading group has been mentioned, the inclusions and omissions in the second category have necessarily been to some extent arbitrary, since the number of those who have played first-class solos at some period in the history of recorded jazz runs into the thousands.

After all the dust of critical controversy has settled, it will be found in due course that the musicians whose contributions deserve to be remembered will survive regardless of how they fared at the critics' hands (witness the cases of Gillespie and Parker, both crucified in print at the time of their struggle for a break-through to esthetic acceptance). It will also be found that no matter where we draw the lines between jazz and popular music, classical music, Afro-Cuban, Latin-American and all the other musical forms that impinge upon jazz in varying degrees, the music that has in it an honesty and freshness of conception, allied with conviction and musicianship and integrity in its execution, regardless of whether or not it be called jazz, will survive in the record collections of our children and of the generations to come.

° Nor have I padded the pages with recitals of biographical facts, which can be found in my own reference books, *The Encyclopedia of Jazz* and others, published by Horizon Press and Bonanza Books.

CHAPTER 2

BEGINNINGS

A wave of vulgar, of filthy and suggestive music has inundated
the land. Nothing but ragtime prevails. . . . No seaside resort this
summer has been without its ragtime orchestra, its weekly
cakewalk . . .

Worse yet, the fashionable idle folk of Newport . . . have
been the chief offenders. Society has decreed that ragtime and
cakewalking are the thing, and one reads with amazement and
disgust of historical and aristocratic names joining in this sex
dance, for the cakewalk is nothing but an African *danse du
ventre*, a milder edition of African orgies, and the music is
degenerate music . . . Ragtime rhythm is nothing new, but its
present usage and marriage to words of veiled lasciviousness
should banish it from polite society.

—*The Musical Courier*, 1899

Jazz was not born in New Orleans.

Jazz is a social, not a racial music.*

Jazz is written as well as improvised.

Jazz can be played in four-four time, waltz time or any other
time.

These views run counter to the concepts of jazz established
by most of the early experts. The tendency has been to localize
the music in the sporting houses of New Orleans' Storyville, to
Jim-Crow it as a form in which all white artists were interlopers
and imitators, and to segregate it still further by labeling it as

* It was the segregated American Negro, not "the Negro," who contributed most of its essential characteristics.

8

folk music that could never be documented, and by insisting on
the necessity of a binary meter. Some jazz authorities still hold
these views, though to an ever-diminishing degree.

—At least half the greatest jazz artists have been Negroes; the
proportion among the definitive style-setters is far greater, perhaps ninety per cent. Jazz was the product of a specific social
environment in which a group of people, the American Negroes,
largely shut off from the white world, developed cultural patterns of their own. As soon as the rigid segregation under which
they had lived began to soften, it became obvious on the basis
of a freer interchange of ideas that anyone could play jazz,
according to his environment, his ability and his talent as an
individual, not as white or Negro. Place an infant from Australia,
China or Siam in the care of a jazz-oriented New York family
and he will have as good a chance as any other infant in those
circumstances of growing up to be a great jazz musician. Take
the infant son of a famous and universally respected jazz
musician and rear him in a non-musical setting among the
people of a distant country; the chances that he will ever
develop any jazz interest or talent are remote.

They are less remote, however, than they would have been a
few years ago; for as the jazz world has in one sense grown,
in another it has shrunk. Today it is so small that an idea
created one month by a saxophonist in California may be expressed with a similar power of inspiration a month later by a
record-buying jazzman in Stockholm. Jazz ideas are imported
as well as exported; the pianists and guitarists who have been
influenced by Shearing and Reinhardt, the saxophonists who wait
eagerly for the release of Tubby Hayes' next LP, attest to the
increasing degree of international interchange and to the theory
that jazz at present is not local, not regional or racial, but natural
—natural to any musician, regardless of his geographical circumstances, who may be within reach of a phonograph, a radio,
or another musician.

That this interchange was impossible at the stage when jazz
was crystallizing must certainly be taken into account in any
assessment of its origins. Moreover, the documentation of this
early period has been thoroughly and painstakingly undertaken

only since the early 1940s, when most of the original performers
were dead, or at an age that enabled them to take credit for
contributions they may not in fact have made. The quantity of
wishful thinking, deliberate misstatement and contradiction in
the stories that have been readily accepted by historians makes
it impossible to determine who the real progenitors of jazz were
and what the quality of their contribution was. To cite one
example, though Bunk Johnson has been widely publicized as
Louis Armstrong's mentor and as a member of Buddy Bolden's
band, much of the information he supplied was contradicted
by other New Orleans musicians; Louis Armstrong has consistently maintained that his sole musical influence was Joe
"King" Oliver. Since there was no phonograph recording of any
jazz until 1917, and no substantial recording of Negro jazz until
about 1922, the accuracy of these early values will never be
determined.

It is thus equally difficult to decide when the stage was
reached at which music was being played that could be called
jazz. It seems improbable that anything thus definable was
heard before the late 1890s, but here one is hampered both by
the lack of recorded evidence and by the lack of a stable definition of the term itself. The music we recognize today as jazz is a
synthesis drawn originally from six principal sources: rhythms
from West Africa; harmonic structure from European classical
music; melodic and harmonic qualities from nineteenth-century
American folk music; religious music; work songs and minstrel
shows.

Dr. Marshall Stearns, in his absorbing study of what he calls
the "pre-history of jazz", poses and answers one major question:
"What is the connection between jazz and West African music?
Perhaps the most obvious similarity is the rhythm . . . take a
tribal ceremony in Dahomey . . . the main instrument . . .
is the drum—usually a set of three drums . . . At its peak, the
sound may seem like a combination of disordered pneumatic
drills. The music is polyrhythmic . . . A common foundation
for West African music is a combination of 3/4, 6/8 and 4/4
time signatures . . . something of this engaging rhythm that
identifies a lot of jazz for us came from West Africa. It's a

survival—diluted, to be sure. There's nothing quite like it in Europe, the source of most of the rest of our music."[1]

Leonard De Paur, long a student of Afro-American musical origins, and director of a distinguished Negro choir, points out the fallacy of oversimplification in ascribing "African" rhythmic origins to jazz. "You can break down the pure African influences into many, many divisions, some of greater and some of lesser culture. To trace the rhythmic family tree completely you would have to comb through all the influences in various parts of Africa, define them, then go into Latin America, find out where these influences break off and where they merge with Latin rhythms from Spain and Morocco and trace them to the Delta area, to the Gulf of Mexico, sometimes by way of the Caribbean and Latin America. The levels of culture varied greatly too: even the French and Spanish emigrants brought over were not in all cases educated people—often they were emptied out of jails to colonize."

There is disagreement concerning the relationship between African music and later American forms related to jazz. According to Ernest Borneman: "Up to the time when slavery first brought Africans into extensive contact with alien civilizations, African music, from the Ivory Coast to the Congo, had remained without any development of a native harmony. Even today, wherever natives have remained untouched by alien music, chords are only produced as accidental meeting points of three or more lines of melody."

Rudi Blesh and Harriet Janis affirmed a connection, at least on the rhythmic level. Outlining the early impact of Negro ragtime in Chicago in the 1890s, they pointed out that at the same time the ragtime players were congregating in Chicago "the Dahomeans were startling World's Fair visitors in 1893 with the original African form of the same rhythms."[2]

Barry Ulanov, referring to André Gide's *Travels in the Congo* with its apparently perceptive reaction to African music, has a conflicting theory: "The music that Gide describes is vaguely related to jazz, but is by no means the same thing; it has only a general resemblance to many different kinds of primitive music, European as well as American . . . a comparative analysis of

African and American music does not yield clear parallels. For one thing, jazz is a measured music, the structure of which depends upon fixed beats, occurring in rhythmic patterns as unmistakable and immediately identifiable as the pulse of a metronome. African drumming, submitted to the most painstaking of auditions, simply does not break down into a structured rhythmic music; there are shifts of time and points and counterpoints of rhythm that make accurate notation impossible. As for the melodic qualities and quantities of African music, these too are shaped by a tonal and rhythmic conception entirely outside the Western diatonic tradition. To speak of the blue notes— the flatted third and seventh—as they are inflected against their natural position within a fixed key, or the alterations of pitch of jazz singers or instrumentalists, or their swooping glissandos, as American developments of African music is to talk unlettered nonsense. The basic chordal and melodic and rhythmic structure of the blues and of the jazz that has developed out of the blues is firmly within the orbit of Western folk music. There is far more of the sound of jazz in Middle-European gypsy fiddling than there is in a corps of African drummers."[3]

One fusion that apparently took place with the importation of slaves from Africa to the new world was the blending of Spanish folk music with the West African songs. Cuba gave birth to the habañera; to the rhumba, supposedly named after a West African dance step; and to the bolero, the tango and other forms, while calypso, conga and beguine rhythms sprang up in Trinidad and other islands. Many of these folk music developments that had originated in the mid-nineteenth century were ultimately to impinge upon ragtime, early blues and jazz, all of which showed occasional French and Spanish influences.

While the slave ships from Africa brought with them some of the Negro cultural patterns, there were developing in many parts of the United States songs that had the melodic and harmonic characteristic of what was known much later as ragtime, jazz and/or the blues. *Frankie and Johnny,* a song of obscure origin, was known in St. Louis in the 1880s, according to one source; originated in 1850 and was sung at the siege of Vicksburg, according to a second historian: a third writer dates it back as far as 1840. This song is important because structurally it has the classic twelve-measure format of the blues (see Chapter 18), with the first four bars on the tonic and the next on the chord of the subdominant, and so on through the regular 1-4-5-1 blues pattern. Considerable doubt exists whether *Frankie and Johnny* was of Negro or white origin; but it seems certain that the harmonic formula it represented was common in American folk music of both races a century ago, just as the majority of popular songs of the nineteenth century had a simple harmonic base that had been in general use among European composers since Bach's day. The twelve-measure form can even be found in English and French balladry as far back as the thirteenth century. Though this may be coincidence, there can be little doubt that the blues structurally is of white origin, though melodically and harmonically it is the product of an American Negro environment.

The work song is a jazz antecedent of unquestionable folk origin, born in slavery and raised in protest. "Fearful of the silence of the slaves," Duke Ellington has theorized, "their masters commanded them to raise their voices in song, so that all opportunity for discontented reflection or plans for retaliation and salvation would be eliminated."⁴ The work songs, of which *Old Man River* is a modern travesty, originated in chain gangs, on plantations and among levee camp and railroad workers. Though the stories told by the lyrics have no direct bearing on the musical qualities of jazz, they are a significant reflection of part of its social background, as even some of their titles indicate: *Nine-Foot Shovel, Chain Gang Bound* and *Told My Cap'n. (Cap'n, cap'n, you mus' be cross; six 'clock in Hell 'fo' you knock off . . . raised my hand, wiped de sweat off my head, cap'n got mad, shot my buddy dead . . .).*

The plantation work song might center on the boll weevil, or on the physical prowess of some legendary hero such as John Henry. Often in the work songs one finds examples of the "chant-and-response" form, a pattern that has occurred throughout jazz history, from the blues laments of Bessie Smith, answered by the ad lib obbligatos of a trumpeter or trombonist, through the simple reeds-versus-brass riffing of the early swing bands in the 1930s; the orchestra repeating the piano's explosions in Lionel Hampton's *Boogie Woogie* in the 1940s; and the new outburst of instrumental and vocal juxtaposition along call-and-response lines in the commercialized rock 'n' roll ceremonies of the 1950s. Some of the traditional work songs have been recorded by the late Huddie Ledbetter, better known as "Leadbelly," and in a slightly more urbanized style by Josh White.

Contemporaneous with the development of the work song was the religious music of both Negro and white Americans. Barry Ulanov points out that: "A comparison of the so-called white spirituals and the so-called Negro spirituals shows enormous exchanges of melody, rhythm, and lyric."[5] Fortunately this area of jazz genealogy is more adequately documented than most. An 1881 edition of *The Story of the Jubilee Singers,* documenting the career of the Fisk University choral group, provides a fascinating and relevant case history. The Jubilee Singers almost singlehandedly spread the spiritual and the work song from a limited audience in the southern United States to a peak of international acceptance that did much to spread the influence of this music with its peculiar melodic implications.

Opened as a school in 1866, Fisk was chartered the following year as a University. George L. White, the treasurer, organized a school chorus that gave its first public concert in 1867. Four years later the group, composed of six female and five male students, left Nashville on a fund raising tour and ultimately attracted so much enthusiasm, despite many racial obstacles, among white church and lay organizations, that within a year or two the group was on its first tour of England and performed for Queen Victoria. For decades the Jubilee Singers remained a symbol of the branch of music they represented.

An examination of the music reproduced in the book devoted to their story, transcribed from their hitherto undocumented performances, reveals that many of the tunes are simple diatonic melodies that must have gained their quality from the accent and rhythmic nuances of the performances. As the book's editor points out, a noticeable feature of the songs is the rarity of the occurrence of triple time, which he attributes to the "beating of the foot and the swaying of the body which are such frequent accompaniments of the singing. These motions are in even measure, and in perfect time; and so it will be found that, however broken and seemingly irregular the movement of the music, it is always capable of the most exact measurement. In other words, its irregularities invariably conform to the 'higher law' of the perfect rhythmic flow." He also notes that the melodies are in the same scale as old Scottish music forms, with the fourth and seventh tones almost completely omitted. As Leonard De Paur has said, a comparison might also be drawn with Greek modal forms; "or you could say this is a deficiency of the western ear, because you can go to things that are being recorded in Africa and find evidences of twelve-tone scale usage." The presence of the flatted seventh, endemic to the blues, can be observed in only a few of the 112 songs reproduced, among them *Roll, Jordan, Roll.* De Paur feels that the jazz use of such notes developed separately from the spiritual: "The blues was purely an urban development and didn't come into existence until the Negro had been exposed to some urban living of a peculiar sort, in that he was no longer a servant— at least not an indentured servant; he was still an economic slave, but he lived pretty much to himself in his own civilization within the confines of this urban area. Out of this came the blues and out of that the development of jazz. All of these things had a high degree of white origin. People don't like to admit this, because they like to think in terms of complete purity. The forms of the spirituals, too, can be traced directly to the hymns these slaves were taught, and other forms of gospel music— expressions of a fundamental sort generally, because the slaves were considered too simple-minded to absorb more organized western culture. They adapted things they had been taught or things they had heard. Only the rhythmic origins are purely Negro."

There can be little doubt that the work songs, whether or not they derived from West Africa, and the Negro and white spirituals, which evolved in part from English hymns and ballads, overlapped with, and were in effect first cousins of, the blues. But even today there are religious singers who reject the idea of association between spirituals and blues. Interviewed by Mike

Wallace during a television program in 1957, Mahalia Jackson was asked: "You've heard the traditional blues songs of Bessie Smith and other artists . . . How do they differ from gospel songs in the way they make you feel when you hear them or sing them?" Miss Jackson's answer was: "Anyone who sings the blues has a broken spirit—they are burdened and they sing the blues to relieve that feeling that they have. Being oppressed or worried about something and not knowing God, they've sought a way of trying to relieve themselves . . . you get relief from spiritual songs, but you don't get real relief when you sing the blues because the spiritual song has divine power behind it and lifts man up, but the blues makes you feel moody and sad and makes you cry."

Wallace said: "You are now in great demand as a gospel singer, but back in the 1920s a good many ministers prohibited that kind of singing in church—isn't that a fact?" Miss Jackson answered: "Well, not too many. In any race of people there are some that like the hymn, some like the spiritual and some like the one that has the jolly beat like the kind I like to sing—one that I say is full of fire."[6]

The last of the six principal elements from which jazz derived is the minstrel show, which began about 1800 when a young singer from Germany, Gottlieb Graupner, did a blackface act at a Boston theater, introducing himself as "The Gay Negro Boy." All through the nineteenth century and into the first decades of the twentieth, the full-sized minstrel show was a firmly established form of entertainment in which, by developing parodies and satires of various Negro characters, the white performers in effect evolved folk music approaches of their own, which in turn were taken back and used in altered form by Negro performers.

Composers of the mid-nineteenth century whose work had the greatest impact on this field included Daniel Decatur Emmett, composer of *Dixie's Land*, better known as *Dixie* (written and composed expressly for Bryant's Minstrels) and Stephen Foster, whose works have an unmistakably ragtime flavor. Basically *Oh! Susanna, Camptown Races* and *Old Folks at Home* (better known as *Swanee River*) have the same simple harmonic structure as the early ragtime and jazz pieces.

It must be borne in mind that none of the contrasting areas in which these jazz antecedents grew—religious and secular, North and South, folk and urban, even white and Negro—developed in a complete vacuum. There was considerable mutual encroachment, as a result of which it is impossible to determine the exact point where any one form originated or was fused with another. This is true also of the nomenclature of various jazz forms such as ragtime, blues, Dixieland and New Orleans. Even ragtime, once firmly established as a pre-jazz piano style, later became a diffuse term applied to orchestral forms.

Ragtime, an energetic precursor of the music that is played today by exponents of a commercialized style generally called "honky tonk piano," grew up in the 1890s with Sedalia, Missouri as its unofficial headquarters. According to some historians the first and greatest of the ragtime pianists was a pale-skinned, slight youngster whose features were more Indian and Spanish than Negro: Louis Chauvin, who died at 28, leaving no testament but three published compositions and the memory of contemporaries who recalled the exquisite originality and beauty of his work. Chauvin, like many of the ragtime men, was from St. Louis, the home for many years of Tom Turpin, whose *Harlem Rag* (1897) was credited by Rudi Blesh and Harriet Janis as the first published Negro rag.[7] A story in *Jazz Magazine* in 1942 conjectured that many of Chauvin's ideas may have been incorporated in the *Original Rags* published under that title in 1899 by Scott Joplin, who as the writer of *Maple Leaf Rag* (published in Sedalia in 1899) was the best known of the ragtime composers.

Writing of Sedalia's role as the birthplace of ragtime, Blesh and Janis pointed out that the town treated Negroes with more enlightened fairness than was then customary, that good schooling and good jobs were plentiful, but that "it was not the respectable Sedalia that supported the beginnings of what was to become the classic ragtime: East Main Street, with its honky-tonks, clubs and bawdy houses, was the patron of syncopated music. . . ."

In Sedalia and throughout the United States, both Negro and

white pianists drifted from town to town playing embryonic ragtime. All were close to folk music sources and formed a virtual folk academy as they met at Tom Turpin's Rosebud Cafe in St. Louis, at the Frenchman's in New Orleans, at Johnny Seymour's Bar in Chicago, at the Maple Leaf Club in Sedalia, and in Louisville, Nashville, Little Rock, Indianapolis, El Remo and the Oklahoma Territory, "and only the sporting world and husbands secretly out for a fling were there to hear the music."[8]

Soon after the turn of the century ragtime became known to a wider public and even reached the stage at which a ragtime opera was presented—Scott Joplin's *A Guest Of Honor*, seen in St. Louis in 1903. Joplin moved to New York in 1907; *Treemonisha*, another opera, was produced at his own expense for a single performance in Harlem in 1911. The ragtime piano vogue lasted well into World War I and continued for a while after Joplin's death in 1917. Some of the men who played it had the misfortune never to come within reach of either a player piano roll or a phonograph, but diligent research by Bill Grauer and Orrin Keepnews enabled them to present a few years ago a series of records dubbed from piano rolls made by Joplin, Tom Scott, Joseph Lamb and Tom Turpin. Because of the limitations of the piano roll in recreating the subtleties of dynamics that may have been an important part of the original performances, these recordings give an incomplete though absorbing idea of the work of these ragtime pioneers. They were issued in the album on the Riverside label.

How far ragtime overlapped into jazz is another debated point. Dave Dexter, in *Jazz Cavalcade*, avowed flatly: "Jazz is not ragtime; ragtime is not jazz." But Grossman and Farrell, in *The Heart Of Jazz*, state: "As jazz developed alongside ragtime, a very large measure of this music [ragtime] seeped into what is believed the younger form, being particularly noticeable in the piano styles of many band players. All the work of the Original Dixieland Jazz Band shows a marked ragtime influence." According to Frederic Ramsey, Jr., "Ragtime has touched jazz all along the way of its development, and more than a mere echo of ragtime is to be found in many exhilarating jazz performances."

Whether the two forms overlapped slightly, extensively or

not at all, this much is certain: at the dawn of the twentieth century, while America listened and danced the cakewalk to ragtime, singers in rural areas, accompanying themselves on simple string instruments, were developing the sad, slow songs that came to be known as the blues, and the faster, less melancholy folk themes that were soon to be blended with ragtime. Contemporaneously another interrelated branch was developing that played a vitally important part in framing the background of jazz: the music of the brass band.

CHAPTER 3

BIG TOWNS AND BRASS BANDS

"People don't realize," says the trombonist and bandleader Wilbur De Paris, "that in the early days brass band and orchestral playing were very closely related. The musicians I remember from my childhood were mainly brass band men, because there weren't many jobs for strictly orchestra men." To De Paris, "orchestra" in this context refers to the dance band. Born in 1900 in Crawfordsville, Indiana, De Paris, who toured with his musician father from infancy, can recall many of the groups that played in the brass band style, in many parts of the United States, during his childhood. The conventional instrumentation included one or two cornets, a clarinet, a trombone, guitar, bass and drums. Their polyphonic interpretations, according to Louis Armstrong and others who heard them, had some qualities in common with the jazz of the later day.

The Negro bands played at picnics, rode in advertising wagons and frequently marched through the urban streets. White musicians were developing bands along parallel lines. Jack "Papa" Laine, who formed his first band in 1888 and claims to have been one of the first to perform ragtime, led the Reliance Brass Band, which played for parades and carnivals. The most widely publicized of the brass bands were all led by trumpeters or cornetists. The most powerful, both in the strength of his legend and in the reputed clarity and carrying power of his horn, was Charles "Buddy" Bolden, born in 1878 in New Orleans. Bolden, with whom music may have been a sideline (his other activities included the editing of a scandal sheet and the operation of a

barber shop) organized what was possibly one of the first real
jazz bands around the turn of the century. According to the
tangled evidence available, Bolden played traditional themes that
combined ragtime with brass band music in the first primitive
statements of jazz; beyond any doubt, too, he played the blues.
Bolden's fate, as it turned out, was neither fame nor fortune,
but dementia praecox. He ran amuck during a parade, was committed to a state hospital and spent twenty-four years there,
dying in 1931. Some of Bolden's contemporaries in brass were
Freddie Keppard's Olympia Band, the Original Creole Band, and
the Eagle Band, with Mutt Carey and Bunk Johnson.

There were many other areas far from New Orleans where
this primeval jazz was being performed by brass band musicians.
Asked whether he could recall some of them, Wilbur De Paris
replied, "I've always felt that though New Orleans was a focal
point of the South, most of the large cities in various parts of the
country also made their contributions and helped to set styles.
For instance, the type of trumpet playing that came to be identified later with Bix Beiderbecke was quite common in the
Midwest among Negro musicians. I came from Indiana, and I
can name half-a-dozen trumpet players who were playing that
style. Charlie Hart, one of the trumpet men in a road show called
Old Kentuck', was one; another was Frank Clay of Indianapolis,
who led a military band as well as a theater pit orchestra. Then
there were the Wolfscale Brothers, and Roy Pope, the Hoosier
cornetist; and there were clarinetists like King Phillips, who
wrote the *King Phillips Rag* and the *Florida Blues*. These were a
blend of brass band and orchestra men, and they played dances;
and they played jazz.

"There was a whole other school that should complement the
New Orleans school, and that was the school I came up in.
Basically, these men were better, musically and technically, than
most of the New Orleans musicians. They got their foundation
from amongst the teachers, Italian and German, across the
country, throughout the Middle West. They were equivalent to
jazz, and this wasn't necessarily the same thing that we know
as ragtime. Jazz was growing up in different parts of the country
without one part necessarily knowing what the other part was

doing—that is, aside from these musicians that I came up with. We knew what was going on in other parts of the country because we travelled a lot, but a lot of people didn't know about New Orleans at all until much later."

A principal aspect of the first social and geographical settings of jazz, not yet fully documented, is the use of syncopated music at Negro funerals.* Most historians, like many novelists who have been concerned with the colorful sociological roots of the music, have placed this custom almost exclusively in New Orleans. It would be more accurate to estimate that rhythmic funerals were taking place, some years before the turn of the century, all over the South, and, indeed, wherever there was a substantial Negro population.

Eubie Blake, the early ragtime pianist-composer, recalled that in the late 1880s and early '90s, when he was a child in Baltimore, funerals of this kind frequently took place. "Joe Blow would die, and maybe he belonged to some society, so they would get the money together and have a band for his funeral. Those fellows couldn't read, but they sure played ragtime on their horns on the way back from the graveyard—tunes like *Bunch of Blackberrries*. Those trombone slides would be going like crazy. My mother said that nothing but low people followed the parades, and she used to whip me because we played ragtime coming back from the graveyard.

"The bands in Baltimore had all the regular instruments, and they had alto horns, or peckhorns as we used to call them, and euphoniums. Charlie Harris was one of the fine musicians who played in those bands; in fact, he was my teacher, and sometimes when I was a kid and those fellows used to get $2 to go out and play an excursion, they would give me a dollar and I would play second cornet to Charlie.

"There were dozens of fine musicians who played ragtime in the parades and at the funerals. Trumpet players like Pike Davis and Preston Duncan; a musician named Emil Daverage, who

* A recreation of one of these ceremonies, with the band playing solemn music on the way to the graveyard and stepping into a lively march on the way back, was presented as a prologue to the motion picture, *Pete Kelly's Blues*, released in 1956.

played the euphonium. We called the music ragtime, whether it was a piano or a band playing. We never heard the word 'jazz' until many years later, long after I came to New York."

W. C. Handy, the cornetist and band master later famous as the composer of *St. Louis Blues,* confirmed the growth of jazz-related forms in many southern states during the 1890s. Born in 1873 in Florence, Alabama, he toured as a young man with Mahara's Minstrels, as cornet soloist and musical director. The following conversation took place in 1957 between Mr. Handy and the author:

Mr. Handy, when you were a young man, did you hear anything about the New Orleans musicians that jazz historians are writing about today, such as Bunk Johnson and Buddy Bolden?

No, I didn't hear about them, but I had associations with others; my best trombone player was from there, and I carried New Orleans musicians with me when I had a band in 1896 and '97 all over the United States.

Did the jazz musicians come from New Orleans, then, or from all over the South, or all over the country?

From all over the country. Fewer of them were from New York than any place. You could get them from Philadelphia, but you got your best musicians back in the '80s and '90s from Shreveport, Baton Rouge, Vicksburg, Jackson—Mississippi and Louisiana. Alabama had some, also Florida and Tennessee.

Don't you think that jazz and ragtime and the blues all had something in common and overlapped to some degree?

I think they are separate things in this: ragtime you played as it was written, but in jazz you had improvisation. And ragtime had very little melody—it was mainly rhythm. The blues had a good melodic line. But they did sometimes overlap.

Who were some of the musicians that you associated with jazz, and where did they come from?

It would depend on what you call jazz.

I would like your interpretation of the word.

Well, I played with a fellow in Bessemer, Alabama, and they called him Lard Can Charlie and he made good jazz out of a lard can. See what I mean? I played with another fellow in Huntsville, Alabama. He played with a long iron pipe and the people would rather dance with him playing that iron pipe than with him playing string bass. So I've played with many novelty musicians. We had an E Flat cornet player with Mahara's Minstrels, Elmore Dodd from Nashville, who filed his mouthpiece down so he could make an E Flat cornet sound like a piccolo, and that was a sensation. Even in the minstrel days we played music similar to jazz, but we didn't call it jazz. We called it faking. Just pick up a piece like *A Hot Time in the Old Town Tonight* and sporting house songs and put any interpretation we would want to put, but we didn't call it jazz—we didn't know anything about that word.

When did you first hear the word "jazz" used?

Not until I went to Memphis, after I had written the *Memphis Blues*. A book came out called *The New Negro*—J. A. Rogers wrote an article about me and this new music called jazz and gave me credit for it.

How about the early songs that you documented—did they come from New Orleans?

When I lived in Bessemer, Alabama in 1892 or '93, we used to sing a song, *Careless Love,* and they claimed that song came from New Orleans. But I moved to Kentucky, along the Ohio River, where I found that the governor's son had been killed over an unhappy love affair and the Negroes made up a song called *You See What Careless Love Has Done.* So *Loveless Love* floated down the Ohio River with roustabouts and *down* the Mississippi to New Orleans. Can you see what I mean? So much of our folk music just drifted on down the river—like *Joe Turner. Joe Turner* started in Memphis and I kept it alive, but it could have gone on down to New Orleans and have been called something else, but the same tune in New Orleans was called *Goin' Down the River 'Fore Long.*

Do you think anything equivalent to jazz or ragtime was being played up here in the East around the turn of the century?

Well, some of our singers in certain illiterate churches were breeders of what we call jazz today. They put in their music, in their singing, something that instruments do today. So that when a boy got to be able to play clarinet or trumpet, he put into his music the same thing they put into the shout songs—not the spirituals.

Do you think this went on in churches all over America?

I wouldn't say all over America, but wherever slavery was practiced.

The Southwest, too, undoubtedly was a proving ground for the same syncopations and improvisations that had begun to prevail in other regions by the turn of the century. All around Texas, Oklahoma and neighboring states there were parade bands patterned along the traditional ragtime lines: a typical group was one in Oklahoma City that included Jim Bronson on clarinet, Andrew Rushing on trumpet (his son, born in 1903, is the ex-Basie blues singer, Jimmy Rushing), Millidge Winslett on trombone and George Sparks on peckhorn (E Flat horn).

The seldom-discussed role of the East in the creation of jazz is emphatically confirmed by one of Duke Ellington's early piano idols, Willie "The Lion" Smith. Born in 1897 in Goshen, New York, Smith recalls hearing jazz from early childhood and contests the theory that all its developments had drifted up from New Orleans, whose musicians were, he says, unknown to him and his contemporaries during the period up to and including World War I. The following conversation with "The Lion" took place a few years ago in New York:

When and where do you remember hearing the first jazz played?

Well, they always played jazz. We had a famous club in New York called the Clef Club. That was the greatest club in the world.

How far back did that go?

Oh, man! That goes way back before the first World War; I was a member then and am still a member.

Were there any equivalents around here of the Bunk Johnsons and King Olivers of New Orleans?

Yes, we had guys around that could play the hell out of a horn. We had a trumpet player that was with me by the name of Major; later he was with the first Mamie Smith band. He was a pistol. We had another guy that gave everybody a fit in New

York; his name was Jack Hatton. He was a cornet playing fool. He did all that growling like Bubber Miley and those guys tried to do later. Of course, that was long before phonograph records. There are musicians around who are 75 to 80 years old who used to be tops. We always had jazz bands; we had them at a place in Brooklyn called Coners. The guy who played piano there was called Kid Griffith and he wore tight pants . . . a little, short good-looking guy. They had a jazz band—they had to have jazz bands. This was before the first war. I had a jazz band at LeRoy's before the war, too. It was a 12-piece band, and who do you think was singing there with me—Mamie Smith. Talk about jazz bands—My God! They had better guys playing jazz than a lot of these guys trying to play it, because those guys knew what they were doing.

Did you ever hear about the musicians from New Orleans?

I never heard of the guys—never heard of them. There were only two guys I saw from the West. One was a guy by the name of Johnny Williams, whose wife poisoned him. He was a better cornet player than Louis Armstrong ever thought about being, and anybody in the West will tell you that. He was from out West, but not from New Orleans. The only guy I knew to come from New Orleans was Louis Armstrong and the only time I saw him was when I went out there.

How about this legend about New Orleans' being the birth-place of jazz?

It's the writers. If you don't think I know what I'm talking about, just look in those books these fellows have written, and see guys like Danny Barker and all of them talking about the bands on the Mississippi riverboats. Man, they've got riverboats all over, right here in Haverstraw, New York. Ever since I can remember, there's been jazz played.

The kind of rhythmic qualities that came to be known as jazz were growing up all around the country, then?

That's right. Now you're hitting it. The rhythm—you know I've been associated myself with synagogues and Baptist churches all my life and they had the greatest rhythm you ever heard.

How about the blues? Was that always around?

Always the blues, ha! ha!

That wasn't always in the South, either?

No, sir. Here's one that'll kill 'em. The blues comes from the brickyards in Haverstraw, New York, where those colored people worked in the brickyards. They sang blues all day. Men older than I will tell you that.

Luckey Roberts, another ragtime pianist numbered among Duke Ellington's first influences, came to New York from Philadelphia in 1898 as a child actor in *Uncle Tom's Cabin.* Roberts' earliest recollections concern ragtime musicians, particularly pianists, who were active in the East and had converged on New York from at least a dozen states:

"There were some great piano players. There was Dude Finley from Florida, and One Leg Shadow, and One Leg Willie. They played all over the country. And Jack the Bear, whose real name was Jack Wilson; he was around Pennsylvania and Ohio. And Bud Howard out of Detroit—and did you ever hear of Benden Boots? He played fine piano and was out of Baltimore. Then of course Pike Davis and Preston Duncan on trumpets; Pike was one of the best attack men I ever heard. He came from Baltimore in one of the first groups that started reading music."

The "One Leg Shadow" mentioned by Roberts was the late Walter Gould, a legendary ragtime pianist. Born in Philadelphia in 1875, he told Rudi Blesh of even earlier performers: "Old Man Sam Moore was ragging the quadrilles and schottisches before I was born. He was born 'way before the war. He doubled on bass and piano." Not long before his death in Albany, N.Y., "Shadow" at 83 was vocal and alert, as stubbornly convinced as most of his Eastern contemporaries that the New Orleans legend presents a one-sided story. "I begged Blesh not to believe all that stuff about everything happening in New Orleans," he said in 1957. "You know what started everybody believing that? Louis Armstrong and King Oliver coming from there, that's what did it. And yet when there was dozens of great musicians in the East, you couldn't find but two or three good piano players in the whole of New Orleans."

Evidently Gould's plea to Blesh did not go completely unheeded. The latter's first book, *Shining Trumpets,* placed a heavy accent on New Orleans; his second, four years later *(They All Played Ragtime,* 1950) receded a little from this position ("Eastern ragtime has as long and honorable an ancestry as the others . . . it focused at first in Virginia and the Carolinas and then spread up into Maryland and down the coast into Florida, Georgia and Alabama."). By 1953 Blesh, at a seminar attended by jazz experts and anthropologists, spoke of Mississippi and Eastern Texas origins, of an Eastern Seaboard style that "didn't just start with Ellington and Henderson but came from something else," and added that he was "trying to deal with the assumption that jazz began only in New Orleans. I used to think so; I once wrote along those lines. I don't think so any longer."[2]

Leonard De Paur recalls: "My mother, who was born around 1887, was completely conversant with jazz as it was practiced by nomadic bands such as the Jenkins Orphanage Band from Charleston, South Carolina. I remember when I was a child there these kids used to come up as far north as Trenton and just play on the street corners in the most nondescript uniforms you ever saw—some sort of jacket with brass buttons and pants with stripes. They would just stand around in a circle and the leader was somebody who could dance like hell—he didn't have to have any talent more than the ability to say 1, 2, boom! and then go into a routine of his own which would highlight the performances. But they did move around all over the country and they played the most positive ragtime you have ever heard. My wife was from Charleston and she said she had known about this orphange organization as a child there and my mother, when she first saw them, said, 'Oh, my God, there's Jenkins' Orphanage Band! I haven't seen them since I was a little girl.'

"This was strictly low-brow stuff—right-thinking people who went to church with starched neckbands on Sunday didn't admit to the existense of this type of thing, but there was an element which really lived on this music; and they played funerals—on the way and back from the graveyard in South Carolina. Even if the graveyard was right around the corner, they would have the band travel all over town advertising this funeral with this band doing what we now call tailgate trombone.

"But the boys who chronicled the development around New

Orleans did a much more effective job than the people who were East, and it also seems that the whites were more aware of its value around new Orleans and they really did a job of promoting. There are evidences of this kind of activity that go back to the very time it was supposed to be incubating in New Orleans. I've heard Hall Johnson, in whose choir I used to sing, make the same comment. He came from a very literate family; he's from Georgia, and he knew of the existence of jazz very far back, and he is over seventy now. New Orleans just happened to get the publicity."

Eubie Blake once told this writer: "I'm 74 years old, and when I was a kid, around ten or eleven, this kind of music was already around then. I was playing it myself in Baltimore from 1898, and we called it ragtime." Blake, who came to New York soon after the turn of the century, confirms that jazz, both in its ragtime piano form and in musically similar brass interpretations, was a firmly established entity at that juncture, and that the musicians from New Orleans were practically unknown until about 1915, when Freddie Keppard visited New York with the Original Creole Band.

The picture that emerges from a synthesis of the statements cited in the preceding pages, of the recollections and revelations of ragtime historians and musicians from various centers, and of the constantly documented histories of the New Orleans musicians, can only point to one conclusion. Jazz, which by the first World War was an acknowledged and organized facet of the music scene, and which for many years has been localized and pinpointed by writers to a degree clearly at variance with the facts, is a child neither of Louisiana nor of Pennsylvania, owing no more allegiance to the Confederacy than to the Union. Jazz simply was born in the United States of America.

CHAPTER 4

NEW ORLEANS—MAINSPRING OR MYTH?

> Specialists have built up a doctrine according to which the
> superiority of the pioneers over their successors is admitted
> *a priori* . . . True, the effort of the New Orleans pioneers to
> form a new language still deserves respect. Esthetically, however,
> their work was a failure.
>
> —André Hodeir[1]

New Orleans was the seat of many procreative forces; the
most important in terms of talent and influence were the trumpet
players (Oliver, Armstrong, Red Allen) and the clarinetists
(Picou, Noone, Bechet, Bigard, Edmond Hall, Irving Fazola).

Beyond doubt Storyville, as the scene of much early jazz
creativity, was one of the many areas in which this music was
formulated. While the musicians listed above have shown indisputably the validity of their work, there are others, to be
discussed in the ensuing pages, the importance of whose roles
has been at least debatable. Their advocates, numbered by the
scores among traditionalist jazz experts and by the tens of thousands among similarly oriented jazz fans, have built up a cult
of such mystic qualities that myth and legend have replaced
music and leger-line in an assessment of true values. To them,
any impartial subjective or objective appraisal of any of these
early jazz figures, for whom their special pleading has done
much to shape the documentation of jazz history, would smack
of iconoclasm.

In the following pages will be found a series of illustrations
of the extraordinary dichotomy that has existed for some 20 to 25

years between, on the one hand, the non-musician advocates of some of these New Orleans jazz personalities, and on the other hand, professional musicians who have listened to jazz played by early New Orleans musicians, frequently under the subjective and therefore prejudice-free conditions imposed by a "blindfold test" for which they were given no information about the performances. These musicians represent every period from the 1920s to the present and (except for the New Orleans style itself) every school and phase of jazz, from Dixieland through swing to the new era. The name of André Hodeir is included in the musicians' column because, as Wilder Hobson has pointed out, Hodeir is "at once a trained musical analyst, a composer, and an experienced performer of jazz" and is therefore primarily a musician and secondarily a critic.

The musicians discussed below are the pianist and composer Jelly Roll Morton; the trombonist Kid Ory; trumpeters Bunk Johnson and Kid Rena; clarinetists Johnny Dodds and George Lewis. All were prominent in New Orleans at some point before 1925; all but Dodds, who died in 1940, were part of the "revivalist" campaign launched by enthusiastic critics, whose efforts brought the musicians recording sessions and, in several cases, unprecedented prominence during the late 1930s and early '40s.

CRITICS' VIEW:

Jelly Roll Morton's playing is the definitive jazz piano and represents the highest development of and from ragtime . . . he broadened the expressive power of ragtime, infusing it with the hot elements of jazz and the Blues, making ragtime piano hotter and bluer . . .

—Rudi Blesh[2]

In Armstrong and clarinetist Dodds the greatest one-two

MUSICIANS VIEW:

That's a tuba in there, isn't it? Oh, and a slap tongue tenor solo! Ouch! I don't recognize this, but it sounds like something from the '20s. Even the Dixie they're playing now doesn't sound like that. . . . No beat at all—can't even imagine how they danced to it. What does it lack? It lacks music! No stars.

—Mary Lou Williams (re Jelly Roll Morton record, *Red Hot Pepper*).

Louis Armstrong cannot be compared with his sidemen in

punch of all time was in operation. In addition, Kid Ory was unquestionably the best trombonist of his time . . .

—George Avakian

Johnny Dodds . . . whom some venerate as perhaps the most inspired artist ever to record . . . shows a basic restraint and a lyrical approach.

the early Hot Five, whose rhythm is extremely weak. Listen to Dodds' alto solo in *Come Back Sweet Papa.* Isn't it an excellent sample of not getting the notes in the right place, rich in rhythmic faults and anti-swing if anything ever was? . . .

Ory [is] sometimes very interesting as a soloist . . . primarily bent toward ensemble playing, an art at which he is certainly most adept. It is doubtful whether any other recorded trombonist has shown himself Ory's master in this regard.

—Wm. Grossman-Jack Farrell[3]

. . . How stiff Kid Ory is and how heavily he leans upon the beat . . . Johnny Dodds' rudimentary technique does him a disservice; I can't help feeling uncomfortable when I listen to his fumbling on *Big Butter* . . .

It is not a question of disparaging Dodds and Ory, but simply of setting things straight. The shortcomings of these two musicians are not merely technical; both are deficient musically as well.

—André Hodeir[5]

Bunk's gift of ceaseless variational invention seems to derive from a perpetually youthful inspiration. No one has ever excelled him . . . his recorded band work exemplifies the dissonant tendency of the classic style.

—Rudi Blesh[4]

Do you have to play this all the way through? . . . This music stands for something, but as it is now, it seems quite a bit webby . . . time has just walked right by these guys. . . . I won't rate this one.

—Count Basie (re Bunk Johnson record, *When I Leave the World Behind*).

With a new trumpet Bunk played as well as ever—a grand old man of jazz. He was always clear and melodic.

—Stephen Longstreet[6]

I don't know what to say. I'm prejudiced against people who are trying to take music back forty years. I think that just to make money, some people forget

about music. The solos are not
even good for that type. Musi-
cianship? I didn't hear any.
—Mary Lou Williams (re Bunk
Johnson record, *When the Saints
Go Marching In*).

Bunk's solos show a degree of
melodic invention which places
him in the genius class of jazz
improvisors . . . they possess that
high degree of art which is always
expressed in classic simplicity.
—Frederic Ramsey, Jr.

These writers can't react to
music the way a musician can,
because they simply don't know
what it is . . . they listen to all
that old time stuff because they
like to have their own private
pleasure out of things. They want
something they think nobody else
can appreciate, instead of something they're sharing with the
whole public. That's why they
don't appreciate people like
Benny Goodman and prefer to
listen to Bunk.
—Max Kaminsky

. . . the rhythm is simple and
uncluttered throughout. Kid Rena
was the victim of a stroke sometime prior to the making of these
discs . . . his pleasing middle
register performance is, therefore,
a truly remarkable accomplishment. Rena's approach is very
straight-forward, showing considerable respect for the melody
"as written". (Louis) Nelson
(shows) the full, warm tone and
simple yet liquid style that was
a tremendous influence on many
other New Orleans clarinetists.
—Grossman & Farrell[7]

If this is a recent recording,
those men must have wonderful
photographic memories. This says
absolutely nothing to me, emo-
tionally; it doesn't speak in my
idiom . . . The musicians aren't
artists in the same sense of today's musicians; if they did have
real artistry it would project itself
to me somehow . . . all the same,
these musicians are less ridiculous
than the fans who idolize them.
How can they be sincere? It's just
one of those esoteric cults. No
stars.
—The late Dave Tough (re Kid
Rena record, *Lowdown Blues*).

The group's creativity in jazz
is . . . very considerable. The
leader's clarinet is played in a
liquid style with much of the

They were doing the same
thing over and over. All of them
were. Every once in a while
they'd stop and the clarinet

Creole influence in evidence, but the blues manner also is present. . . . George Lewis plays many passages that require great dexterity in execution. His style contains a level of emotion that is obviously inspired.

—Grossman & Farrell[8]

It is certainly dangerous to bring back figures of legend, well past their prime, and expose them to the harsh light of reality. But things worked out remarkably well . . . Bunk was on occasions quite magnificent, and even when he faltered, the combination of what he was trying to play and the overwhelming aura of nostalgia and romance felt by his audiences was enough to make it quite clear that this particular noble experiment had been a most valuable one.

—Bill Grauer & Orrin Keepnews[9]

Jelly Roll Morton was an extraordinary pianist . . . the music he wrote . . . contains some of the greatest jazz literature of all time.

—George Avakian

The significant thing to remember about Jelly Roll is that

player would play by himself . . . they didn't show too much imagination and I've heard records that sounded like they were made as far back as this that had a lot of imagination—a lot of Armstrong and Bix . . . rhythm section played on the same level all the time. I didn't like the clarinet —it sounded like an exercise book. I'd rate it one star.

—Jimmy Giuffre (re George Lewis record, *Fidgety Feet*).

Much has been written about the New Orleans revival. The praises of toothless and winded cornet players have been sung by zealous partisans of early jazz, for whom oldtime jazz is necessarily better than classical, and primitive jazz better than oldtime. Even if these musicians had been able to recapture the skill and enthusiasm of their youth, they would still have remained no more than useful but humble precursors whom many others had surpassed.

—André Hodeir[10]

In the early days, the great piano players were always on the East Coast; Jelly Roll Morton played piano like one of those high school teachers in Washington; as a matter of fact, high school teachers played better jazz. Among other things, his rhythm was unsteady.

—Duke Ellington[11]

Well, I suppose the fellows did the best they could with that

he was a genius.
—Bill Grauer & Orrin Keepnews[12]

piece . . . I really don't want to rate that at all. This is a lot of hodge-podge; I wouldn't even be particular about listening to that anymore.
—Coleman Hawkins (re Jelly Roll Morton record, *Grandpa's Spells*).

One important conclusion can be adduced from several of these quotations: the musicians, judging these early jazz artists on a purely subjective basis, their minds completely free of any prejudice that might have been instilled by an identification of the performers, were unanimous in their verdict. They did not find this music valuable or even listenable. In sharp contrast the critics have found genius in the creators of these performances and masterpieces in their recordings. The Grauer-Keepnews quote on Bunk Johnson is especially significant; it is tantamount to an admission that nostalgia and cultism were governing factors rather than the audience's ears.

Hodeir's views are most important, since he cannot be accused of a complete lack of sympathy for the New Orleans-style musicians (on the contrary, he has written of the emotion, sincerity and "admirable warmth" of Dodds and his ability to play slow blues solos); what strikes one most forcibly is his capacity not only for observing what is lacking in the work of these performers, but also for analyzing it in musical terms. One of the most absorbing and impressive passages of his book is an analysis of a blues solo by Mezz Mezzrow (a musician who, though not from New Orleans, is greatly admired by some adherents of this school) which he promptly contrasts with a Charlie Parker solo "to show the gulf that separates the musician of limited gifts from the improviser of genius." In contrast with this realistic attitude one finds, among the quotations in the left hand column, a consistently hyperbolic enthusiasm which the authors, unable to speak in musical terms as jazzmen, cannot explain or analyze.

A few critics have attempted to present the musicians' viewpoint; on the other hand, aside from the New Orleans jazzmen themselves, very few musicians have supported the critics' side in this disagreement. Thus the two columns of comments do not represent any selective or slanted quotation. As far as it is possible to generalize one may say that they reflect the predominant attitudes of these two groups. Nor can it be claimed that the musicians are receptive only to music from their own particular field, since all are well known for the breadth and perception of their jazz interests and are capable of understanding and appreciating every phase of the art.

It should be axiomatic that music can best be judged in terms of how it sounds to the human ear. This was the only standard used by the musicians in the above judgments; the factors of age and historical perspective were not allowed to distort their instinctive reactions. When jazz is truly timeless, as are the 30-year-old solos of Armstrong or the Ellington masterpieces of the 1930s, it calls for no special pleading, no extrinsic considerations on the part of either the critic or musician; it continues to stand on its musical merits.

True musical merit can hardly be said to govern the emotions of the listener who grows ecstatic over the tremulous exercises of a group of jazz primitives. His reaction, rather, is comparable with that of the observer who, overhearing a group of children going through the customary juvenile procedure on *Row, Row, Row Your Boat* or *Three Blind Mice*, gasps in disbelief and exclaims: "Listen! They're singing a canon!"

The argument so often used among jazz traditionalists that "you don't need to reject Bach and Beethoven just because you understand Stravinsky and Schoenberg" uses a palpably false analogy, implying as it does that jazz has come no further in its brief life than classic music has in two or three centuries.

In order to provide a true parallel for the early jazz of Buddy Bolden and Bunk Johnson it would be necessary to retrogress to the chaotic stage in which music found itself before the first true codification and the development of the Gregorian chant. One does not hear much sixth century music being played nowadays, for the valid reason that it would sound unlistenably crude and formless to the present-day ear, just as the early jazz sounds to the present-day jazz musician.

A truer analogy could be drawn between the pre-Gregorian

music, circa 590 A.D., and the pre-jazz that was played around the end of the last century.

A period from the 11th to the 14th century, bringing the earliest and most primitive forms of counterpoint and the first attempts to document music with a system of notation, would correspond with the jazz of the first World War and the early recording era of the 1920s, when jazzmen stepped from semi-illiteracy to the first stages of consciously coördinated development, of early attempts at jazz orchestrations. The birth of the modern music era and of the symphony, represented by Bach and Haydn, would be equivalent to the development of the swing bands, and of smaller groups that stepped from Dixieland polyphony to the symphonious planning of the Teddy Wilsons and John Kirbys—all events of the 1930s.

The late Beethoven works, with their attempts to depart from complete adherence to tonality, would provide an approximate parallel for the efforts of Gillespie, Parker and the other innovators of the early 1940s, who freed jazz from a harmonic and melodic straitjacket. The nineteenth century composers such as Brahms and Tchaikowsky would find their jazz equivalent in the degree of progress, though not in actual musical content, with the Kenton band, while the 1950s' experimental jazz would roughly parallel the innovations of Debussy. (Some of the work of the Modern Jazz Quartet, ironically, takes us back to Bach, not merely in analogy but in actuality.) So we find that a period extending from 590, when Gregory became Pope, until 1918, when Debussy died, produced developments in music for which a corresponding degree of development in jazz was accomplished between about 1905 and 1965—a ratio of more than 1300 years against 60, which means that jazz has been evolving more than 20 times as fast. Thus it could hardly be expected that a 1965 jazz musician would derive any more emotional pleasure from the products of the Bunk Johnsons and George Lewises than a contemporary concert composer might from the quality of early Christian music created before the establishment of bar lines, meter and scales.

As André Hodeir pointed out in the observation quoted at the head of this chapter, one must respect the pioneers for what they attempted to do; nevertheless contemporary annals as well as the future of recorded jazz must depend not merely on the limited efforts of the beginners, but on the positive achievements of those who succeeded.

CHAPTER 5

JAZZ AND RACE

In Hollywood, California, a motion picture company substituted two white musicians for the two Negroes in Charlie Barnet's band during the filming of a picture. The Negroes played for the soundtrack but did not appear in the visual portion of the movie.

In Gadsden, Alabama, the musicians' union refused to let three white members of Fletcher Henderson's orchestra play an engagement unless they blackened their faces with burnt cork. They complied with the union and played in blackface.

In Mount Pleasant, Tennessee, a white mob stormed a motion picture theater and halted the showing of an all-Negro film, *Cabin in the Sky*, featuring Duke Ellington and Lena Horne.

In Boonville, Missouri, Hazel Scott, the singer-pianist, wife of a Congressman, was told in a local restaurant that she would have to eat in the kitchen and was made to stand at the counter to wait for sandwiches to take out.

In New York City, a white taxi driver refused to take a Negro musician to Harlem. The musician asked to be driven to the nearest police station, where he complained to the officers on duty. He was arrested and beaten in his cell.

These incidents took place in America during the 1940s and '50s. Apparently unrelated to each other and seemingly having no direct bearing on musical history, they form a jagged mirror of the ugly, menacing atmosphere in which much of jazz saw its cultural birth. No study of jazz can be complete without a consideration of the socio-racial factors that determined the associations and the frustrations of the man who created it.

Today we pride ourselves on the absence of racial lines: show business in general and jazz in particular, we claim, acknowledges talent without regard to ethnic origins. Yet the freedom of which we so wishfully boast is often illusory. In the United States of America, the breeding ground of an art that more than any other has contributed to a diminution of anti-American emotions overseas, the domestic tension persisted as recently as the late 1950s, when the following took place:

A vote among members of Local 6 in San Francisco rejected a motion to amalgamate with the all-Negro Musicians' Local 669. San Francisco thus chose to remain one of about fifty locals in the American Federation of Musicians whose members were segregated by skin color. Even Chicago, Boston, Buffalo and New Haven kept their Negro musicians herded into small separate unions.

At a conference held in the offices of one of the two biggest television networks, the name of a distinguished Negro bandleader, who for years has nourished an ambition to launch his own series of programs, was submitted for consideration. After a brief discussion the suggestion was rejected on the grounds that the Southern affiliated stations would be displeased. A white bandleader of immeasurably less musical stature and achievement was given the assignment.

At another network, a nationally popular Negro singer and instrumentalist was rejected in the casting of a big TV musical show because the role might have involved implications of social mixing and even dancing with the show's blonde leading lady.

In Birmingham, Alabama, playing before a segregated audience, Nat Cole was assaulted onstage in mid-performance by a gang of hooligans representing a local White Citizens' Council.

In Knoxville, Tennessee, Louis Armstrong's mixed combo was playing a dance when a bomb thrown from a passing car landed outside the hall.

In Houston, Texas, where he had insisted on playing to a non-segregated audience with his "Jazz at the Philharmonic" concert unit, Norman Granz, along with several members of his troupe, including Ella Fitzgerald and Illinois Jacquet, was arrested on trumped-up charges.

The incidents continue even in the 1960s, some subtle, some violent. In its corroding cumulative effect on the mind of the victim, the first class is more vicious and noxious than the second, for one can legislate against violence, but there is no legislation to govern the poison in the human mind.

Jazz lives in this race-ridden world. There is no musician of stature, white or Negro, who is not touched directly or indirectly by episodes such as these: none who at some point in his life has not faced the problem of having been unable to offer or to accept employment, of having seen employment denied to him or to a personal friend or musical idol for racial reasons. Jazz, on whose lofty peak we fly the flag of democracy like a slightly soiled shirt, fights the noble fight and chips the granite of prejudice, but too often it is fight beyond the endurance of men who must live at peace with themselves and their families and their tax-collectors. Until the story of racial mixing in jazz is more fully told and more widely understood, there will continue to be misapprehensions concerning the physical and psychological characteristics of the jazzman.

Most of us no longer speak of "white jazz" and "Negro jazz." The myth of race, a curious distortion of Hitler's theories, almost disappeared in jazz until the stirring of a chauvinistic theory that Negroes are the only real "blues people" caused an alarming new rift. It remains a scientific fact that there are no jazz genes. Despite southern white claims, the Negro is *not* "born singing and dancing" with a natural gift in which education plays no part.

Long before he was able to think of music in terms of a professional livelihood, the Negro turned to music as a solace and relief from the tyranny of slavery, an outlet in which he was more likely to be encouraged than punished. Decades later, while his chances of becoming a lawyer, banker, successful businessman, Army officer, architect, senator, judge, were limited to an incalculable degree by the handicap of his color, music was one area in which he was comparatively free to pursue the chance of a livelihood. Since music in many cases had been a part of the constricted life of his parents, many of them slaves

or recently freed, and since this gave him advantages of environment and heredity, the Negro became a musician.

Almost immediately, through his music, he was able to establish with some of the more liberal-minded whites a rapport never
before possible. Though Jim Crow and music have been partners
for decades in a shotgun wedding, with Uncle Sam in charge
of the arsenal, the alliance has been an uneasy one from the
start. As early as 1880 J. B. T. Marsh, in *The Story of the Jubilee
Singers,* wrote that "People who would not sit in the same church
pew with a Negro, under the magic of their song, were able to
get new light on questions of social equality." Nevertheless, even
during the Reconstruction years, the singers had to submit to an
endless round of dining room and hotel accommodation refusals;
it was only during their triumphal tours abroad that they were
allowed to feel like completely free and equal human beings.

While there is no agreement among theoreticians concerning
the birthdate of ragtime, of the blues or even of the first music
known as jazz, it is commonly accepted that white performers,
from the beginning, were playing similar though not identical
music. Though the white and Negro musicians heard each other,
there were few opportunities to play together. In a few rare
instances light skinned Negroes or Creoles "passed" into white
bands. Early examples were Achille Baquet, the clarinetist who
once worked in a jazz band led by Jimmy Durante, and trombonist Dave Perkins, who along with Baquet was a member of
Jack Laine's Ragtime Band in the early years of this century.

Generally, though, in the first two decades of ragtime, Negroes
and whites lived apart, worked and played apart, thought apart,
and thus grew culturally apart. That two separated bloodstreams
were flowing in the veins of jazz can be confirmed by a comparison of the records of Duke Ellington or Louis Armstrong
with those of Ben Pollack and Red Nichols. A Jim Crow society
had produced Jim Crowed music, and it was to take a full generation for the blood lines to reunite.

The appearance of a Negro musician with a white band, even
in the seclusion of a recording studio, was a rarity until as late
as 1933, a commonplace among small jazz combos by 1937, still
an exception among large studio orchestras through the 1940s.

The participation of a white musician in a Negro record date was rarer. So unusual were events of this kind at one time that the sessions were talked about for years among record collectors as examples of an extraordinary phenomenon, "a mixed band" •

White musicians worked on their well-padded side of the fence, securing the most lucrative dance hall and radio work, while Negroes for the most part were confined to the "race" record lists aimed at a Jim Crow market, and found that the majority of jobs most valuable to them in terms of money and prestige were hopelessly out of reach.

Benny Goodman's hiring of Teddy Wilson in 1935 was an historic precedent, the magnitude of which can hardly be appreciated today in correct perspective. At that time the appearance in public of a Negro musician with a white band was thought so radical that Wilson was allowed only to appear as an "act," a special adjunct rather than a regular member of the organization; the same treatment was accorded Lionel Hampton when the Goodman Trio became a quartet the next year, though later Hampton played drums in the regular orchestra for brief periods.

Integration crawled along for almost a decade after Goodman had broken the checkerboard ice. Every incident was a curiosity: Billie Holiday's eight months with the Artie Shaw band in 1938;

° For one of his Chocolate Dandies dates in 1928, Don Redman assembled an almost-all-white band including the Dorsey Brothers. In 1929, Louis Armstrong made his memorable *Knockin' A Jug* with Teagarden, Joe Sullivan and Eddie Lang; Fats Waller used Condon and Teagarden on one or two dates; Lang and Hoagy Carmichael joined with Lonnie Johnson, King Oliver and Clarence Williams for a unique pair of sides released on Okeh under the pseudonym "Blind Willie Dunn's Gin Bottle Four."

Scarcely less remarkable and remarked about were the mixed dates under white leaders: a single tune on a Hoagy Carmichael date in 1930 for which Bix Beiderbecke and Bubber Miley sat side by side; several Eddie Condon sessions, two under the Mound City Blue Blowers name, using Coleman Hawkins and bassist Al Morgan, in 1929 and 1931; two under Condon's own name, using Leonard Davis, Happy Caldwell and George Stafford (1929), Alex Hill and Sid Catlett (1933). Jack Teagarden and Ted Lewis hired Fats Waller for dates in 1931 and 1932. It is also claimed, though not firmly established, that Jelly Roll Morton played on a New Orleans Rhythm Kings session in 1923.

Of the thousands of jazz sides waxed between 1917, when jazz recording began, and 1932, the above are literally the only interracial examples of any significance.

Fletcher Henderson, Charlie Christian, Cootie Williams with Goodman in 1939-40; Joe Sullivan's mixed sextet at Café Society in Greenwich Village in late 1939; June Richmond's alliance with the Jimmy Dorsey band; Flip Phillips' appearance as clarinetist with Frankie Newton at Kelly's Stable in 1940; then, in 1941, the four months spent by Lena Horne as Charlie Barnet's vocalist, Hot Lips Page's several months on trumpet with Artie Shaw, and the beginning of Roy Eldridge's long association with Gene Krupa's big band.

It took considerably more courage for a Negro bandleader to hire a white sideman, and for a white musician thus to expose himself to racial problems in reverse. Partly as a result of the wartime shortage of musicians, the walls crumbled early in the 1940s, in the West Coast band of Benny Carter, and in the Eastern band of Lucky Millinder. Carter's sidemen as early as 1943-4 included Joe Albany, Hal Schaefer and, briefly, Buddy Rich. Among Millinder's first white sidemen were Freddie Zito, Leon Merrian and Roy Harte.

"I toured all over with this band—even in the deep South," Millinder recalls. "At one point I had nine white and eight colored musicians. Of course, everybody in the band understood that we were out to make money, not trying to make history. When the white musicians would reach a town, they would avoid walking around with their instruments, in case the question came up whose band they were with, which could have led to trouble.

"Usually the evening was half over before anybody noticed anything, and then it was too late for them to do much about it. In some towns I knew the Chief of Police, which helped. Often the musicians would have to pass for Puerto Ricans. I remember one night, when I had a drummer who looked unmistakably Jewish, the cop kept asking questions while the band was playing. After the set he walked up and looked the drummer straight in the eye for quite a while. Then he said, 'Yeh, he's a nigger all right,' and walked away satisfied. We never had a major incident, though we came pretty close a couple of times."

In many of the Southern towns where the Millinder band played, interracial appearances were legally proscribed.

The record of the principal jazz orchestra leaders in integrating their personnel has varied greatly from band to band. Benny Goodman has continued to mix his orchestras and combos freely; before his 1962 U.S.S.R. tour his personnel is said to have been deliberately integrated for psychological reasons.

Tommy Dorsey, who hired Sy Oliver as staff arranger in 1939 and occasionally presented him as vocalist, had Charlie Shavers as a band member off and on from 1945 until Dorsey's death in 1956; Paul Gonsalves played with the band briefly in 1953.

Charlie Barnet used Negro sidemen consistently from 1941, when he hired Dizzy Gillespie for a few weeks; during the 1940s he was responsible even more often than Goodman for the presentation of an integrated ensemble.

Les Brown and Bob Crosby have generally used all-white personnels. Woody Herman at one juncture showed signs of mixing his band indiscriminately (in 1949-50 he had Gene Ammons, Ernie Royal, Shadow Wilson, Milt Jackson, Oscar Petti-ford) but abandoned the practice as a result of some discouraging experiences.

Count Basie has used white sidemen from time to time: Georgie Auld, Serge Chaloff and trumpeter Al Porcino were with him for short periods in 1950, Buddy De Franco was a member of Basie's septet for a year (1950-1); Johnny Mandel, Don Rader, Sal Nistico and Sam Noto are also Basie alumni.

Duke Ellington hired the non-Negro Juan Tizol, a Puerto Rican, in 1929, but by the queer standards of American racism his was a borderline case. The first affirmative break was the use of Louis Bellson on drums, in 1951-3, followed by another white drummer, Dave Black, in 1953-5. During these periods Ellington, who had often described his contribution to jazz as representative of "Negro music" but who by now was more concerned with its value simply as music, experimented with several other white sidemen. Notable among them was Tony Scott, who quit the band after a month, despite Ellington's protests, in 1953, and whom Duke has since described wistfully as "the only musician who was ever forced out of my band by race prejudice." Scott admitted that the hostile attitude of one or two band members was not conducive to his staying.

Probably the most genuinely interracial of all, simply because no racial thinking of any kind was involved, was the big band assembled by John Gillespie early in 1956. Originally there were four white musicians; at times since then there have been as many as seven, at other times none, but at no point has there been any question of a quota system.

Gillespie's racial record is a long and honorable one; as far back as 1942 he had Stan Levey working with him in Philadelphia, and throughout the natal years of bop white musicians intermittently formed a part of his personnel.

It was in the field of small combos such as Gillespie led during that period that the racial lines began to crumble. The clubs of West 52nd Street, then the jazz mecca of the world, opened their doors belatedly to Negro customers and their bandstands to mixed combos.* While talent agencies screamed that they could not book a mixed group, while night club owners whined that their patrons would object, the forces on either side of these barriers—the public and the musicians—saw eye to eye. Little by little the mixed combo, once an exception, became the rule. Today most of the remaining all-white and all-Negro combos retain their monochromatic format more through chance, laissez-faire or social relationships among the members than through any active desire to protect racial solidarity. Some Negro leaders understandably hire Negro sidemen because, realizing that the opportunities for the white musician still are much broader, they feel that he may need the job less than a Negro musician of equal skill. Some white leaders hire only white sidemen simply because they live in the same neighborhood or attend the same parties or play golf together. But as the social obstacles disintegrate, the professional and economic barriers slowly fade away.

A survey of combos during the past decade shows that Louis Armstrong has invariably had one or two white musicians in his sextet, and that all the others of any consequence have at one period mixed their personnels: the Shearing Quintet, the Brubeck Quartet, the groups of Eddie Condon, Jimmy McPartland,

---

* Cafe Society, the Greenwich Village night club, had paved the way, from 1938, by encouraging integration both in its clientèle and its entertainment.

Charlie Ventura, Nat Cole, Lennie Tristano, Miles Davis, Stan Getz, Gerry Mulligan, Chico Hamilton, Charlie Parker, Buddy De Franco, Red Norvo, Terry Gibbs. There was a precedent-setting example of dual interracial leadership when Jay Jay Johnson and Kai Winding formed their quintet in 1954.

The stubbornest barrier of all, involving implicit defiance of the mongrelization tabu against which Southern politicians had inveighed in the race for white votes, fell in 1952. Helen Merrill, unmistakably blonde, sang for three months with Earl Hines' Sextet (her white saxophonist husband also was a member of the combo). The following year Lionel Hampton, who has made free use of white musicians, took on Janet Thurlow, an inconspicuous brunette who doubtless was assumed by Southern audiences not to be white; for it is inconceivable to the white cracker mentality that a red-blooded, white, true-blue American girl singer would of her own volition join a Negro band.

The result of the freer association of white and Negro artists on a professional level (and of the greater social mixing occasioned by such factors as the gradual opening up of hotels to Negro patrons in many cities) was, predictably, a breaking down of stylistic lines. Less and less, with the passing of the postwar years, could "white jazz" and "Negro jazz" be said to exist. Roy Eldridge, returning from a long sojourn in Europe and imbued with some of the cultural confusion still manifest in critical circles in France, made a bet with the author that he would be able, in a blindfold test, to distinguish white musicians from Negroes. At the end of the test he admitted that he had been wrong; he had failed even to achieve the 50% ratio of correct guesses to which the law of averages entitled him.

Eldridge at that time, embittered by his experiences with white bands, vowed never again to play in one; the traumatic, nerve-wracking events that are part of a Negro's life in a predominantly white orchestra were described in an interview with this writer for *Down Beat:*

"We arrive in one town (with Krupa) and the rest of the band checks in. I can't get into their hotel, so I keep my bags and start riding around looking for another place where someone's supposed to have made a reservation for me. I have a heavy load

of at least a dozen pieces of luggage . . . when the clerk sees
that I'm the Mr. Eldridge the reservation was made for, he
suddenly discovers the last available room has been taken. I lug
all that luggage back into the street and start looking around
again.

"By the time that kind of thing has happened night after night,
it begins to wear on my mind; I can't think right, can't play
right. At the Palladium in Hollywood I had to watch out who
I could or couldn't sit at the tables with. If they were movie
stars who wanted me to come over, that was all right; if they
were just the jitterbugs, no dice. And all the time the bouncer
with his eye on me, just waiting for a chance . . . on top of
that, I had to live way out in Los Angeles while the rest of the
guys stayed in Hollywood. It was a lonely life . . . one night
the tension got so bad I flipped. I could feel it right up to my
neck while I was playing *Rockin' Chair;* I started trembling, ran
off the stand, and threw up. They carried me to the doctor's. I
had a 105 fever; my nerves were shot. . . ."

At Norfolk, Virginia, barred from the washroom the other
musicians were using, Roy was handed a bucket of water. Riding
on the Norfolk ferry with some musicians on the top deck he
was told: "We don't allow no niggers up here." When a complaint about this remark was made to the captain, he commented:
"Well, if you can stand him, it's all right with me."

"Just as if I had leprosy," said Eldridge.

In Youngstown, Ohio there was no room in the hotels, no service in the restaurant; even Krupa's offer to let him use one of the
twin beds in his own room could not console him. Eldridge
abruptly left town; it was a week before he could be talked into
rejoining the band.

In 1944, working with Artie Shaw, Eldridge ran into the same
problems. No food, even in a small Mexican restaurant in Del
Mar, California, where the white musicians walked out with him
in sympathy. No admission to the local dance hall even though
his name was up in lights outside as a featured attraction with
Shaw.

"When I finally did get in, I played that first set, trying to
keep from crying. By the time I got through the set, the tears

were rolling down my cheeks. . . . I went up to a dressing room and stood in a corner crying and saying to myself why the hell did I come out here again when I knew what would happen?

"Man, when you're on the stage you're great, but as soon as you come off, you're nothing. It's not worth the glory, not worth the money, not worth anything."

Despite the willingness of Eldridge to admit the fusion of white and Negro styles, there remains among certain critics and fans a persistent legend that jazz still must be the subject of a dichotomy in every analytical discussion. Continental jazz writers, even those who in other respects are thoroughly reliable and well informed, cling to the racial labeling of musicians. Ironically, the belief of the condescending white southerner that the Negro has instinctive musical gifts (which in the southerner's mind places him in a class with the well-trained poodle) is shared by many foreign jazz audiences; this has resulted in an attitude diagnosed, in an acute monograph by Barry Ulanov, as "Crow Jim." According to this theory jazz, as the property of the Negro, can only be played by whites to the extent that they have assimilated the "Negro idiom." As recently as 1953 it was impossible for any white American musician (even Benny Goodman) to win a French jazz poll. The height of impudence was reached when one French critic, in a book of biographies, branded as "of the white race" those few white musicians who were considered worthy of inclusion, while the Negro musicians were unidentified by race—a reversal of an equally obnoxious racial labeling that still obtains in some parts of the United States when crime stories involving Negroes are reported. (In the United States edition of the book these racial labels were removed.)

The automatic assumption of the Negro's supremacy may, indeed, smack of poetic justice; it can easily be understood why many jazzmen, visiting France and other countries where this attitude is prevalent, have decided to take advantage of it by making their homes there. But to the more mature musician, who would rather be accepted as a man than lionized as a Negro, it is uncomfortable to observe some of the manifestations of Crow Jim.

Joachim-Ernst Berendt, a brilliant and well-informed writer, is Germany's leading jazz critic. His survey *Das Jazzbuch* is illustrated by a series of genealogical tables, one to each instrument, in which are shown the relationships of various styles. In almost every case two main lines are traced, one labeled "*schwarz*," the other "*weiss*." The result is a tangled skein of non-sequiturs in which, to take one example at random, Harry James stems directly from Bix Beiderbecke, while Rex Stewart forms a link between Bubber Miley and Buck Clayton. Common sense, memory and the human ear recall that James' real influences were Armstrong and Spanier, and that Rex at one time copied Beiderbecke choruses note for note.

Even André Hodeir has a blind spot on the race question. To him there is a greater natural relaxation among Negroes which manifests itself not only in their jazz performances but in the events at the Olympic Games. This pseudo-scientific gobbledygook led M. Hodeir to some curious mathematical equations in an examination of two Miles Davis recording sessions on Capitol. On one, he observed, there were seven white and two Negro musicians; on the other the proportions were almost reversed. Ergo, the second swings more. One wonders whether M. Hodeir would have picked out the four tunes on the second session as swinging more had he had no prior information concerning the racial make-up of each group.

In England the same attitude is prevalent. An otherwise excellent survey of modern jazz, written by Alun Morgan and Raymond Horricks, constantly refers to musicians b / their color, employing such phrases as "meanwhile, among the white musicians . . ." or "the Negro trombonists, on the other hand . . ." One wonders again how this attitude would have held up under blindfold conditions.

The final proof of the absurdity of this race-conscious view of jazz lies in its arbitrary method of segregating the musicians. By what scientific standards, for instance, do Hodeir, Berendt, Morgan and Horricks assign Willie Smith to the Negro side of the fence when the saxophonist clearly, by any but the most Hitlerian of standards, is white? In which branch of their split family tree do they place an equally white trumpeter named Carl

"Bama" Warwick, or the noted bandleader of the 1930s, Willie Bryant, or Ernie Royal, who is lighter and less a Negro than many musicians of Latin origin whom these critics consider white? And what was their attitude when Barney Bigard applied for (and was refused) a transfer from the Negro to the white local in Los Angeles before the two unions were amalgamated? Is Miles Davis, a very dark-skinned Negro, more authentically a jazzman than was John Kirby, who may have had three white grandparents?

The critics are in an untenable position, just as are the white supremacists who enact different laws in each state determining what percentage of "Negro blood" (there is, of course no such thing) determines a citizen's racial status. They would do well to examine a colloquy between John "Dizzy" Gillespie and Mike Wallace on the latter's television program in April, 1957. Wallace asked: "I would like your opinion of the Negro's success in jazz. Is it because, as some people say, the Negro has more music, more rhythm, more beat in him than the white people?"

Gillespie's reply was "I don't think God would give any one race of people something that the other one couldn't get if they had the facilities . . . You probably could take a white kid and subject him to the same things that one of us was subjected to and he'd probably stomp his foot just like we do. *It's not a matter of race, but environment.*"

Counterposed against the attitude of the "Crow Jim" critics is the position taken by Stan Kenton, who on reading the results of the 1956 *Down Beat* critics' poll sent the magazine a telegram expressing his "complete and utter disgust" with the results and sarcastically deducing that there was now a "new minority group, white jazz musicians." Kenton's telegram brought a flood of protesting mail; his chauvinistically pro-white attitude seemed as indefensible as that of the Crow Jim critics. There is no proof that Kenton was motivated by actively anti-Negro feelings, however; his band had included Negro musicians occasionally. Nothing was proved on either side except that the color question remains inflammatory.

In the late 1950s and early 1960s, when race relations and integration in jazz seemed to have reached a high point, the situation took a sharp turn for the worse.

Two interrelated factors were involved. The first was the reverse racial prejudice long prevalent among French and other European critics and fans, which began to find its way into American circles. The second was the rising tide of the Negro revolution. Self-awareness and pride in their heritage induced in some Negro musicians a bitterness at the sight of the white tail wagging the black dog in jazz. They resented having played so small a role in managing a music they had helped to create, and sharing so meagerly in the credit and profits. Along with this attitude came the concept of the Negro as "soul brother," of the funkier forms of modern jazz as soul music, and such statements as the following, made by a noted jazzman to a Swedish journalist in 1962:

"The Negro has a long inherited tradition in jazz. It's his music. White people have no right to play it. It's a colored-folk music. White society has its own tradition like the polka. This is the kind of music they should concentrate on and try to bring up to date. Although white musicians are aware of jazz they don't know the reason behind it. Everyone outside America should in my opinion play his own music."

The theory that claimed jazz as the Negro's own music, and as a reflection of American racial history, was rarely preached or practiced until the late 1950s. (Duke Ellington's *Black, Brown and Beige,* described as "a tone parallel to the history of the American Negro" and first presented at Carnegie Hall in 1943, was a remarkably effective early example of jazz as social program music.)

With the emergence of the new African nations, and with mounting domestic tension, jazzmen produced from about 1959 a growing library of suites, symphonies, concerti and tone-poems dedicated either to their African ancestors, their present-day African cousins or their embattled brothers at home.

Black pride of origin sometimes spilled over into black nationalism, with fascistic overtones. Though it was no secret that black nationalist leaders and the American Nazi Party had a relationship of mutual respect, that both had expressed similarly antagonistic views on the Jews, and that they had shared a lecture platform with Fuehrer George Lincoln Rockwell at a rally in Chicago, some jazz musicians nevertheless expressed sympathy for the nationalists and chose to ignore these aspects of their activities. One celebrated jazz artist who has applauded speeches by the black separatists has had a close and successful artistic and social relationship with several Jewish musicians.

It would seem to be an inescapable fact that some of the most valuable jazz of recent years has been produced by interracial teams: Miles Davis-Gil Evans, John Lewis-Gunther Schuller, Dizzy Gillespie-Lalo Schifrin, Sonny Rollins-Jim Hall. If black nationalism nevertheless was common in some jazz circles by 1960, the path to this gloomy doorway clearly had been paved by the myopia and hypocrisy of America's white power structure. Crow Jim was the bastard child of Jim Crow.

Although even some of the most militant Negro musicians have employed whites, there are some Negroes who have exercised strong pressure, in recent years, against integration in jazz.

A Negro pianist, Jaki Byard, playing in the predominantly white orchestra of Maynard Ferguson, underwent a typical experience when Negro fans asked him: "Why do you play in this band and help to make these white cats sound good?"

Don Ellis, the white trumpeter who was a colleague and close friend of Byard in the Ferguson band, later led his own combo and reported: "It is almost impossible for a new white leader to make it in jazz today, and things are going to get worse before they get better. A booking agent told me recently the only possible way for me to make it was to use an integrated group. Now I believe in this as a matter of principle, but the other day my bass player, the only colored member of the group, dropped out on me at the last minute with no warning, just before we were to open a New York club. He left to play with an all colored group—perhaps the pressure was too much for him."

Ellis added that his experience was in ironic contrast with the days when it took courage for a white leader even to assume the economic and social risk of hiring a Negro.

Cannonball Adderley, having decided that Victor Feldman was the ideal pianist for his combo, felt obliged to submit his other sidemen to a "blindfold test." Not until they had accepted Feldman on unidentified recordings were they informed that he was white. Had they known in advance, the instinctive prejudice of Crow Jim might have forced Adderley to hire a Negro in his place.

In 1961 Ralph Gleason wrote in the *San Francisco Chronicle* that "racial lines are now drawn in many instances much more strongly than ever before in jazz. Jazz clubs are reluctant to hire any white groups except the top few (Shearing, Previn, Brubeck), because they will not draw the jazz fans. The latter come out in force these days only for the Negro groups."

Fortunately, many jazzmen of both races still reject the notion that jazz is a racially exclusive art. They agree that it is as wrong to exclude whites from jazz as to forbid Negroes to play Bach or Stravinsky—or, for that matter, the polka. They also point out that jazz is based almost entirely on the European scale system, and on European harmony. Billy Taylor, the pianist, observed: "Crow Jim is a state of affairs that has to be remedied. Jazz can never again be music by Negroes strictly for Negroes any more than the Negroes themselves can return to the attitudes and emotional responses that prevailed when this was true."

Partly because of the hostility among some of the angrier Negro jazzmen and because of the lines that have been drawn, consciously or subconsciously, to limit integration among leading combos, today's jazzmen are more often distinguishable by race than those of Roy Eldridge's blindfold test.

The hard bop groups such as Art Blakey's Jazz Messengers, and the hard-blowing tenor men of the John Coltrane school, are almost always identifiable as colored, while the saxophonists influenced by Stan Getz and Zoot Sims are more likely to be white (but for such exceptions as Buddy Collette and Eddie Harris). On the other hand, integration both of personnel and of musical cultures can invariably be found in the orchestras of such composers as John Lewis (Orchestra U.S.A.), Quincy Jones, Gary McFarland, Oliver Nelson, Gil Evans and Gerald Wilson, all of whom represent a scholarly approach to jazz that incorporates many European techniques.

Bossa nova, the popular music imported from Rio with American jazz additions in 1962, has been largely a product of white musicians, though it has involved one outstanding Negro artist, the Brazilian guitarist Bola Sete.

Bola Sete offers a reminder of another important rule to which he is an exception: most Negro jazzmen in other countries, notably in Britain, are not and never have been any more adept than their white colleagues at developing the feeling for the jazz beat that seems to be second nature to so many Americans. Every style of jazz has evolved as a result of environmental influences.

The rapid changes in the social climate and their effect on the world of music cannot prevent jazz from remaining basically an interracial art form. If one had to choose between (a) losing the force of character and basic identity of jazz, because of racial mixing, and (b) maintaining its dual nature as a product of two segregated societies, it would be better for society (and for the jazzman) if jazz were to perish; but happily this choice seems less and less likely to present itself.

Despite pressures from the disenchanted and the dissidents, who are sure only of what they are against, most jazzmen today are mainly concerned with what they are for. They are for the right to work, play and live together on equal terms. Their "third stream" and *cosa nova* ("new thing") experiments show that they favor comparable amalgamations of musical styles and cultural influences.

White and Negro jazzmen in the past have played a laudable part in breaking racial barriers. Those of today and tomorrow, no matter what the current skirmishes seem to indicate, will certainly carry forward the initiatives of their predecessors.

CHAPTER 6

THE PIANO

Like the blind student who develops an uncannily keen sense of hearing, the piano throughout jazz history has compensated for its failures and absences in certain areas by showing amazing strength in others. Because of its immobility, it was absent from the early ragtime crews that played in street parades and rode on advertising wagons; but because a house is not a home without a piano, it was the first instrument available, the first studied and mastered for jazz, in thousands of houses (many of which were also not homes). New Orleans' Storyville bagnios, the honky tonks of Sedalia and Washington and Brooklyn, relied on their "professor" to keep up a rolling, tumultuous background of rags, stomps and blues while the customers were entertained —upstairs or down.

Again, while the piano is incapable of the glissandi, "smears" and tonal distortions that lent jazz its original vocal and local color, it compensates by providing the soloist with the outlet for triply rich expression in the fields of melody, rhythm and harmony, while all the horns, capable of but one note at a time, are limited to the first two of these.

Curiously, the piano's history has been retrogressive in this respect, for during the past twenty years there has been a tendency to treat the keyboard as if it were a horn; many soloists have played a single-note horizontal line with the right hand and have limited the left hand almost entirely to occasional rhythmic punctuations. A counterrevolutionary movement, though, has been observed in the work of Erroll Garner and others, who seem conscious of the fact that God and the keyboard have conspired to endow the pianist with unique facilities. Equipped to play as many as ten notes at once, he can enact the part of a lone or auxiliary bass player, through the normal function of the left hand, as well as those of several horn players through the work of the right.

It is impossible to separate cause and effect in examining the original function of the piano. Perhaps it was because the ragtime artists struck single notes or octaves with the first and third beats of the measure, and filled in with chords on the second and fourth, that the fuller sound of these chords gave the music a syncopated quality, as if the weaker second and fourth beats, because of their richer harmonic content, were being deliberately accented. Or perhaps this apparently ragged rhythmic imbalance (leading to the spontaneous development of the term "ragtime") was an effect deliberately sought as a result of some quality already inherent in the music as played on guitars, cornets and trombones.

Whatever the reason, ragtime piano provides us, through the medium of early piano rolls transferred to LP discs, with a glimpse of syncopation in its most primitive stage of development. As far as one can generalize about a phase that produced thousands of pieces of written music, it may be said that the typical ragtime composition (ragtime was more composed than improvised) involved, in the right hand, alternations of single notes, simple chords and syncopations. Though the left hand maintained the "ump-cha, ump-cha" feeling of what was in effect a four-four time, the right hand used eighth notes extensively. The syncopation in the left hand might divide the four beats into two dotted quarters followed by a quarter, for variety, and in the right hand would often use such simple devices as the hesitation, omitting half the first beat in favor of an accent on the second (Ex. 1):

There were scores of capable exponents of the piano rag, all of whom are dealt with comprehensively by Rudi Blesh and Harriet Janis in *They All Played Ragtime.* The most important were Scott Joplin, composer of the first famous ragtime piece, *Maple Leaf Rag;* James Scott, Joseph Lamb, Eubie Blake, Tom Turpin, Jelly Roll Morton, Luckey Roberts and Tony Jackson. (Many others who played ragtime overlapped into other pianistic phases and will be discussed later.) White ragtimers came into the picture early, Blesh and Janis point out: one of the first was S. Brunson Campbell, a friend and admirer of Joplin and other leading Negro ragtimers. Campbell started to play and compose professionally about 1898, a year before printed ragtime got underway effectively with the publication of Joplin's *Original Rags* and *Maple Leaf Rag.*

Though the most widely publicized pianists are the few who gravitated toward St. Louis and Sedalia, Missouri, there is ample evidence that keyboards everywhere in America were resounding to ragtime during the same period. Luckey Roberts, the Philadelphia born ragtime pioneer, recalls that there were experts in the East who developed their own styles quite independently.

Roberts also pays tribute to Ike Randolph, the march king—"he played marches in syncopation"—while Willie "The Lion" Smith, who came up a decade after Roberts, asserts that Kid Griffin and Sam Gordon, both from Trenton, New Jersey, were among the finest technicians in early ragtime.

Since there was no phonograph recording and only limited access to ragtime on player piano rolls, most of the interchange of ideas in the tidal wave of ragtime mania (ca. 1897-1912) took place when these musicians went on the road, and through the vast quantity of sheet-music that brought ragtime, amateur or professional, to every parlor during those heavily syncopated years.

The next piano style to develop after ragtime, which became obsolescent during and after the first World War, was "stride piano," so called because it made even more emphatic use of the after-beat left hand effects shown in Ex. 1. During the 1920s there were developments along these lines that amalgamated the elements of ragtime with the general jazz style heard at that time on other instruments.

Close to the core of ragtime but certainly linked to a later era as the father of the stride pianists was James P. Johnson (best known in the pop-music field as composer of the song *Charleston*), some of whose player piano rolls were once transferred to LPs on Riverside. As Orrin Keepnews observed, Johnson "very obviously began in the ragtime tradition; to this he added a substantial feeling for the blues, a touch of the brittle gaudiness of Broadway, a great deal of the rollicking spirit of the crowd that gathered around the party piano. . . . His vigorously striding, joyous style set the pace at the all-night doings that took place as often as possible in just about every Harlem apartment that owned a battered upright . . ."

Johnson, who had been playing professionally for a decade before World War I, considered Luckey Roberts his major influence. In addition to the piano rolls, he was heard during the 1920s on many records, on tours with Negro revues, and in early sound movie shorts with Bessie Smith and others. During those years New York was firmly established as the mecca of jazz piano, the city in which Willie "The Lion" Smith, one of the subtlest of the stride artists, would coax his gentle, wolf-in-sheep's clothing variations on lacy, spring-airy themes from Harlem keyboards; when Duke Ellington, at the vortex of this piano school, idolizing the Lion, would sit down and try to follow him at the Capitol Club, 140th and Lenox, and when Fats Waller, who brought James P.'s ecstasy to a sharper edge and ultimately to a far wider audience, would follow Johnson around and study the superb symmetry and rounded beat that made every chorus swing.

Stride piano was the left-hand technique that obtained in jazz all through the '20s and most of the '30s. Though men like Johnson and Waller were directly associated with it, there were others whom it served as an occasional or frequent prop in a more variegated style, among them Cliff Jackson, a blues expert still prominent in the New York clubs of the late 1950s; Count Basie, a Waller disciple who later leaned toward a simpler, single note style that depended for much of its success on the

rare art of ellipsis; and Art Tatum, whose chronological place
in this sequence belongs a little farther along.

Though the great pianists of jazz are legion, the number of
those who were pace-setters, milestone-makers, is relatively
small. After the ragtime archetypes and the stride pioneers, the
next giant, emphatic both in his influence and in the vigorous,
flamboyantly rhythmic nature of his approach, was Earl "Fatha"
Hines. Famous first for the records he made with Louis Armstrong
and Jimmie Noone in 1928 and heard in his epochal first solo
session during that year, he made dynamic use of octaves in the
right hand, often with a tremolo for dramatic sustaining effect,
and was capable ambidextrously of tying himself into the most
baffling of rhythmic knots and of successfully extricating himself
every time. Though "the Houdini of jazz piano" might have been
a more fitting name, he was often called "the trumpet style
pianist," because the octaves on single note lines in the right hand,
in contrast with the emphasis on chords that had predominated
among the ragtimers and early stride pianists, lent the solos a
bright and brassy quality that brought to mind the impact of a
horn. Actually Hines was much more than a pianist imitating
a trumpeter, as the slogan falsely implied. He was essentially
pianistic in his approach, in the sense that the left hand, far
from playing a subsidiary role, was used more obliquely, with
more diligence, taste and technique than had ever been heard
in jazz piano before.

Hines' work in the areas of light and shade, of perspective,
form and impact, and the influence left in his wake, can find
its analogue in the paintings of Giotto, whose full impact was
felt long after his own day. Hines in 1965 was still active,
but less prominent and less directly influential on the young
pianist; it is in the Hines-motivated work of innumerable other
pianists that we can see how long his contribution is bound to
last. Nat Cole and Stan Kenton showed distinctly the image
of Hines in their piano work; Tatum, Basie, Jess Stacy, Joe
Sullivan were as much in his debt as in Waller's. The Hines
influence is directly discernible today in the occasional jazz
appearances of Mel Powell, though Powell clearly spent many
early listening years at the feet of another pace-setter, the next

in line after Hines. This was Teddy Wilson, who in 1933, having indulged in a brief Hines-style fling of his own, startled the jazz piano world, when John Hammond and Benny Carter brought him to New York, by developing something still fresher and, in terms of the standards of that time, quite radical.

Wilson kept the beat going more evenly, indulged in few dynamic fireworks, achieving a neat, quiet symmetry mostly through the use of single-note lines in the right hand. A more deliberately horizontal style than Hines', it was the first step toward the bop era's ultimate rejection of the use of the left hand for steady rhythm and concentration on the right for horn-like improvisation. Curiously, Teddy Wilson could more aptly have been called the trumpet-style pianist than Hines.

The Wilson approach was belittled by some experts as lacking fire and concentrating too much on academic precision, yet his slow-tempo performances in particular evidenced a great warmth and an approach that compensated in dignified, swinging simplicity for what it lacked in Hines' brilliant and sometimes flashy variety.

The Wilson influence was heard in scores of piano works of the late 1930s. Billy Kyle contrived to develop a personal quality directly out of the Wilson style, perhaps by restoring a little of the Hines sense of dyamics. Mary Lou Williams, a respected figure throughout the 1930s as the pianist-arranger with Andy Kirk's band, successfully blended Waller, Hines and Wilson touches and established herself as the first feminine jazz pianist of lasting importance.

Many other pianists came up in the Wilson era. A little of Teddy had rubbed off on all; a suggestion of Waller and Hines was reflected in many. There were Joe Bushkin, a prominent combo and big band sideman in 1935-40; Eddie Heywood Jr., who reached his jazz peak with the Benny Carter band of 1939-40 and with his own jazz sextet three years later; Herman Chittison, a largely unappreciated major talent whose trio decorated the New York night clubs of the 1940s and who, like Kyle, reflected himself rather than Wilson; Kenny Kersey, who followed Mary Lou into the Kirk band and revealed a harmonically progressive mind, using chord patterns no 1940 jazzman had a

right to know; Marlowe Morris (today a Hammond organist);
Sir Charles Thompson (with the first big Hampton band in
1940) and the Napoleon brothers, Marty and Teddy, both
engaged in their first name-band forays in the early '40s.

Practically simultaneous with the discovery and development
of the Wilson school was the emergence of boogie-woogie, a
piano form that enjoyed a forest-fire burst of exposure during
a five-year stretch (1936-41) before leveling off into comparative obscurity. Originally known among Negro musicians simply
as "walking bass", boogie-woogie was a piano style characterized
not by the use of eight beats to the bar (though the majority
of its exponents used this rhythm almost constantly in the bass)
but by the employment, in the left hand, of *any* repeated rhythm
that makes any use at all of eighth notes. (Ex. 2, which clearly
is not "eight-to-the-bar", is none the less one of the most famous
of the boogie-woogie rhythms, used in *Yancey Special* and
others, while Ex. 3 offers a more typical sample of the kind of
repeated bass "riff" usually associated with boogie-woogie.)

EXAMPLE 2

EXAMPLE 3

The white public remained completely unaware of boogie-
woogie for many years, though there is evidence that the use
of similar figures, on piano or guitar, goes back as far as 1912.
The earliest and best of the pianists were Jimmy Yancey, who
though immortalized in others' versions of *Yancey Special* did
not himself record until 1939; Cow Cow Davenport, who toured
as a vaudevillian from 1914 until 1930; and Clarence "Pinetop"
Smith, who fortunately recorded two sessions shortly before his

death in a Chicago dance hall brawl in 1929. Cleo Brown recorded her own interpretation of Pinetop's *Boogie Woogie* in 1935; it was during this year that John Hammond, after a year-long search for the creator of a 1929 record called *Honky Tonk Train Blues,* which had deeply impressed him as a new departure in jazz piano, found his man, Meade Lux Lewis, washing cars in a Chicago garage, and promptly salvaged him for the record industry and posterity. Lewis" new versions, recorded early in 1936, triggered a national boogie-woogie fad. Two other pianists who became Hammond protégés, Albert Ammons (then leading a jumping sextet at Chicago's Club De Lisa) and Pete Johnson (Kansas City partner of the blues-singing Joe Turner) were teamed on a series of records and in appearances at Café Society and Carnegie Hall.

Boogie-woogie had a great advantage in its relentless intensity and drive, but this was at once its severest handicap, for the repetitions, both in left hand figures and the corresponding right and chordal patterns, tended toward automation. What was once improvised became anesthetized; the dynamic degenerated into the static. As soon as it became obvious that any musician with a mild feeling for jazz could play competent boogie-woogie, the end was near. Tin Pan Alley moved in and decreed boogie-woogie versions of popular songs, instead of the twelve-bar blues on which it had always been based; Bob Crosby's band recorded boogie-woogie in big band arrangements, Bob Zurke played boogie-woogie piano with savage accuracy, and by 1940 the Will Bradley-Ray McKinley band (with Freddie Slack handling the piano chores ably) had parlayed it into a commercial formula, adding lyrics and scoring popular successes with such tunes as *Beat Me Daddy Eight to the Bar.* Boogie-woogie, killed by kindness, survives today only as an occasional sideline indulged in by pianists who have other courses to offer and are not obliged to present it as a steady diet. The best souvenirs of the phenomenon are a few records by Count Basie, always a humorous and light-fingered eight-to-the-bar man; Jay McShann, a Kansas City band pianist whose boogie-woogie solos are raw, rhythmic meat; and Sammy Price, a Texan who has led his own band here and in

Europe and who retains the forceful authority of the early boogie-woogie catalysts.

In the years preceding and concurrent with the rise of boogie-woogie there came to prominence a pianistic phenomenon unlike anything that had preceded it, and certainly not replaced since its recent disappearance from the scene. Art Tatum, who recorded his first piano solos in 1933 and his last a few weeks before his death in 1956, was the first musician to play jazz piano with complete technical command. His brain and fingers moved so fast that he expressed in one measure more ideas, more subtleties of phrasing and dynamics and harmony, than could most of his predecessors in four.

Graced by Tatum's gossamer touch and articulation, the keys became feathers. Every style known to keyboard jazz was at his command. Unaccompanied, he might veer from a joyous sequence of stride-piano measures to a sudden outburst of boogie-woogie. His blues could express more completely and exquisitely the essence of a blues mood than any horn, any other pianist, any singer ever born. His interplay with the members of his trio (for the last 13 years of his life he usually worked with a guitarist and bassist) showed grace and humor as the three dovetailed in consummate cohesion.

Tatum was not a standard by which jazz piano could be judged, nor an objective toward which others would aim; the cliché "in a class by himself" applied so clearly in his case that other pianists, after sitting for hours in awestruck silence, would go home determined not to try to emulate Tatum, but to give up the piano forever.

Thus there was no Tatum school of piano, no Tatum style to copy, no neo-Tatum to compare with the original. The ideas of Waller, Wilson and Hines at least were potentially within reach of the aspiring youngster while Tatum's remained the envy of his most gifted contemporaries.

If any individual can claim to have been to the 1940s a jazz influence comparable with Teddy Wilson of the '30s, the claimant could be none but Earl "Bud" Powell.

Powell has been the *éminence grise* of modern jazz piano. Even in the comprehensive book *Hear Me Talkin' To Ya* there is no tribute, no discussion of the plenary and pervasive control that made his the most meaningful as well as the most imitated piano style of the decade. A patient at mental hospitals intermittently since 1945, he has demonstrated in his lucid intervals an imagination, fluency and utterly personal articulation that established him, figuratively and at times literally, as a member of the small band of geniuses that invested bop with its essential qualities from the outset. The others, Gillespie and Parker, Johnson and Roach, ultimately earned some measure of the respect that was their due; Powell remains almost unknown to the millions for whom Gillespie is a household name. Already past his most creative years, still sick of mind and weary of soul, he is the symbol of a goal toward which a thousand pianists have striven since his first appearances along 52nd Street with the small combos of the mid-40s.

Bud Powell's gifts are threefold. As a composer he has shown himself capable of instilling within a three-minute framework a pattern of somber majesty, of incisive and bitter beauty encased by a superb sense of form: *Glass Enclosure* is the finest example. As an improvising jazzman he brought the horizontal, single-note-line approach of Teddy Wilson under a newer and brighter floodlight. Where Wilson might have played with a keyboard composed entirely of gray keys, Bud's were unmistakably black and white, edged with a sharp, percussive attack so exceptional that he himself has had difficulty in recapturing it in late years. At his rare optimum, Powell was capable of rivaling Tatum in speed of conception and execution. Often he would use the left hand only for an occasional incisive punctuation, but once, when his ambidexterity was challenged, he played an entire performance with his right hand behind his back and none of the facility was missing.

The Powell style having become the paragon for almost every young pianist, a long list can be drafted of those who have developed successfully in his direction. Only a handful of pianists could play authentic bop with any real conviction at the time of Powell's emergence, most of them men who worked at one time with Gillespie, Parker or both: Al Haig, Duke Jordan, Lou Levy, George Wallington and Billy Taylor.

Contemporaneous with Powell as an arbiter of bop, but more important as a uniquely creative composer than as a pianist, was Thelonious Monk, sometimes called the "high priest of bop", whose approach in many ways was directly opposed to Bud's. Monk has always favored an economy of notes, a tendency to work along vertical lines that are as thought-provoking as Powell's are numbing. Monk, like Powell, has composed melodies of great harmonic charm. In his improvisations he is given to the unpredictable use of two-part intervals and has a predilection for seconds; he has made frequent use of whole-tone scale runs and has an almost pathological aversion for playing the awaited chord at the expected moment. Though he has worked exclusively with bop musicians and is harmonically compatible with the boppers, Monk is beyond classification as a pianist of any sect.

Though Monk has been the fountainhead of inspiration for a number of pianists and composers (notably Randy Weston), the influence of Powell has extended longer and deeper. There are unmistakable Powell traces even in the graceful, almost stately swing of John Lewis; in the powerful drive of Hampton Hawes (himself a strong influence on such fellow West Coasters as André Previn); in the Detroit school, from Hank Jones to Barry Harris, and in the Horace Silver school, to be discussed later.

An important jazz piano technique that matured in the 1940s was the locked-hands or block-chord style, in which the two hands moved in parallel lines, the left hand playing extra notes in the chord or duplicating the right, instead of supplying the bass line. This style was initiated about 1943 by Phil Moore, the arranger, and by Milt Buckner, then Lionel Hampton's pianist. George Shearing brought it to national popularity in 1949. (Shearing, at his best a first-rate Powell-derived pianist, will be discussed in the combo chapter.) Block-chording has been applied effectively to modern styles by Red Garland and others.

Chordal techniques of extraordinary harmonic originality were employed in the late 1940s by Lennie Tristano. Rarely heard in public or on records, Tristano has been a powerful force as a teacher of many young pianists and as an indirect influence on others. Miles Davis credits Tristano with having created the first genuine avant-garde movement after bop, and the first successful experiments with atonality in improvisation.

Horace Silver, like Tristano, used Powell as an early source but soon created an autonomous style. Silver mixed bebop's harmonic additions with the regressive "funky" tendency to strip the chords of all but the essentials and to state them in open fourths and fifths in the right hand, along with very basic Powell-like single-note lines. This blend of antique and modern was often found later in the work of Mose Allison, Ray Bryant, Ray Charles, Wynton Kelly (one of the most flexible soloists in this area), Junior Mance and Bobby Timmons, and in the commercialized heavy-soul gambits of Les McCann and Ramsey Lewis. These artists sometimes placed a stronger reliance on earthy blues chords than on the harmonic deviations of the boppers.

Erroll Garner, first heard in New York in 1944, when he had already formulated the style he later brought to perfection, has a regally emphatic touch and a unique right-hand rubato. His many personal traits include the occasional guitar-like strumming of four chords to the bar in the left hand; the romanticist use of spread chords in ballads, and an extraordinary ability to translate a horizontal eight-hand melodic line into harmonic terms, by playing sequences of eight chords to the bar. Garner, the only well-known modern jazz pianist who cannot read music, brings to these cascades of chords a singularly happy quality. He has enjoyed his greatest successes not as a performer of jazz works but as an engaging interpreter of popular songs, including a few of his own melodies (notably *Misty*).

Dave Brubeck, a controversial figure, has been accused of "senile romanticism" but has also been called by the distinguished British pianist-composer Steve Race, "the most uniquely significant jazzman of our time." Though his touch seems very heavy at times, he is capable of building solos to a pitch of climactic excitement. Whether or not he swings has been angrily debated. Certainly he is an accomplished pianist and composer and has exerted a powerful influence.

Oscar Peterson, whose influence in U.S. jazz circles was first felt in 1950, a year after Norman Granz had brought him from Canada for a New York concert, is the most consistently swinging pianist in modern jazz and technically the logical heir to Art Tatum. A masterful rhythm generator, he has an unsurpassed gift of vitality. This quality gives invigorated meaning to a style that seems to have incorporated the best parts of Powell, Tatum and a few earlier artists (not excluding the Waller stride school).

Probably Peterson's only competitor, in terms of swing, inspiration and technique, is Phineas Newborn, a phenomenally agile performer whose long periods of illness have limited his activity and popular acceptance.

Bernard Peiffer is another underrated virtuoso. Born in France, a U.S. resident since 1954, he has been accused of swinging synthetically; but there is no doubt that his harmonic and melodic conceptions are among the most individual in jazz. Another French pianist, Martial Solal, displays a superb touch and a sonorous, adventurous approach to the piano that has established him firmly among the avant-garde of the 1960s.

Two pianists rose to national prominence in the late 1950s. Stylistically they have nothing in common; their bond is the often-reiterated admiration for both expressed by Miles Davis. They are Bill Evans, who was a member of Davis' Quintet in 1959, and Ahmad Jamal, leader of a Chicago-based trio.

Jamal swings in a manner best characterized as light, airy and even, at times, cute. His technique, though admirable, is rarely put to ostentatious use; often he uses the ploy of understatement, leaving unexpected gaps in his simple, lacily charming lines. At his best he displays an unusual blend of embellishment and economy.

Evans has brought piano jazz forward to a new plateau of lyrical beauty. He has a touch of phenomenal gentleness, a fine facility with the pedals for dynamic contrast, and most important of all, an ability to voice chords so ingeniously that the placement of the notes, the question of which notes are doubled, which struck softly and which heavily, may be far more important than the basic identity of the chord.

Though Evans' swinging fast-tempo playing is admirable, it is the slow chordal work that has earned him his reputation. The style has been called experimental, authoritative, romanticist, brooding, introspective, reflective, perfectly articulated, rhythmically controlled. It is all of these and much more; Evans is the first genius of the piano since Art Tatum. He is also, as one might expect, a composer of exceptional talent.

Evans did not attract widespread attention among musicians until 1959, but within five years he had become, in effect, the father of a new and subtle school of pianists who copied not only his unique voicings but also his remarkable left-hand technique, in which rhythmically unpredictable punctuations, instead of cursorily filling an auxiliary role as they had too often among the bop pianists, now became an essential part of the two-handed whole.

Russ Freeman and other West Coast pianists showed the Evans influence; Toshiko Mariano, the extraordinary pianist-composer from Japan, began to display touches of Evans. Herbie Hancock, Clare Fischer, Denny Zeitlin and many other gifted pianists fell into the new pattern of oblique harmony and more carefully controlled dynamics.

Two important artists emerged from obscurity in the early 1960s: McCoy Tyner and Cecil Taylor.

Tyner's most personal attribute is the ability to work in modal terms. Modes (varying arrangements of the diatonic notes of an octave, most easily identified by starting with any white note on the keyboard and running up an octave in white notes) began partially to supplant chords as a basis for improvisation in 1960. Because Tyner was a member of the quartet of John Coltrane, who was among the first jazz soloists to make extensive use of modes, his style, as introverted and moody in its way as Evans', dovetailed excellently into Coltrane's. By 1965 he had become a favorite of a new generation of pianists.

Tied neither to the chord bases of the boppers nor to the modes of Tyner, Cecil Taylor has become a symbol of total freedom in piano jazz, or rather in piano improvisation played by a musician with a jazz background. As Whitney Balliett observed in a *New Yorker* review of one of his concerts: "He is a hammer and the keyboard is an anvil. His single notes and chords and runs ring and clang and thunder... His solos are virtually forged. Part of one might go like this: A legato passage, made up of well-spaced, high-register single notes, struck all around the beat and chosen to form a lingering, discordant lyricism, will idle by, and then, after a pause during which one can just about hear Taylor's computer whirring and clicking, he will leap to the bottom of the keyboard and let loose a terrific two-handed tremolo, which swells into a volcanic shudder, and then start a series of irregular, pounding left hand chords which his right hand shoots effortlessly through an ascending-descending run that may end in a skidding glissando. Abrupt silence. He may then fire a splintering salvo of staccato chords in the middle register, allow his hands to move apart and into different rhythms and dissonant chords, suddenly drop his volume, and, after another stark silence, swim nonchalantly back into another legato pool. The intensity in each Taylor solo is unbelievable . . . "

Taylor's innovations serve to point up the phenomenal changes that have evolved at the keyboard since the first ragtime tunes were played more than 70 years ago. The next developments may lie in his direction, or in Evans' or Tyner's, or along some other path not yet charted. Certainly for the student seeking diversification there can be no more fecund source than the past, present and probable future of jazz piano.

CHAPTER 7

THE TRUMPET

Ever since small combo and orchestral jazz began, it is the
trumpet that has usually carried the burden of leadership. The
leader may be a pianist, clarinetist or saxophonist, but he must
cede his authority for every ensemble, every rousing tutti that
lends the group its power and its true voice to the trumpet.

During the first decade or two the leader almost invariably
was the musician who played trumpet—or, technically, the
cornet. The difference between the two is largely academic.
"I remember once when Lu Watters was sick and tired of all
this cornet versus trumpet nonsense," Turk Murphy has recalled.
"He went into another room and played a cornet and then a
trumpet for some of these romantics. And none of them could
tell one from the other."[1] There are, nevertheless, musicians and
critics who claim that the cornet has a more rugged, mordant
sound while that of the trumpet is fuller and more brilliant.
Personally, having heard Bobby Hackett and others in recordings on both instruments, I have often found them impossible
to distinguish and advise the reader not to be embarrassed if he
feels inclined to treat them as in effect the same instrument.

Louis Armstrong played both cornet and trumpet, concentrating on the latter from 1928 on. Bix Beiderbecke was a cornetist;
Rex Stewart, Muggsy Spanier and many others have usually
played cornet. The visual identification can easily be made, as
the cornet is shorter.

The singing, soaring tone of the trumpet (for the remainder
of this chapter the word will be used to denote either instru-

ment) is one of the most flexible sounds in jazz. Its range stems from a concert F, a fifth below middle C, up two or three octaves beyond middle C, the exact ceiling being determined by the lip, embouchure, lung power and general physical equipment of the performer. In the early Armstrong era, when Louis made a practice of building tension by climbing a scalar ladder to a high note finale, the climax that staggered his audiences usually stayed close to a C two octaves above middle C. Eddie Tompkins and Paul Webster, in the Lunceford band of the mid-1930s, began to push the horizons, only to be topped in the 1940s by Cat Anderson of the Ellington band and later by Maynard Ferguson with Kenton; but their high notes were more often achieved for melodramatic effect than for any intrinsic musical part in the performances. It has been said that Anderson plays notes only a dog can hear, because nobody else would care to.

The trumpet is flexible, though, in another important respect: its tone and volume can be modified by a variety of mutes. A sharp, biting quality is obtainable from the straight tin mute; a softer and rather mellow sound, often used by Buck Clayton, is offered by the cup mute; a quiet and almost ethereal tone, especially effective in section work by trumpet teams, stems from the so-called Harmon mute; and the growl or "wa-wa" effect is produced by the rubber plunger. Trumpets also make use of derby hats for a reduction of sound, and for a special crescendo effect derived from the waving of these derbies in front of the horn; the felt hat or felt cloth mute has the effect of damping the tone in a mellifluous manner.

The trumpet is a B Flat transposing instrument, i.e. a piano part written in B Flat would have a corresponding trumpet part written in C.

The early jazz trumpeter-leaders have been the heroes of countless legends in jazz history books. The first on whom we have enough recorded evidence to form any judgment are Nick La Rocca, of the Original Dixieland Jazz Band, and Joe "King" Oliver, Louis Armstrong's mentor. The styles of La Rocca, Sharkey Bonano and other New Orleans pioneers may be said to have led indirectly to that of Bix Beiderbecke; however, Ben Pollack and others have stated that Bix was just "a poor imitation of Emmett Hardy". The latter, who played on the Mississippi riverboats with clarinetist Leon Rappolo, died in 1925 at the age of 22 but undoubtedly was Beiderbecke's informal teacher and influence.

Similarly the style of Louis Armstrong in his early years owed much to his apprenticeship with Oliver. Armstrong reached his peak with a superb series of recordings with a small band in 1928-9. During the 1930s, backed by a big band whose saxophone section he tried to model after that of his favorite orchestra, Guy Lombardo's (the influence is unmistakably present on a number of records), Louis began to play more commercially and to aim his high-note finales and comedy effects at an ever wider audience; but to this day, in his more sincere moments, Louis retains the qualities that endeared him to musicians and led other trumpet players in the 1920s to imitate not only his playing but even his walk, his speech and personal mannerisms, just as other young trumpeters twenty years later followed the behavior patterns of Gillespie. Armstrong's greatness lay in the purity and beauty of his tone, his ability to sustain notes with an exquisitely controlled vibrato, his subtle use of syncopation and rubato, his faculty for combining a basic simplicity of approach with an unremittingly swinging beat. One should no sooner look to Armstrong for harmonic complexity, for brilliant cascades of sixteenth notes against a rapidly changing chord pattern, than to a Palestrina Mass for the intricately fragmented motifs, the dissonances and complexities of Schoenberg. Armstrong's limitations are his strength; it is no mere nostalgia that has preserved, for thirty years, the beauty inherent in records that have little else to offer by any standards.

Louis today, as a man who has passed from the epicenter of jazz into the world of popular entertainment, is a figure in whom, at intervals, the embers of jazz still are occasionally rekindled. He is at once the king and the court jester; the majesty of his tone and phrasing make endurable the long intermissions for clowning and comedy vocals.

Of Armstrong's contemporaries, a few others have withstood the test of time; the late Joe Smith, according to the evidence of his records with Bessie Smith and Fletcher Henderson, could have endured for many years as a giant among jazz trumpets, as could Bubber Miley, whose "growl" specialties in the Ellington band preceded Cootie Williams' better-known incumbency in that chair. Muggsy Spanier, one of the first trumpeters to gaze enraptured at every Armstrong bandstand, evolved a style that made effective use of the plunger while retaining some of the qualities of both Armstrong and the white Dixielanders; Jimmy McPartland, following Bix in the Wolverines, inherited his mantle and still brings Bix back to life today.

Red Allen, playing during the period 1929-34 with the Luis Russell and Fletcher Henderson bands, was probably the first trumpet player to escape from the sometimes stultifying effects of symmetry, of phrasing in terms of one or two bars at a time. Allen's longer melodic lines, mosquito-like tone and narrower vibrato opened up a new road, one that was followed during the 1930s by such bearers of even newer tidings as Roy Eldridge, Buck Clayton and Charlie Shavers.

Eldridge, whose primary era of influence was 1935-42 (in person with Teddy Hill, Fletcher Henderson, his own band and Gene Krupa; on records with Teddy Wilson, Billie Holiday and Mildred Bailey) brought to jazz a quixotic, loosely-phrased style; a tone that might be called bright gray, a little akin to Allen's; and an approach that showed, especially at slower tempi, the ubiquitous imprint of Armstrong. Clayton, prominent in the Basie band from 1935-43, showed a less volatile and smoother approach than Eldridge, characterized mainly by his wider and well-controlled vibrato and frequent use, to superb effect, of the cup mute. Like Eldridge, he was a frequent visitor to the Teddy Wilson-Billie Holiday record sessions that were an exciting component of New York jazz in the late 1930s.

Charlie Shavers probably has combined in one style a greater variety of qualities—good and bad but never indifferent—than any other trumpet personality. Mainly known as the sparkplug of the John Kirby band from 1938-44, he remained an important influence for several years during his sporadic association with Tommy Dorsey. Shavers' attributes include a darting, leaping range that throws high notes as a fighter throws sneak punches, a clear and personal sound, with sentimental overtones on slower tempi; a remarkably flexible sense of dynamics, and an extraordinary overall technique. Despite his occasional lapses from taste he may be the most successfully versatile of all jazz trumpeters; whether involved in a pianissimo soufflé with Kirby or a triple-forte ensemble finale with Dorsey, he has never failed to adapt himself to the requirements of the setting.

The '30s, a rich decade for jazz horns, were the halcyon years for Cootie Williams, an Ellington giant both in growl style and with full-toned open horn; Bunny Berigan, the lyrical beauty of whose work was more impressive in the lower register of the horn (*I Can't Get Started,* with his own band, earlier passages) than in the upper brackets (*Marie* with Tommy Dorsey); and Harry James, who, before Tin Pan Alley put him on a bland diet, was better known as a jazzman, with Ben Pollack (1936), Goodman ('37-8) and his own pre-strings band, eloquently saluting Spanier and Armstrong in his crackling, hard-driving solos.

Frankie Newton, an unappreciated, long-forgotten artist who died in 1954, earned a small but faithful following in New York around 1937-41 with John Kirby and later with various groups of his own. His style had much of the intensity of Eldridge; he made effective use of a strange contraption known as the "buzz mute", which sounded like the product of an illicit meeting between a trumpet and a kazoo.

Tommy Ladnier, who like Newton died in obscurity and was not too well represented on records, has shared the fate of Beiderbecke in that his posthumous acceptance has surpassed any recognition earned during his lifetime. Some authorities have likened Ladnier at his best to the early Armstrong.

The turning point in trumpet styles was, of course, one that was to prove no less significant to the whole of jazz, the advent of Dizzy Gillespie. His style, growing out of what had at first been a Roy Eldridge influence, found its mooring in harmony rather than in any essentially different approach to the instrument. (Gillespie's tone, rather anemic and much criticized in the early years, was unimportant: for once the familiar Sy Oliver axiom "Tain't whatcha do, it's the way thatcha do it" was reversed.) Where earlier trumpeters had expressed themselves, say, mainly in eighths and quarter notes, and where the swing era musicians had tended to broaden this approach with the more frequent use of triplets, Gillespie was able, through an unprecedented alliance of imagination and technique, to unleash a glittering waterfall of sixteenth notes, simultaneously implying, through his choice of notes, a more complex harmonic structure. The newly gained complexity was supplemented by the contrasting effects of long pauses, of notes held for a measure or two, of an austere beauty in the spelling out of a ballad.

The first major figures in Gillespie's bop trumpet generation were Howard McGhee, Kenny Dorham and Red Rodney; Fats Navarro (1923-1950); Miles Davis, who was to found a dynasty of his own in the 1950s; and later Clifford Brown (1930-1956), in whom the influence of both Gillespie and Davis seemed to be brewing an exciting new approach before an automobile accident abruptly ended his burgeoning career.

Important non-boppers of the 1940s included Emmett Berry, a product of the Henderson bands, and Bill Coleman, a lyrical and fluent artist who has lived overseas for most of the last 30 years. Jonah Jones, once with Cab Calloway's band, later found a commercial quasi-jazz niche; Harry "Sweets" Edison, a Basie alumnus, was famous for his lachrymose bent notes but had a swinging conception that few fully appreciated. The swing era qualities were still heard in the '40s and '50s, and even more recently, in the highly individual work of Ray Nance, the warm tones of Harold "Shorty" Baker and the Clayton-like Ruby Braff. Wild Bill Davison retained his Armstrong-like directness and beauty of sound. Bobby Hackett, hailed as a "new Bix" in 1938, continued for the next quarter-century to display a highly melodic and smooth sound on cornet and trumpet. Joe Newman is a versatile veteran ex-Basie man on the border between swing and bop, often with touches of humor.

Miles Davis reduced the searing flame of Gillespie, his mentor, to a low-glowing introverted manner often expressed through a Harmon mute. A master of understatement, Davis carried over bop's harmonic essence into the so-called cool school and was later responsible for the pioneer work in modal jazz.

Davis took to doubling on the fluegelhorn, an instrument of the trumpet family but slightly larger in appearance, fuller in sound and deeper in range. The fluegelhorn became suddenly fashionable and in the 1960s was in general use by Chet Baker and Art Farmer (both alumni of the Gerry Mulligan Quartet) and by most of the other jazz trumpeters, including such West Coast Davis descendants as Shorty Rogers. Farmer, a soloist of exquisite taste and discretion, was by far the most accomplished of the post-Davis fluegelhorn soloists.

The cornet, obsolescent since Dixieland days, was revived by Nat Adderley, a dartingly fluent soloist in his brother's combo, and by Thad Jones, an ex-Basieite and neo-bopper.

The era of hard bop brought to prominence a series of technically adroit trumpeters, all capable of loose-jointed, spirited statements. Among the first and most successful were Donald Byrd, heard with Art Blakey in 1952; Lee Morgan, with Gillespie and Blakey, whose composition *The Sidewinder* brought him to national prominence in 1964; and Blue Mitchell and Carmell Jones, successively with the Horace Silver Quintet.

The new movements in jazz during the 1960s, encompassing atonality and freedom from rhythmic, harmonic and metric restrictions, were reflected in the work of Don Ellis, an ambitious and versatile trumpeter-composer; Freddie Hubbard, a highly qualified hard bopper with a most attractive tone, who moved into more capacious fields on forming his own group in 1964; and Don Cherry, featured on a so-called "pocket trumpet" with the Ornette Coleman Quartet, of whom Donald Byrd observed: "Cherry is a good musician, but quite unpleasant to listen to. He is trying something new—but it's something disagreeable for the ears."

Underrated soloists whose commercial studio work has limited their jazz acceptance and activity include Clark Terry, an Ellington alumnus and a brilliant, humor-tinged fluegelhornist; Doc Severinsen, Snooky Young, Ernie Royal and Joe Wilder in New York; Bobby Bryant, Jack Sheldon and Conte Candoli in Hollywood.

CHAPTER 8

THE TROMBONE

No instrument has undergone a more thorough evolution in its jazz use than the slide trombone. It was used in the early days of jazz mainly as a rhythm instrument, pumping out two or four notes to the measure in a role that was more rhythmic than melodic; in fact, to some extent it complemented or substituted for the brass bass. The expression "tailgate" trombone originated when brass bands playing ragtime or early jazz were loaded onto advertising trucks and the trombonist, in order to give free play to the full length of the slide, had to stand near the tailgate of the truck. The reason for the simplicity of the trombonist's original role in jazz was basic; most early jazzmen had comparatively little formal training. The notes on the trombone are produced by placing the slide in one of seven positions. In order to lead to a melodic creation of any real substance, the manipulation of the slide and the control of the embouchure must be expert and highly professional.

The normal range of the trombone runs from F, a twelfth below middle C, up to a sixth or seventh above middle C and even higher—as with the trumpet, musicians in recent years have shown extraordinary technical mastery and increased the upper range considerably. The trombone (which, contrary to popular belief as propagated by the movies, is never known among musicians by such terms as "slushpump" and "sliphorn", but is frequently known simply as a "bone") is subject to modifications of its tonal quality through a variety of mutes, plungers, etc., all of them similar to those used for the trumpet. Music for the trombone is written in the bass clef but in the same key as music for the piano; in other words, no transposition is necessary.

It is self-evident from the records of early jazz that none of the pioneer trombonists had a complete mastery of the instrument. It was a trombonist, Kid Ory, who led the first Negro jazz band ever to make a record. Ory, highly regarded as a tailgate trombonist, capable also of taking solos, was prominent as a member of the King Oliver unit, of his own band, and the small Louis Armstrong group of the 1920s. Two other New Orleans musicians, Honore Dutrey, also heard with Oliver and Armstrong, and Preston Jackson, heard in Chicago in the 1920s, were among the other early exponents of a similar style, while "Daddy" Edwards of the Original Dixieland Jazz Band and George Brunis of the New Orleans Rhythm Kings provided the first tailgate notes of significance in white jazz.

The history of the trombone as a completely controllable instrument for melodic jazz solos may have begun with "Miff" Mole. A member of the Memphis Five in 1923, Mole was a close associate between 1925 and 1930 of Red Nichols, and was Glenn Miller's early idol. The Mole style represented the change to a new conception of the trombone in which each solo was the master, not the servant, of the seven positions of the slide. Tonally, Mole symbolized a flight from the harsh sounds, powerful but rough and limited in emotional scope, of the early soloists. Mole was capable of a beautifully soft, velvet-edged sound. His solos with Nichols on records made thirty years ago do not sound corny even today.

On the blues records of that period, some of the more imaginative trombone creations were the work of Charlie Green, the trombonist heard on a number of Bessie Smith records; Joseph "Tricky Sam" Nanton, whose rubber-plunger muted effects were to the Ellington trombone section what Bubber Miley was to his trumpet team. Another early trombonist, highly regarded by traditionalist jazz fans today, was Jimmy Archey, a Virginian who made his New York debut with Edgar Hayes in 1926. This was the year, incidentally, that a musician was first heard in Fletcher Henderson's band who, according to surviving contemporaries who remember him, was the harbinger of the modern era of the trombone. He was Jimmy Harrison, born in Louisville and raised in Detroit, dead at the age of 30 in 1931. Harrison lent the instrument a warm, glowing sound, with a vibrato of unprecedented finesse; his range was extraordinary and it was said that at times he was mistaken for a second cornetist.

Kaiser Marshall recalled, in *Hear Me Talkin' to Ya,* that Jimmy Harrison was a good friend of another trombonist with whom there was a frequent interchange of ideas, and that sometimes there would be jam sessions at Marshall's house with Coleman Hawkins on tenor sax, Kaiser on a rubber pad that he used as a substitute for drums, and Hawkins and the two trombonists taking turns at the piano. The second trombonist, a big, easy-going youngster who had arrived in 1927 after working around the Middle West, was Jack Teagarden (1905-1964).

In any genealogical tree of the jazz trombone family, Teagarden would have to be listed as a blood brother of Jimmy Harrison, for his style had much more in common with Jimmy's than with that of "Miff" Mole or any of the white trombonists from whom he might normally have been expected to derive his influence. Though he was never heard to deliver, in machine-gun style, a bombardment of sixteenth notes in the manner associated with such modernists as Jimmy Cleveland, Teagarden was credited unanimously by fellow musicians with an extraordinary technique and staying power, a tone that was unmistakably his own, and a style that varied from the earthiest of blues— generally considered his forte—to such technically challenging items as *Lover*, which he played *allegro risoluto* without ever running out of breath or ideas.

J. C. Higginbotham was the supreme example of the trombone as shock treatment in big band jazz. His forceful gutbucket style, with its powerful tone and attack, were best known as a feature of the Luis Russell band in 1928-31 and later in the '30s with Fletcher Henderson, Lucky Millinder and Louis Armstrong. Working in a small group with Red Allen, Higginbotham retained his popularity with both fans and musicians through the early '40s, when he won several polls. He has been in comparative obscurity for the past decade.

Jimmy Harrison and Jack Teagarden were the late 1920s' greatest gifts to jazz trombone. During the next few years a number of other fine musicians, many of whom had already been on the scene for quite some time, demonstrated their facility and originality, though in no case could it be said that the impact and influence was comparable with that of these two masters. Front-rank trombonists of the '30s included Benny Morton, whose main affiliations during that period were with Fletcher Henderson, Don Redman and Count Basie, and whose vibrant, intense style with its attractive vibrato had a great deal in common with Jimmy Harrison; Tommy Dorsey, a smooth-toned expert in Dixieland jazz whose reputation veered toward a more commercial brand of popular music after his first record of *I'm Getting Sentimental Over You*, in 1932; and Dickie Wells, a greatly underrated artist heard with Henderson, Teddy Hill and Basie. Wells, whose legato style was spiced with a darting sense of humor, was the subject of a lengthy and enlightening analysis by André Hodeir.[1] Comparable in many respects with Dorsey (they were always mutual admirers) was Lawrence Brown, a member of the Duke Ellington team from 1932-51, whose best known jazz performance with that band was the politely bouncing *Rose of the Rio Grande*, though most of his successful solos were played in a strictly melodic vein less close to jazz.

A popular favorite with jazz fans in the late 1930s was James "Trummy" Young, best known for his work in the Lunceford band from 1937-43. Lunceford combined semi-humorous glissandi with melodic passages that evinced a unique vitality His biggest hit with Lunceford was *Margie*, which he has been performing in recent years as a member of the Louis Armstrong combo.

The late Fred Beckett, heard briefly with Lionel Hampton's band in 1941, has been described by Jay Jay Johnson as "the first trombonist I ever heard play in a manner other than the usual sliding, slurring, lip trilling or 'gut bucket' style. He had tremendous facilities for linear improvisation." The only evidence of Beckett's early eminence, to the writer's knowledge, is a superlative solo on a record called *A La Bridges* by Harlan Leonard's orchestra, with which he visited New York in 1939-40. At this writing the disc is unavailable.

A consistent favorite with jazzmen of all schools is Vic Dickenson. Though he was born in 1906 and was on public display in reasonably well known bands as far back as the depression years, it was not until the 1940s, when New Yorkers observed him in the bands of Benny Carter, Count Basie and Eddie Heywood, that Dickenson attracted national attention. He is the homespun philosopher of the trombone—a master of the blues, a sly humorist, an intensely rhythmic performer who seems miraculously to have discovered his own way of phrasing pairs of dotted eighths and sixteenths. Like many capable soloists unable to find suitable employment in the dwindling rank of the big swing bands, Dickenson for years has been forced to work in predominantly Dixieland combos, though his style and reading ability fit him for a role affording considerably more scope.

After Dickenson, the first new trombonist to arouse excitement among musicians was Bill Harris. Jet-propelled from obscurity to national eminence on the strength of his membership in the 1944-6 Woody Herman band (Ralph Burns' work *Bijou* was built as a framework for his best known solo in that orchestra), Harris created a style that was frequently imitated. The qualities that combined to make Harris' style provocatively new were his tone, which sometimes gave one the impression of listening to him through a veil; his vibrato, slow and mournful on ballad performances; and his savage attack and choppy rhythmic alternation of strong and weak accents on the faster tempi.

New and important though Harris was, the contributions of two other musicians whose impact was felt almost simultaneously turned out to be more influential. They were Jay Jay Johnson and Kai Winding, both of whom pioneered separately—each unconscious at first of the other's contribution—in the difficult task of transferring the technically complex requirements of bebop to the incompatible medium of the slide trombone. Though it has been a natural tendency of critics to draw the inference that one copied the other, both Johnson and Winding confirm that their styles stemmed naturally from their respective musical environments. Though Johnson played with Benny Carter and Count Basie, while Winding worked with Benny Goodman and Stan Kenton, both made their really important contributions through record dates and night club gigs with small combos, starting around 1946.

Johnson, in his early alliances with Dizzy Gillespie, Bud Powell and the other bop originators, managed to play passages, both improvised and arranged, that most musicians, particularly those of an earlier era, would have branded as impossible. The rapid sequences of eighth notes that were called for in the new jazz produced, in Johnson's early solos, *tours de force* that many listeners swore must have been played on a valve trombone. That Winding was his musical soulmate in this vaulting of a major obstacle on the track for jazz trombonists was most clearly demonstrated when they teamed to form a unique combo, the first of its kind, with which they toured successfully for two years, in 1954-6.

Almost all the important trombonists to have achieved international recognition since Winding and Johnson are those who have clearly been influenced by the pattern they established. Among the most accomplished of the modern school- are Eddie Bert, the amazing Jimmy Cleveland, Carl Fontana, Matthew Gee, Benny Powell, Frank Rehak, Frank Rosolino and Earl Swope. Not directly indebted to Johnson and Winding, though their styles show certain characteristics in common with the two bop pioneers, are the brilliant Benny Green, who might be called a modern Benny Morton; Urbie Green, who has absorbed a variety of influences and is one of the most versatile of modern trombonists; Lou McGarity, who perhaps bears to Teagarden the relationship of Green to Morton.

The old style tailgate trombone tradition, meanwhile, still lives in the performances of traditionalist jazz groups led by Wilbur De Paris, Turk Murphy, Conrad Janis and others, though in De Paris' case this was a style adopted when he happened to fall into a commercially successful format; he is a fluent soloist who has been heard playing far more involved roles in bands such as Duke Ellington's.

Throughout the history of the trombone in jazz a parallel role has been played by the valve trombone, which in tone and range differs little from the slide trombone. This instrument, in which the manipulation of the slide is replaced by the depressing of the three valves, facilitates the playing of fast multi-note passages. Juan Tizol, composer of *Caravan,* popularized the valve trombone in Duke Ellington's band in the 1930s and '40s. Bill Harris and J. J. Johnson have doubled on it; Billy Eckstine, in his bandleading days (1944-7), played adequate bop-style valve trombone.

The brusque, jagged, often humorous valve trombone of Bob Brookmeyer reintroduced the horn in the 1950s in performances with Stan Getz and Gerry Mulligan. At the same time Curtis Fuller, a Detroit musician, came to prominence as a modern soloist on slide trombone in a style strongly influenced by J. J. Johnson. Others who bridged the gap between bop and the "new thing" in the 1955-60 period include Slide Hampton, with Maynard Ferguson and with his own groups; Wayne Henderson of the Jazz Crusaders; and the eclectic yet brilliantly original Jimmy Knepper, hailed by Whitney Balliett as "the first original trombonist in the modern idiom since J. J. Johnson."

Phil Wilson displayed remarkable control and a gift for surprising high-note forays in the Woody Herman band of the early 1960s. Grachan Moncur III, son of a noted bassist, was the first avant-gardist to transpose effectively to the trombone some of the qualities of the 1960s' new jazz wave.

A variety of instruments related to the trombone made their way into jazz during the 1950s and '60s. The bass trumpet, its sound akin to that of the valve trombone, was played by Cy Touff, Dave Wells and others. The trombonium was featured briefly by Johnson and Winding; the mellophonium, newly invented, was featured in a whole section of Stan Kenton's 1963 band. The alto horn was played by Dick Cary with Bobby Hackett's band in the late 1950s; Tom Stewart played the tenor horn on an ABC-Paramount LP and Gus Mancusco the baritone horn, which was also featured by Maynard Ferguson. The French horn and mellophone will be dealt with in the chapter on miscellaneous instruments.

CHAPTER 9

THE CLARINET

A shrill and exuberant voice in the early marching bands, still heard in the sword-crossing improvisations of the early jazz ensembles, was the sound of the clarinet. For years it ranked with cornet and trombone as one of the three principal horns in jazz, reaching its zenith with the glorification bestowed on it by Benny Goodman.

But the extraordinary musicianship of Goodman made further progress on the instrument a challenge almost impossible to meet. By the late 1940s, when there were hundreds of able saxophonists and trumpeters embellishing the jazz stage, the number of comparably gifted clarinetists could be counted on the rings of one instrument. As jazz evolved and placed ever greater technical demands on the performer, the role of the clarinet moved in an inverse ratio.

Part of the difficulty lies in the fact that in a sense the clarinet is two instruments, each played in a different register. The lower, known as the chalumeau register, is by far the easier to play and produces a rich, sonorous quality that can be changed from a gentle murmur to a bullfrog croak. With all rings and holes uncovered the clarinet makes a sound equivalent to F above middle C on the piano; as the fingers depress the rings and cover the holes it descends a tenth to D below middle C. The upper register (reached by pressing a ring under the left thumb) extends from F above middle C, upward for two more octaves. Only an exceptional musician can hit the higher notes with unerring accuracy of pitch and with acceptable tone; in addition, the notes marking the transition between the lower and upper registers (known as the break) are sometimes tricky to execute in rapid improvisation. The clarinet, like the trumpet, is a B Flat instrument; music is written for it a whole tone higher than it sounds on the piano.

In skillful hands the clarinet is capable of dazzling chromatic runs and arpeggios, and of glissandi that may seem impossible to a lesser artist (Barney Bigard, of the old Ellington band, was a master of the slow and steady upward glissando).

Two kinds of clarinet, each with a different fingering arrangement, have been in general use in jazz: the Albert or "simple" system, and the Boehm system.*

Alphonse Picou was probably the first important jazz clarinetist; certainly he and George Lewis, also from New Orleans, have given us the only recorded examples of the earliest solo and polyphonic styles, though neither recorded until the 1940s, when they were well past their prime. First to establish any widespread impact and influence via recordings were Leon Rappolo of the New Orleans Rhythm Kings, Larry Shields of the Original Dixieland Jazz Band and Johnny Dodds of the King Oliver band.

A family of clarinetists by the name of Tio (Lorenzo Sr. and Jr., and Louis) has been remembered with fervor by contemporaries, but except for a few obscure and unenlightening records by Lorenzo Jr. the Tios left no evidence to posterity.

During the 1920s jazz produced several musicians whose control over the clarinet enabled them to express themselves with a variety of tonal shadings and, in some instances, with great emotional scope. Jimmie Noone, possibly the first true jazz giant in his field, had Benny Goodman, Frank Teschemacher, Joe Marsala and every other clarinetist in Chicago spellbound at the

* Ironically, the so-called simple system seems to most clarinetists harder of execution than that invented by Boehm. Among the leading clarinetists the Albert system adherents have included a number of the New Orleans veterans (Shields, Dodds, Bechet, Bigard, Simeon, Hall) as well as Russell Procope and Jimmy Dorsey. Those who have played Boehm clarinet (which, according to Buster Bailey, makes certain passages easy that are impossible on Albert) include Goodman, Teschemacher, Nicholas, Russell, Herman and Shaw. Bailey generally plays Boehm but is also fluent on the Albert clarinet.

Apex Club as he wove blues and fast legato stomps into well conceived and cleanly played patterns. The Noone tradition was perhaps best upheld by Marsala, a greatly underestimated musician.

Teschemacher was one of the intense members of an informal cabal known as the Austin High School Gang. Originally inspired by the New Orleans Rhythm Kings, he shared Rapollo's poignancy, his tendency to bend and crush high notes until they screamed in pain, and a thin-toned but warm sound that was, one hears, at its least effective in the recording studios.

Pee-Wee Russell is the clarinetist most closely identified with what has been called the "dirty" tone. His smeared notes, glissandi, choked-up effects, sometimes producing a sound that was half B Flat and half saliva, had much in common with "Tesch". This capricious spirit and odd phrasing, which at times resembled the stammering of a woman scared by a ghost, compensated for whatever may have been his technical problems. Russell is still wailing today in the same sweet-and-sour manner.

The King Oliver band was the incubator for a series of fine clarinetists of the liquid-toned, blues-grounded school, among them the magnificent Barney Bigard, who went on to fame with Duke Ellington in the '30s; Omer Simeon, who spent most of that decade in Chicago with Hines; Albert Nicholas, whose '30s were spent chiefly in the Luis Russell band; and Sidney Bechet, who had been with Oliver in 1916 and spent much of the postdepression decade with Noble Sissle, later gaining international fame as a soprano saxophonist.

In a different class (though also an Oliver alumnus) was Buster Bailey, an academically trained musician who shared Benny Goodman's teacher. Bailey, in a full decade with Fletcher Henderson and another with John Kirby, played in an adroit style with a correct tone, somewhat thin and reedy when compared with Noone's, but masterfully fluent.

Jimmy Dorsey, in his years as a fledgling jazzman, was one of the better clarinetists; such early solos as *Prayin' the Blues* reveal a degree of passion never heard in the later years of comfortable financial success. Though never a major influence, Dorsey was admired and respected by many musicians.

For the record mention will be made here of Mezz Mezzrow, the technical, melodic, rhythmic and harmonic nature of whose work were assessed with such devastating accuracy in an analysis by André Hodeir[1] that it would be redundant to go into any further details.

Edmond Hall, though a jazz veteran, came late to recognition, having languished obscurely in unimportant big-band jobs until, at the age of 38, he was presented to a jazz-seeking audience as a member of Joe Sullivan's band at Cafe Society. Heard in the 1940s at the same club with Red Allen, Teddy Wilson and then with his own sextet, Hall later spent six years at Eddie Condon's club, playing in a style that proved most invigorating in a generally conventional setting of white Dixieland jazz. Hall has a sharp, reedy tone with a peculiar vibrato, a method of attacking the notes and a manner of phrasing that give his work the mark of complete originality. Best known for his work in Louis Armstrong's sextet, Hall in recent years has been free-lancing, mainly in and around New York.

The words "jazz" and "clarinet" became almost synonymous in the public mind when Benny Goodman, in 1935, became a national name. Though he had listened to Noone, Dodds and others, his style by now was unmistakably his own, making frequent use of the high register, in which his tone and control were of an unprecedented smoothness; of grace notes, variations in dynamics and contrasting uses of tension and relaxation that combined to give jazz one of the most imitated styles of the decade. Though today it may be possible to play (even for an audience of experienced musicians and thoroughly trained critics) a record by Peanuts Hucko, Sol Yaged, Johnny Mince or some other Goodman-inspired clarinetist and convince the listener that Goodman himself is playing, the agreeable musical atmosphere that these men can evoke owes everything to the style that Goodman created.

Far less influential was Artie Shaw, whose peak of fame was reached in 1938. A master of the higher register, he brought to the clarinet a jazz style technically comparable with Goodman's, though sometimes accused of lacking the latter's fire, and occasionally tending to sound mechanical. Shaw was at his best with his band playing a climactic blues arrangement behind him; but most of his work has been consistently adroit and melodic. Of the other clarinetists generated by the swing era, Woody Herman was perhaps the most stylized. Given to occasional artificial forays into the upper register with notes that outstayed their welcome, he has often been most effective playing in the chalumeau register; like Shaw, he has made some first-class blues recordings.

Little known as a clarinetist, though his role could have been a major one had he cared to concentrate on the instrument, was the tenor saxophonist Lester Young, who played clarinet in a liquid, nervous style on a record session for Commodore with the Kansas City Six in 1938. To this day there are jazzmen who name Young among their favorite clarinetists.

Jimmy Hamilton, Duke Ellington's clarinetist since 1942, has always impressed jazzmen with his articulate, well-schooled sound, as correct and dignified as his own personality on the bandstand. Hamilton might be called a low-blood-pressure Goodman, but with boppish modern overtones.

A revolution was brought about in jazz clarinet by Buddy De Franco, who during his tenure in the Charlie Barnet and Tommy Dorsey bands in the mid-1940s made it clear that he had accomplished for the instrument what Gillespie and Parker had achieved for the trumpet and alto saxophone. De Franco was the first to show the astonishing flights of fancy to be accomplished by a wedding of the ultimate in clarinet technique with the new harmonic approach with which bop had revitalized jazz. The perfection of his execution was comparable with that of few other jazz musicians irrespective of instrument; possibly no soloist since Tatum had combined technique and taste to such stunning effect.

De Franco for a long time had little competition; it was a full decade before Tony Scott, another product of the Parker-Gillespie jazz generation, broke what had appeared to be a monopoly. Scott, who in early years had a tendency to try to play more than his fingers allowed and to reach for high notes with a somewhat shrill tone, had ironed out these problems by the middle 1950s to become a first-class modern jazz clarinetist, playing with verve and conviction. But by 1959 Scott had found few outlets for his talent. He left for the Orient and remained out of touch with the U.S. jazz scene for several years.

Others who have flirted with the clarinet in the past decade include John La Porta and Bill Smith, both avant-garde composers and fluent soloists; Rolf Kuhn, one of the best disciples of De Franco, who lived in New York in the late 1950s but later returned home to East Germany; and Jimmy Giuffre, the ex-saxophonist who moved from modern swinging big band jazz to folk jazz combos and later to some of the most experimental atonal music ever performed in the jazz clubs by an artist with a jazz reputation.

Two outstanding clarinetists rose to prominence in Sweden in the late 1940s: Putte Wickman and Stan Hasselgard. Wickman, heard briefly in New York in 1959, was originally inspired by Goodman but developed a modern style of his own. Hasselgard earned the unique distinction of playing second clarinet in a Benny Goodman Sextet, in 1948. Closer to De Franco than to Goodman in style, he could have developed into a major soloist but was killed in an accident later in 1948.

Pete Fountain, a New Orleans clarinetist, achieved television prominence as leader of a Dixieland unit for Lawrence Welk in 1957-8. Later he bought a New Orleans night club and played on best-selling albums with his own sextet. The combo's style, like his own solo work, recalled the Benny Goodman era of the early 1940s.

Although such saxophonists as Phil Woods, Zoot Sims and Paul Horn have doubled on clarinet, by the 1960s the instrument had all but dropped from sight as a solo medium for younger jazzmen.

The bass clarinet, pitched an octave lower than the regular (soprano) clarinet, has been played now and then by Harry Carney and was one of the media of expression of the late Eric Dolphy (1928-1964), a respected avant-gardist. In 1965 Buddy De Franco took up bass clarinet and recorded an album for Vee-Jay. The bass clarinet with its deep purple, often sinister sound may have a viable future in jazz improvisation.

CHAPTER 10

THE ALTO SAXOPHONE

In the jazz age (a period during which the term had hysterical rather than musical overtones) the phrase that seemed to symbolize the *Zeitgeist* was "a moaning saxophone," or some other ululant adjective applied to the same noun. The saxophone, indeed, could have been a part of F. Scott Fitzgerald's coat of arms: two altos rampant on a field of cocktail-shakers. Yet ironically the saxophone was a late starter in jazz. For at least two decades while this music was crystallizing it played a negligible role. Not until the late 1920s, some 85 years after its invention by Adolphe Sax, did it cross the line successfully after decades of identification principally with brass bands.

Despite its brass construction the saxophone is not known among jazzmen as a brass instrument; it is classified as a member of the reed family. Like the clarinet and other reed instruments its sound varies according to the quality, thickness and pliability of the reed in use, and the manner in which the musician blows into the thin channel of air between the reed and the mouthpiece. (Some saxophonists spend all their lives looking for the perfect reed; its ultimate discovery usually is a prelude to the moment when a bystander brushes against it, causing irreparable harm both to the reed and the saxophonist's nervous system.)

The E Flat alto saxophone (so called because an alto middle C makes the same sound as the piano E Flat) has a normal range far narrower than that of the clarinet, starting at E Flat below middle C on the piano and rising to G, a little over two octaves higher. It has a round, gentle and lilting quality that made it

the lady of the saxophone family; not until Charlie Parker's
advent was it apparent that a lady could behave like a vixen.

Don Redman, one of the earliest jazz alto soloists, played
with Fletcher Henderson's band and McKinney's Cotton Pickers,
and on some of the best records by the Armstrong combos of
1928. Jimmy Dorsey was considered one of the "hottest" alto men
by many of his contemporaries; his standard solo on *Tiger Rag*,
repeated in Red Nichols' recording under the title *That's No
Bargain*, was as widely imitated in the late '20s as were the
most celebrated Charlie Parker solos two decades later. Though
Dorsey sometimes sounded as if he were reading a prepared
solo (the *Tiger Rag* instance indicated that this actually happened at times) he was certainly one of the more fluent performers at a time when the alto sax was a stepchild in jazz.

The essential qualities of improvisational greatness—a pro-
fundity of ideas, individual tone, the ability to phrase subtly and
swing constantly, complete technical control in the mouth and
under the fingers—were combined in the alto saxophone of
Johnny Hodges, who was 21 when he joined Duke Ellington's
band early in 1928. Hodges in his early years with the Duke
was a stomping soloist, using an occasional trill or grace note but
basing his solos primarily on eighth notes and making constant
use of syncopation. Not until the middle 1930s did his mastery
of the glissando, the slurring use of quarter-tones, become apparent as he began to assume a more important role in ballad
performances. By the early 1940s, on records with Ellington and
with small contingents from the band under his own name,
Hodges had established a scooping, smearing style that had
substituted saccharine for pepper and tended often to lose most
of the qualities that give any solo its jazz identity. *Passion Flower*
was an example of this fulsome approach; but on the other
hand, a half hour after he had completed it, Hodges recorded
Things Ain't What They Used To Be, a slow, rocking blues. He
has remained a genius of the blues and an incomparable jazz
soloist at any tempo, as the most recent records by his own groups
attest; but in the Ellington band, which he rejoined in 1955 after
a four-year absence, his role too often is confined to routine

performances of straightforward melodic tales a thousand times told, though he still tells them better than anyone else.

Benny Carter, a year Hodges' junior, joined the jazz élite about the same time, recording from 1929 with a series of groups known as the Chocolate Dandies, and from 1933 with his own big band. Though Carter has distinguished himself in a half dozen roles, as trumpeter, clarinetist, composer, arranger, leader, it is the alto saxophone that is his automatic association in the minds of the countless jazzmen whose respect he has gained and retained during the past three decades. Carter's alto has the identical virtues found in Hodges,' yet both are completely themselves and can be readily recognized on any recording. The Carter tone is perhaps even more personal than Hodges', for while the latter has acquired many capable imitators (Woody Herman, Johnny Bothwell, Charlie Barnet) there has never been another alto man comparably close to Benny. In their choice of material they have varied greatly, Hodges preferring slow blues and ballads while Carter, though also an expert ballad performer, prefers his jazz performances in faster tempi, whether blues or not. There is in Carter's work, even in his earthiest moments, a certain dignity and assurance, mirroring the personality of the man: his passion is deep but contained.

Charlie Holmes, of the Luis Russell band, was one of the best of the Hodges school in the 1930s, while Hilton Jefferson, with Henderson and Webb, showed a Carter influence. Arranger Edgar Sampson played alto with Webb in a Carter-Hodges vein.

The most underrated alto player of jazz history was Pete Brown (1906-1963). As with Carter, the style reflected the man. Physically he was a great circle of a man, with a wide-eyed smiling face and a disposition to match; musically he told his story in a staccato, essentially rhythmic manner, like a cumulative series of punch-lines. A familiar and beloved figure with the John Kirby sextet in 1938, later with Frankie Newton, Brown can still be heard on a few recording dates produced by the author, including one with Coleman Hawkins on RCA Victor. His small, wheezy tone and light timbre were a main source of inspiration for Paul Desmond.

Akin to Pete Brown was the soaring jump style alto of Louis Jordan, a Webb alumnus who led his own combo from 1938. So popular as a singer that his playing later became secondary, Jordan concentrated on buoyant, humor-tinged blues to become a multi-million record seller in the 1940s.

A contemporary of Jordan and Brown was Willie Smith, with the Lunceford band (1930-41) and chiefly with Harry James from 1944-63. (He also spent a year with Ellington, 1951-2, in Hodges' chair.) Smith's alto had a floating, flexible sound that was most effectively used in the upper register.

Charlie Parker effected a total change not merely in the approach to the alto but to the entire concept of jazz improvisation. First in 1941 at the Savoy with Jay McShann, then from 1944 around 52nd Street, Parker spoke through his horn like a consumer of basic English who had suddenly swallowed the whole dictionary yet miraculously managed to digest every page. Where others had played in and around arpeggios on a single chord for four beats, he would involve two, three or four chords; where they had moved in eighth notes Parker took command of sixteenths. Parker's timbre, far from the lyrical beauty of Hodges or the sedate lead-alto sound of Carter or Marshall Royal, had a coarser quality that was perfectly fitted to the more liberated style. Parker helped create a new language for jazz, though it is beyond question that similar developments were evolving spontaneously in other areas. Sonny Stitt claims, and many who heard him confirm, that he was playing in an identical manner before he ever met or heard Parker. Stitt followed Parker as a Gillespie combo associate in 1946. The style, a natural and logical evolution from the earlier jazz, was reflected also in the work of Art Pepper, who played often in the Kenton band of the 1940s.

Lee Konitz bore the same relationship to Parker as Miles Davis to Gillespie in bop's evolution to its cool phase in the late 1940s. Konitz played Parker compositions in a Parker style in some 1947-8 Claude Thornhill band records, but soon he was polarized by two magnetic associates, Lennie Tristano and Miles

Davis. Tristano helped shape Konitz's prescient harmonic knowledge and intricate, fluent melodic lines; Davis was the counterpart in Konitz's tone quality, more languid than the boppers'. Exceptionally light in texture and pure in tone, with a quality often characteristic of a soprano sax, is Paul Desmond, a San Franciscan prominent from 1951 with Dave Brubeck. His improvisational lines travel in casual luxury without ever attempting a crash landing, yet Desmond at times can move with a subtly implied dynamic force that becomes evident in the many examples of his polytonal and polyrhythmic counterplay with Brubeck. Combining an exquisite lyricism with a cerebral harmonic-rhythmic complexity, Desmond gained wide acceptance among musicians and won many popularity polls from 1955.

Earl Bostic, a veteran of many name bands, left Lionel Hampton in 1945, formed his own combo, and during the next decade enjoyed tremendous acceptance as a rhythm-and-blues artist with a big, hard tone and florid style that earned him the praise of critics and fans overseas, and of Negro audiences in the U.S. He later modified his style to incorporate a less synthetic, more jazz-oriented flavor.

For several years after Parker's death in 1955, the Bird impact remained strong. Julian "Cannonball" Adderley arrived in New York from Florida only months after Bird's death. Though there were occasional Carter touches in his ballads, the Parker influence was inescapable; later, during his two years in Miles Davis' combo (1957-9), he seemed to absorb some of the modal ideas and rhythmic complexities of John Coltrane, his colleague in the Davis group.

An unspoiled, inspired craftsman who ranks with Adderley among the great alto discoveries of the 1950s is Phil Woods, best known for his work with Quincy Jones' band. Woods' lines seem to flow directly from Parker, as do those of Leo Wright and James Moody (both heard with the latter Gillespie groups), Lou Donaldson and Hank Crawford. The Kenton band of the

'50s displayed the Parker-derived sounds of Bud Shank, then Lennie Niehaus, later Charlie Mariano. Another fluent West Coaster of the period was Herb Geller, who later took up residence in Germany.

An apocalyptically new concept began to mature in 1958 in Hollywood, where Ornette Coleman made his first LPs. From 1959, when Coleman went East and was acclaimed by John Lewis as the first true innovator in jazz since the bop era, his influence grew swiftly. Coleman shrugged off the conventional structural devices of jazz as well as the traditional harmonic system. He flirted with atonality, indulged in suspensions of meter and in small-group improvisations that bespoke total freedom. His rejection of many of the basic rules, not merely of jazz but of all music, did not entail the formulation of specific new rules; consequently his work was wrongly equated by some critics, including the author, with anarchy and nihilism. Despite the technical inadequacies and apparent incoherence of his saxophone playing, it was soon clear that Coleman was vitally important as a composer and general influence on jazz.

The 1960s saw the rise to prominence of Eric Dolphy (1928-1964). A restless innovator, Dolphy once said that the singing of birds and the ragas of Indian music inspired him to use quarter tone intervals. Dolphy's great potential was far short of realization when he died.

Jackie McLean, formerly Parker-influenced, was one of the many whose musical thinking was reoriented by Coleman. From 1962 his records showed an explosively virile, searching style, almost as free as Coleman's from harmonic restrictions.

On the West Coast, the exploratory work of Jimmy Woods was of major interest, while Paul Horn, whose influence was Coltrane rather than Coleman, moved in the modal direction both as composer and player.

Some of the most valuable qualities of Parker and Coleman were combined in the work of Frank Strozier, a youngster from Memphis featured in 1965 with Shelly Manne's group. In England Joe Harriott, the alto saxophonist and composer, became a local leader of the avant-garde. The influence of Coleman was even heard in Leningrad in the work of Gennadi Golstain.

Other capable and prominent alto men in the 1950s and '60s included Gigi Gryce, Jerome Richardson, Buddy Collette, Sonny Criss, Gene Quill; Arne Domnerus in Sweden; John Dankworth and Bruce Turner in England; and in the mid-'60s John Tchicai, a highly regarded avant-gardist.

CHAPTER 11

THE TENOR SAXOPHONE

Measured in terms of quantity or quality, the B Flat tenor saxophone has produced more jazz talent than any other instrument except the piano. Many musicians prefer it to the alto because of its deeper, ampler sound and because of its physical proportions (it is larger and its keys are correspondingly farther apart).

In contrast with the ladylike tendencies of the alto, the tenor sax is virile, rugged, plunging to A Flat, a tenth below middle C, rising to D a ninth above middle C; though at times harsh in the lower reaches it sounds full and rich in the middle register and is susceptible to a wide range of tonal approaches. Between two extremes represented by the manly sonorities of a Coleman Hawkins and the milquetoast delicacy of the cool school's subzero subscribers there are many gradations. A recent survey listed more than 140 tenor men heard prominently on records at one period or another in jazz history. Of these at least 25 merit some discussion here as major contributors.

Coleman Hawkins, who was the only important tenor saxophonist playing jazz when he joined Fletcher Henderson to take his first posterity-bound solos in June 1923, miraculously survived a series of evolutions and revolutions to remain one of the most compelling performers on tenor in the late 1950s. An inspection of his work with Henderson (repugnant to Hawkins himself, whose reaction to anything he recorded more than twenty years ago is a mixture of amusement and self-recrimination) reveals a jumpy, "slap-tongue" technique in which his manner of tonguing the reed gave some of the solos a disjointed effect; but the seeds of greatness already were perceptible. The record generally regarded as the first landmark in Hawkins' career is *Hello, Lola* and *One Hour*, recorded in 1929 with Red McKenzie's Mound City Blue Blowers. The first title is a stomp in which Hawkins' tone, fuller and more rounded, is applied to a savagely swinging attack. *One Hour* gives a forestaste of the exquisite ballad style that was to become his most successful technique. The next Hawkins landmark was *Body and Soul*, recorded in October 1939, a few weeks after he had returned from five years of triumph as a renowned ambassador of jazz in England, Holland and France. *Body and Soul* was the apotheosis of the ballad approach to jazz, its tone demonstrating the body, its phrasing the soul in his ever-sensitive, harmonically and melodically advanced mind.

Hawkins remained undisputed king of the tenor for many years, winning magazine polls as recently as 1947. When the bop revolution came along, instead of fighting it, he joined it, incorporating many of its characteristics in his own style. In 1957 still one of the great stars of his instrument and still active around New York, he had maintained all the qualities that brought him adulation from fellow musicians three decades earlier, when he had been the first to march bodily into an instrumental territory alien to jazz; but in the long interim subtle changes had been wrought in his style. Following a suggestion by Nat Hentoff in *Down Beat*, musicians experimented by playing Hawkins' new record of *There'll Never Be Another You*, with the turntable speeded up from 33⅓ to 45 r.p.m. They were astonished to observe that with the tenor thus raised to the pitch of an alto, his style was the twin of Charlie Parker's.

Hawkins' reign has been long and deeply influential. During the 1930s and '40s a score of tenor men in the big name bands inevitably were judged by the standard he had set, though many developed attractive and highly individual sounds and styles of their own.*

* The following alphabetical list includes in parentheses the names of their most important affiliations and periods of influence:

The late Chu Berry (Cab Calloway, 1937-41), best remembered for his superb ballad version of *Ghost of a Chance;* Don Byas (Andy Kirk, 1939-

Of all these estimable talents, Ben Webster's may well be the greatest. One might call Webster the Clark Gable of the tenors—at once a brute and a hero in his heavy-toned romances with the ballad form—and his saxophone, voluptuously erotic, a physically irresistible woman who wears a little too much make-up. As she slips off her sharps and flats and climbs gently into the first chorus, you are aware of the mascara and rouge before her real beauty strikes you, just as you are conscious of the reedy edges on Webster's slowly vibrated melodic syllables. Not for nothing was one of Webster's finest albums titled *Music for Loving*.

The Hawkins-Webster era of boudoir saxophone had not grown up in a vacuum. A parallel school of jazz tenor was founded by Bud Freeman, who made his first record date as a leader in 1928, distinguishing himself later in the hands of Red Nichols, Tommy Dorsey and Benny Goodman. Freeman's tonal approach to the instrument was notably different from Hawkins', his phrasing symmetrical, yet emotional. In some respects he was able to translate into tenor sax terms what was known as the Chicago style of early jazz. He was the first and almost only saxophonist to be welcomed into the Dixieland clique whose central figure was Eddie Condon; the latter once stated in an interview that saxophones simply didn't belong in jazz, with the sole exception of Freeman. Bud's influence was felt constantly in the solos of Babe Russin, who like Freeman was featured with Nichols,

40; Count Basie, 1941), resident of France since 1946; Corky Corcoran (Harry James off and on since 1941); the late Herschel Evans (Count Basie 1936-9), whose most notable contribution was the Basie record of *Blue and Sentimental;* the late Herbie Haymer (Red Norvo, 1935-7); Budd Johnson (Earl Hines, 1934-42), who moved on to become a pioneer associate of the boppers; Vido Musso (Stan Kenton, 1945-7); Flip Phillips (Woody Herman, 1944-6), best known for his frenetic performances with the Norman Granz concert units in later years, but capable of superior ballad work; Ike Quebec (Cab Calloway, 1944-51); Eugene Sedric (Fats Waller, 1936-42), also much admired for his clarinet work; Buddy Tate (Basie, 1939-49); Joe Thomas (Jimmie Lunceford, 1932-47), one of the most inspired and melodic of the great Lunceford soloists; Lucky Thompson (Basie 1944-5), a warm-toned individualist; Ben Webster (Duke Ellington, 1939-43), and Webster's own most successful follower, Paul Gonsalves (Duke Ellington from 1950).

Goodman and Dorsey; Eddie Miller (Bob Crosby, off and on since 1936) and Boomie Richman (Tommy Dorsey, 1946-52).

Of indeterminate category were several swing era bandleaders. Georgie Auld (Artie Shaw and Goodman, 1938-42), a bandleader intermittently since 1939, showed a Freeman influence on his early records, moved to a Hawkins-Webster mood, and in recent years has shown himself one of the most versatile of tenor men, capable of excellent work in the cool Getz style.

Other tenor playing leaders have included Charlie Barnet, whose volatile solos have been heard with his own band for a quarter-century, and Tex Beneke (Glenn Miller, 1938-42), a soloist of limited ability who enjoyed a tremendous fan following in the early '40s.

The so-called "cool school" of tenor saxophonists, which in the past decade has acquired more adherents than the Hawkins dynasty or the Freeman college, owes its charter to Lester Young, who as a member of the Basie band from 1936-40 exercised an influence as indigenous to his era in jazz as Hemingway's to the modern novel. "Pres", as he is called among musicians, pioneered in the move away from the full, lush tone and the dotted-eighth-and-sixteenth-note-rhythmic approach, favoring instead a hollower, pipe-like and somewhat laconic sound and a tendency to make great use of rubato and to play long passages of evenly-phrased eighth notes. Dick Wilson, a tenor man with Andy Kirk's band, showed similar tendencies in his remarkable solos, and before his death in 1941 showed promise of becoming a strong influence.

After Young came the deluge. The middle '40s marked the period of gestation. Fledgling tenor men, who a few years earlier would have turned automatically to Hawkins for inspiration, now used "Pres" as the model. In the middle '40s there was a preliminary flowering of new tenor men with Young ideas. Among the first were Allen Eager, whose fleet improvisations livened the sets at many a 52nd Street club from 1945; and Stan Getz, whose early records reveal a rougher and thicker sound, though he soon evolved into a successful Young disciple.

Getz was one of a series of young tenor men who made the Woody Herman band an incubator of cool jazz. Though it was

Getz whose work won international prominence and made him a symbol of the cool era, several of the other Herman tenor soloists have since proven themselves no less considerable in an assessment of this branch of the family. Their dates of service in the Herman band are included parenthetically: Al Cohn (1948), Jimmy Giuffre (1949), Richie Kamuca (1954-5), Arno Marsh (1951-3; '57), Bill Perkins (1951-4), Zoot Sims (1947-9), Herbie Steward (1947).

The cool image prevailed on the West Coast throughout most of the 1950s, when the most prominent jazz recording artists included Bob Cooper, Buddy Collette, and several others whose sound was relatively light. Simultaneously, though, several other California residents, more aggressive in style but less successfully in vogue, were intermittently active. Most notable among them were Teddy Edwards and Harold Land.

During the same period Warne Marsh, a pensive and cerebral young student of Lennie Tristano, played in a style not unlike that of Lee Konitz' alto.

More effective in terms of the ultimate direction of the tenor saxophone were a group of extrovert modernists who had begun to come to prominence in the middle 1940s. Though Charlie Parker rarely played tenor, their influence seemed to be as much Parker as Pres. First and most important in this school were Gene Ammons and Dexter Gordon, both members of the catalytic Billy Eckstine orchestra in 1944-6. Both displayed a bolder tone and more volatile ideas than the Getz school. Sonny Stitt, best known originally as a Parker-style altoist, switched to tenor and soon became associated with this group of extrovert moderns.

The most fertile breeding ground for tenor men of the post-Young, post-Parker era was the Count Basie Band of the 1950s. Its members included the late Wardell Gray (1950-1), who combined a strong attack with extraordinary linearity and a manner of phrasing and melodic creation that strongly recalled both Young and Parker; Eddie "Lockjaw" Davis (1952-3), who added a Webster touch as well as a dash of humor; Paul Quinichette

(1951-3), who was known as the "Vice-Pres" because his style and tone most directly resembled Lester's own; Frank Foster and Frank Wess, both Basieites for about a decade from 1953, Foster being the more forceful while Wess was inclined to an occasionally more lyrical sound and style; and such later additions as Eric Dixon, whose work in the Basie band of the 1960s mirrored contemporary influences as well as the early impression made on him by Paul Gonsalves and Lockjaw Davis.

Closely related to the "extrovert moderns" were several fine musicians who, for commercial purposes, stressed a somewhat synthetic excitement of one kind or another. In the case of Illinois Jacquet this was achieved through the use of freak notes and vulgar tonal effects, though Jacquet at his best was a fine musician capable of excellent ballad work and of such stomping, generally exciting performances as the original *Flyin' Home* solo with Lionel Hampton's band. Other tenor men prominent from the mid-1950s included Benny Golson and Harold Ashby, both of whom combine some of the values of hard bop with the softer and richer ballad effects of the Hawkins-Webster days; also Hank Mobley, James Moody, John Griffin, and Charles Rouse.

After Getz, who remained the most influential tenor saxophonist during the period 1950-7, the next significant innovation was that of Sonny Rollins, whose contribution was of paramount importance for two years, 1957-9, until he went into a two-year voluntary retirement. Rollins' technique enabled him to develop fearless, endlessly flowing lines that could lend an unprecedented sense of continuity to a long series of improvised choruses. His basic sound was wan and unlovely, not unlike that obtained by a tyro who picks up the tenor for the first time; his work was also marked by a satirical quality with which he mocked and distorted some of the strangely corny melodies he selected to play; yet his very personal use of grace notes, extraordinary harmonic imagination and structural ingenuity gave a unique value to his solos of this period. When Rollins emerged from retirement in 1961 the continuity and the exacting, incisive qualities were underplayed while his more abstract tendencies were intensified. Often melodically and rhythmically unsettled, Rollins now allowed his mockery to give way to gigantic outbursts of reckless, unsorted, quasi-atonal sounds.

During Rollins' absence the effect of his earlier impact had been greatly mitigated as a result of the arrival of John Coltrane in the front rank of the new tenor men. Coltrane's style, like Rollins', had grown out of the developments of bop and hard bop. During his incumbency in the Miles Davis combo, during most of the 1955-60 period, Coltrane developed an improvisational approach that was as different from Young's as the latter's from Hawkins'. Harmonically he began to reject the by now standardized cycle-of-fifths thinking of the beboppers in favor of a newer and greater linear complexity that began to show the influence of modes, and of Indian music. The attraction of the ragas and the impact of such musicians as Ravi Shankar became more and more dominant. Melodically, Coltrane was given to strong contrast between probing, tortuous phrases, often with a hypnotic, montuna-like quality, and sudden vivid flurries of notes best described by critic Ira Gitler as "sheets of sound." Coltrane's urgent, unflagging dynamism enabled him to sustain these qualities in solos of unprecedented length, often running 10, 20, or even 40 minutes without interruption.

The influence of Coltrane far outweighed that of any other tenor saxophonist in the early 1960s. It could be heard in the work of long-established and talented men such as Yusef Lateef and in the evolution of such relative newcomers as Charles Lloyd and Wayne Shorter. Around 1964 a new wave of the avantgarde, influenced by both Coltrane and Ornette Coleman, became evident in the work of Archie Shepp, Albert Ayler and Pharaoh Sanders.

The hard swinging qualities that had grown out of bop and the extrovert moderns were not totally lost in the deluge of Coltranism. Combining the influence of the new wave with strong characteristics of earlier styles, more directly related to the traditional concept of swinging, were the versatile Roland Kirk, the dazzling Sal Nistico, and such compelling soloists as Booker Ervin, Stanley Turrentine and Joe Henderson.

CHAPTER 12

THE BARITONE AND OTHER SAXOPHONES

The saxophone story did not begin with the alto and end with the tenor. Concurrently with these two familiar models a number of others have been employed, cutting across the broad span from piercing soprano to nethermost bass.

Few musicians have mastered the soprano sax, said to be the recalcitrant child of the family, hard to keep in line when accurate intonation is desired. The only man to make it his permanent mate (deserting it occasionally for a flirtation with his first love, the clarinet) was Sidney Bechet. A legend in New Orleans as a teen-aged prodigy before World War I, Bechet toured Europe with a concert orchestra not long after the Armistice. The shrill voice of Bechet's soprano sax found sympathetic settings at fast tempi in harmonically simple tunes like *Shine* and *Darktown Strutters' Ball*, or in improvisations on standard slow melodies such as *Indian Summer* and *Summertime*. His central personality trait was the vibrato. Frederic Ramsey called it "big and sunny" but Hodeir heard it as "panting in high frequency." Bechet died in 1959 after living for a decade in France, where, like Louis Armstrong in the United States, he had stepped beyond the commercial boundaries of jazz to become a national vaudeville figure, serving up French popular songs sizzling hot, functioning in the music halls of Paris no less diligently than Satchmo in the studios of Hollywood.

The dangers inherent in the term "inimitable" recur in the case of Bechet. Bob Wilber, thirty years Bechet's junior, studied and played with him frequently for a couple of years; the most hardened of New Orleans jazz experts found it impossible to distinguish one from the other on records. Wilber later returned from soprano sax to clarinet, studied modern music and lost his Southern accent.

In the swing decade the best use was made of the soprano sax as the mellow senior voice in five-man saxophone sections. Charlie Barnet did some of his best work topping his reed team in this manner; the same technique was employed by Georgie Auld in his short-lived big band of the mid-1940s.

Johnny Hodges used the soprano in his early Ellington days, achieving a sound much like Bechet's. Steve Lacy, who moved in the 1950s from Dixieland groups to avant-garde associations with Cecil Taylor and Thelonious Monk, was the first important soprano artist in modern jazz. He was followed by John Coltrane, whose Oriental influences were even more apparent in his soprano work than on tenor; by Curtis Amy, a Coltrane-like Californian, and by Roland Kirk, whose manzello closely resembles the soprano in timbre.

In the saxophone family, the C Melody is the Ishmael among Aunt Hagar's children. So named because, unlike the other saxes, it calls for no transposition (i.e. middle C on the piano corresponds with middle C on the sax), it has a range and sound similar to that of the alto. The only exponent who ever concentrated on the C Melody was the late Frankie Trumbauer, whose light yet soulful quality inspired numberless musicians, not the least of whom was Lester Young. Lester recalls: "Trumbauer was my idol. When I had just started to play, I used to buy all his records. I imagine I can still play all those solos off the records . . . I tried to get the sound of a C Melody sax on a tenor; that's why I don't sound like other people. Trumbauer always told a little story, and I liked the way he slurred the notes."

The E Flat baritone, pitched an octave lower than the alto, was for many years a saxophonic Suez Canal through which the right to move freely, in unchallenged solo passage, was restricted to the uniquely plangent sound of Harry Carney. A member of the Ellington band since 1926, Carney by the early 1930s had become the fundamental personality of the Duke's sax section.

He performed a dually brilliant function, lending much of the character inherent in the tonal texture of the reed team, as well as providing solos that were compellingly personal. Carney's big sound on the baritone bore much the same relationship to the efforts of later exponents as the Coleman Hawkins quality on tenor did to the less rigorous tenor men of later years.

What seemed at first like an anti-trust action aimed at Carney and his baritone began when the monopoly was at last broken, first by Jock Carruthers of the Lunceford band and Jack Washington with Basie, and by Ernie Caceres, a capable swing-era clarinetist who doubled on baritone in the bands of Bobby Hackett, Jack Teagarden, and Glenn Miller. But there was no inherently new approach to the instrument until the arrival of Serge Chaloff, a young Bostonian who, at 21, made the imprint of his modernist-oriented horn in the Boyd Raeburn and Georgie Auld bands and was revealed, in a series of small combo records, as the first bop baritone saxophonist. Two years later, in 1947, Chaloff earned national prominence in the Woody Herman band, and by 1949 he was able to dislodge Carney from the official throne he had held for so many years, winning the *Down Beat* and *Metronome* polls. (Chaloff died in July 1957.)

Established not long after Chaloff as baritone men were Leo Parker and Cecil Payne. The latter, heard first on alto sax, was featured with Gillespie on baritone (1946-9), playing a slightly brusquer and no less eloquent reflection of Charlie Parker's influence. The most independent contemporary baritone saxophonist is Gerry Mulligan, whose career could be compared with that of a painter who goes through a cubist period before taking up portraiture. In his early associations with such bop groups as Kai Winding's and Chubby Jackson's, Mulligan appeared to be using the same canvas as Serge Chaloff; later it became evident that he was on display in an entirely different wing of the Museum of Modern Art. Using a pianoless combo as his setting, Mulligan, in whom a strong sense of humor frequently becomes evident, offered a fascinating pastiche of mainstream, quasi-bop and Dixieland-modern.

On the West Coast, great progress in modern baritone was made by 27-year-old Bob Gordon shortly before his death in

1955 in an automobile accident. Several West Coast alto or tenor men doubled on baritone in the 1950s, notably Bud Shank and Buddy Collette.

Gil Melle, using baritone as a reflective and supple medium for the interpretation of his own compositions, was featured at the first Newport Jazz Festival in 1954 but fell into obscurity during the next few years. Sonny Stitt occasionally played baritone. Charlie Ventura, in his years as a bop popularizer, worked more tastefully on baritone than on tenor.

Other baritones of the 1950s included Charlie Fowlkes, a perennial Basie sideman, fine section member and infrequent but expert soloist; Danny Bank, a New York studio jazzman too rarely heard in solos; Marty Flax, whose musicianship and humor graced the international tours of the Gillespie band in 1956; the big-toned, exceptionally facile Sahib Shihab, an expatriate in Scandinavia in the 1960s; and Lars Gullin, the gently forceful Swedish musician who gained respect in the U.S. as a European counterpart of Mulligan in a number of combo recordings.

Just as Serge Chaloff symbolized the bebop approach to baritone and Mulligan the cool, Pepper Adams became the standard bearer for the resurgence of bop, or "hard bop" as it was now called, in the late 1950s. His virile, muscular style and full tone adorned the bands of Benny Goodman, Lionel Hampton and many others, including a combo he has co-led from time to time with an early Detroit associate, trumpeter Donald Byrd.

England provided two superior baritone men in Harry Klein and Ronnie Ross. The latter has made two or three visits to the U.S., including one as a member of the International Band at Newport. His work is quietly intense, showing a tendency to recall the earlier values of Chaloff but with greater melodic and harmonic finesse.

A unique experiment was conducted in 1964 when two Hollywood jazzmen, Jack Nimitz and Bill Hood, led a quintet in which their baritone saxes were the main feature. Despite the thickness of the ensemble sound the group achieved some delightful results, with the help of much doubling on bass clarinet, bass saxophone, etc.

The new generation of jazzmen produced a promising baritone artist in Charles Davis. Originally inspired by Leo Parker's early records, Davis has pointed the baritone in a new direction. Both as composer and soloist he has reflected the exotic flavor of Indian influences (via Coltrane and Lateef). Though he refuses to be labeled an avant-gardist, Davis foresees an emancipation for the baritone in terms of sound, color and range.

The bass saxophone, possibly because it is the least portable member of its family (and the least likely to be found in a bargain basement), has had few practitioners. This patriarch of the reed clan can plumb unusual depths. Its range is an octave below that of the tenor sax. It is more resilient and lends itself better to fluent improvisation than other instruments in or around this register (notably the tuba).

Adrian Rollini (1904-1956) specialized in bass sax from 1924 until 1935. Heard on hundreds of important discs with Red Nichols, Bix Beiderbecke, Frank Trumbauer and Joe Venuti, he earned a unique niche in jazz history with his great flexibility and eloquence in this unlikely medium. Rollini's mantle was inherited by Joe Rushton (1907-1964), a West Coast figure featured with Nichols from 1947 until shortly before his death.

The bass saxophone was also well used occasionally by Charlie Ventura. In recent years some traditionalist combos have added color to their Dixieland performances by including bass sax, less as a solo voice than as a means of replacing or supplementing the tuba or string bass.

CHAPTER 13

THE GUITAR

The role in jazz history of the guitar and related instruments (banjo, etc.) has been overshadowed by the greater dominance in later years of the piano as a medium for ragtime. Yet long before the seeds of ragtime as a piano art were sown, primitive banjos and guitars were in use in the hands of itinerant folk singers deeply rooted in the blues. In homes that could scarcely afford furniture of any kind, let alone a piano, the heart of the musician, seeking a manual release, found its outlet not at the keyboard but on any plank of wood or metal across which a few wire strings could be arranged in simulation of the rough, vigorous sounds of the minstrel show's banjo and the wandering laborer's guitar.

The theory has been advanced that ragtime itself was a tributary of the early flow of banjo music. The piano, according to this hypothesis, was employed in ragtime to imitate one or two banjos; indeed, a very early published rag entitled *New Coon in Town* (1884) is significantly subtitled *Banjo Imitation*. The use of the banjo among American Negroes probably goes as far back as the American Revolution; Thomas Jefferson in 1781 referred to it as an instrument brought here from Africa.

The imitative process was eventually reversed: Huddie Ledbetter, a blues singer more generally known as "Leadbelly", tried to copy on his guitar the left hand of boogie-woogie piano when he heard it around Texas about 1910. Leadbelly represented, vocally and instrumentally, the folk-blues idiom that had a propulsive effect on early blues-ragtime-jazz forms. As a young man in the last decade of the nineteenth century he was one of countless Negroes who, in the post-slavery years, were able to make their own living out of music. Leadbelly, who without urbanizing his style became a successful night club attraction in the North before his death in 1949, was one of the last survivors of an era in which the instruments that told a primitive and potent blues story grew side by side with ragtime and the brass band, interlocking more and more frequently until jazz was born.

In the earliest years of recorded jazz the two parallel forms, ragtime on the banjo and blues on the guitar, were preserved respectively in the work of Fred Van Eps, playing in the minstrel show style typical of the early 1900s, and of Blind Lemon Jefferson, a contemporary and frequent associate of Leadbelly. Both can be heard in the "Backgrounds" tracks of Riverside's *History of Classic Jazz;* they were recorded not long after World War I. This album, unfortunately, is now hard to find.

Little change was effected in jazz banjo during the early 1920s; the guitar for the most part was quiescent. Every band had its banjo man: Will Johnson or Bud Scott with Oliver, Charlie Dixon with Henderson, Freddy Guy with Ellington, Lew Black with the New Orleans Rhythm Kings, Johnny St. Cyr with the early version of Armstrong's Hot Five. Their four-to-the-bar strumming threaded the rhythm section together but added little or nothing of durable solo value. Lonnie Johnson, a guitarist who had played on the Mississippi riverboats with Charlie Creath, became a recording artist in 1925 and soon had to his credit the luster of disc associations with Duke Ellington and Louis Armstrong. With him came the first signs of melodic continuity and tonal depth, of a maturation beyond the metallic plunking that had characterized so many of his predecessors.

Eddie Lang was the first to elevate the guitar to the stature of horns and piano as an adult jazz voice. Lang could play the blues with an earthy feeling that, for some Southern-oriented skeptics, belied his Philadelphia background; but he could also do for the guitar what Bix was doing for the cornet and Venuti for the violin, in the sense that all three combined unprecedented tonal purity with the gently swinging grace of an aerialist. In recording duets with Lonnie Johnson (under the pseudonym of "Blind Willie Dunn", presumably a more authentic name than Eddie Lang for the "race record" market), in duos and quartets with Venuti, and innumerable sides with the small jazz groups and large commercial orchestras such as Whiteman's and Gold-kette's, Lang became one of the most accessible artists on wax; his early death in 1933 left a void that was never filled. At a time when guitarists were strumming simple, unaltered chords, Lang not only expanded the harmonic horizon but developed a single-string solo technique that was a decade ahead of its time, for not until 1939, with the advent of Charlie Christian and the electric amplifier, did the guitar step permanently out of the shadows of the rhythm section.

There were others who accomplished the difficult task of transferring the language of Lang to their own guitars: the late Carl Kress and Dick McDonough were among the most talented, devising well-meshed duets more noteworthy for their slickness than for intensity or depth; George Van Eps and others of that well known plectrist family were early arrivals, but none quite captured the spark that had radiated from Lang.

In the six years that separated Lang's death from the so-called Christian Era of the electric guitar, there were only half a dozen guitarists who left footprints that are still discernible. Two were strictly rhythm guitarists—Eddie Condon, whose banjo or guitar livened many a small-combo jam session but has never yet been heard in a solo role, and Freddie Greene, whose imperative, rock-steady rhythm was tied like a tugboat to the Basie liner not long after it docked in New York. After thirty years with Basie, Greene is still considered unique in his class and still has never taken anything more than a few brief unamplified solos. The other four were solo guitarists: Teddy Bunn lent zest, humor and a beat to the unique combo called the Spirits of Rhythm, featuring guitars and tiples (smaller instruments of the guitar family). Al Casey, a courtier in the Fats Waller palace, stood in a corner while the leader played piano, sang and clowned, but in his occasional short solos revealed an unprecedentedly smooth single-string solo style, and on his only solo record with Fats, the memorable *Buck Jumping*, evidenced a mastery of both chord and single-string solos and deep-bred awareness of the blues.

Django Reinhardt, a Belgian-born gypsy, burst on the scene with the formation in 1934 of the Quintet of the Hot Club of France (violin, three guitars and bass), whose string-heavy sounds, novel and unprecedented though they were, seem in retrospect to suffer from much of the spring-like swing of an over-thick carpet. Reinhardt's gypsy background was reflected in the capricious style, the sudden explosive use of passages in octaves, of flurries of too many notes too soon; very rarely did he manage to swing with complete ease. Yet he was the first foreign musician to have a profound influence in the United States; Les Paul and others listened to his records and copied his style. He visited the U.S. in 1946, toured not too successfully with Duke Ellington, playing electric guitar with the air of one who had to keep up with the times, but the supple tone that had lent his work much of its charm for many listeners was coarsened as a result. Reinhardt, who died in 1953, left a bulky legacy of recordings, of which those taken at an easy ballad tempo seem the most viable.

Some observers in Paris in the late 1930s felt that a contemporary named Oscar Aleman could outswing Reinhardt and was a far superior jazzman, but the French spotlight was not large enough to accommodate two guitarists. Aleman, who made few records, was last heard of in Argentina.

Allan Reuss, with Benny Goodman, showed that the big swing bands had an important place for the rhythm guitarist. In general, however, the swing era was a period of transition for the guitar in jazz. As the spotlight concentrated more and more on large and generally vociferous orchestras in which the strumming of the plectrist was as effectual as a swimmer battling a tidal wave, there were a few tentative attempts to solve the problem of inaudibility. One of these was a tin resonator, which helped to amplify in some small degree the guitar's limited sounds.

One of the first musicians to use the resonator, later the first also to use the electric guitar, was Eddie Durham, the trombonist in Jimmie Lunceford's band who made a hobby of doubling on guitar. Durham was featured on the Lunceford record of *Hittin' the Bottle* in September 1935, probably the first recorded example of any form of guitar amplification. "Lunceford was crazy about the resonator," Durham recalls. "He used to bring the microphone right up to the F hole of the guitar, so that between that and the resonator it was almost like having an electric instrument.

"A year or two later, after the people that made the resonator had gone out of business, I found somebody else who was manufacturing an electrically amplified instrument. I joined Count Basie's band in the summer of 1937 and stayed with him a little over a year. Toward the end of that time I made two sessions with the Kansas City Five and Six, just a few guys out of the Basie band, with Freddie Greene playing rhythm guitar and myself on electric.

"A lot of people thought that was a screwy idea, having an amplified guitar, and the ballroom managers were always afraid you'd blow out their lights. There was DC current all over the place so I often had trouble finding electrical outlets while I was touring with Basie.

"Touring with the band I ran into Charlie Christian in Oklahoma City. He was playing piano when I first saw him, but I never in my life heard a guy learn to play guitar faster than he did. It was around the latter part of 1937, and I'll never forget that old beat up five-dollar wooden guitar that he took to the jam session where I heard him play. I told Charlie the way to sound like an instrument, staccato, was to use all down strokes. Most of the guys at that time played alternating up and down strokes across the strings. The down strokes gave a sharper tone like a saxophone, but when you come back up, while the strings are bouncing back, it gives you a more legato effect.

"I don't think Christian had ever seen a guitar with an amplifier until he met me. It was a year before they got on the market generally, and then he got one for himself.

"I influenced Floyd Smith to get an electric guitar, too. His mother didn't want him to buy an instrument, but one day I went downtown with him and talked him into getting one. I taught him how to tune it. The next time I saw him he was with Andy Kirk."

Both Floyd Smith and Durham experimented with two types of amplified instruments—electric Spanish and electrical steel guitars. Playing the latter, a somewhat strange device capable of quasi-Hawaiian glissando effects, Smith made a record with the Kirk orchestra, *Floyd's Guitar Blues*, in March 1939. A minor sensation, it was a trigger for the whole fusillade of new guitar styles to be issued only months later by Charlie Christian's arrival in New York.

With the advent of Christian, the guitar came of age in jazz. As early as 1938, in small bands around North Dakota, he was using the single-note line of a guitar as a third part, voiced with trumpet and tenor saxophone, thus removing it from the purely rhythmic function and giving it full membership tantamount to the addition of another horn. On his solos, he played with an utterly relaxed, even beat mainly in eighth notes. Occasionally he might play a Reinhardt solo taken note for note from one of Django's records, but basically his style was at an opposite pole, for Christian was the quintessence of swing. Harmonically he was able to experiment with augmented and diminished chords, to weave his own web around some of the better standard tunes such as *You Go To My Head*—a practice beyond the harmonic scope of most other guitarists, indeed of most other jazzmen, in 1938. Rhythmically, according to observers who heard him at that time, his ideas were highly suggestive of what was to be known as bop. That his connection with bop was more than co-incidental was confirmed when, after John Hammond had brought him to New York in the summer of 1939 to join the Benny Goodman Sextet, he spent many nights, after hours, jamming at Minton's in Harlem, where Gillespie, Monk, Kenny Clarke and their fellow-chemists held informal workshops.

Charlie Christian was only a "star," in the Hollywood sense, for two years (he contracted tuberculosis and died early in 1942), but it took only the first few months of this brief span to re-orient the whole concept of jazz guitar. Every guitarist since then can be judged largely in terms of the debt he owes to Christian and how much of Christian's sublime facility he has acquired.

The true Charlie Christian spirit has been captured very closely by Barney Kessel, formerly of the Oscar Peterson Trio, now one of the more preoccupied denizens of the Hollywood recording jungle; by Irving Ashby and Johnny Collins, both of whom were sheltered from public view through lengthy association as unobserved members of Nat Cole's accompanying unit; by Mary Osborne, a young North Dakota girl who bought an electric guitar, sat in with Christian and studied his technique long before he became a New York cynosure; by "Jim Daddy" Walker, who made some remarkable records with Pete Brown in 1944 but has not been heard from since; and more recently by Kenny Burrell, a young Detroiter prominent lately in the New York recording studios.

These are the artists whose lineage goes directly back to Christian; many others, cousins once removed, have evolved from Christian, adding new technical touches. The most agile of all is Tal Farlow (heard with the Red Norvo Trio off and on, 1950-55). Unlike most modern guitarists he is self-taught, in the sense that the phonograph and Christian were his only teachers.

Through the 1940s there were a few others who, without treading directly on Christian's territory, blended his innovations with their own personal qualities. Nat Cole's original trio in 1940 had an exceptional talent in Oscar Moore, who slipped from poll-winning eminence (first place every year in *Down Beat* and *Metronome*, 1945-8) to rhythm-and-blues obscurity. Jimmy Shirley, with the Herman Chittison Trio, made unique use of an attachment, the "vibrola," which lent his solos a semi-Hawaiian twang that should have earned him the commercial success accorded such gimmick artists as Alvino Rey and Les Paul. Billy Bauer (first heard with Herman) brought some of his studies with Lennie Tristano to bear on a series of records with Tristano, Konitz and company. "Slim" Gaillard, a comedian often accepted by the more gullible of fans as a jazz musician, earned a triple distinction: he was the performer with the largest hands, the loudest and most distorted amplifier, and the least taste of all the post-Christianites.

Though most of the Christian-influenced soloists have tended toward single-note horizontal lines in their solos, the potentialities inherent in the six strings of the guitar have not been neglected. (The strings are tuned upward, starting at E a twelfth below middle C to A, D, G, B and E, a basic two-octave span.) The Lang-Kress-McDonough generation had its offspring in George

Barnes, a brilliant studio musician whose duets with Carl Kress, in concerts and on records, offered a modern parallel for the Kress-McDonough work of the 1930s.

The guitarists of the bebop era were as much in Gillespie's and Parker's debt as in Christian's. Tiny Grimes played on Parker's first combo records; Remo Palmier and Bill De Arango distinguished themselves on early Gillespie sessions.

In the 1940s and '50s guitar was a major voice, blended with piano, in the popular King Cole Trio. This led to the formation of the Page Cavanaugh Trio (with Al Viola on guitar), the Art Tatum Trio (with Tiny Grimes), and the Soft Winds, featuring Herb Ellis, a Texan, who displayed the peculiar beat and facility common to guitarists from the southwestern U.S. From 1953 to 1958 Ellis was a galvanizing component of the Oscar Peterson Trio.

During the 1950s the piano-guitar-bass combo format receded from center stage. One superior guitarist, Johnny Smith, became a major jazz figure in 1952 'when his recorded ballads, such as *Moonlight in Vermont,* played in a relaxed chordal style, gained popular acceptance. From 1949 guitar (voiced with vibes and piano) was a cornerstone of the George Shearing Quintet. (15 years later Chuck Wayne, Shearing's original guitarist, became the first plectrist to record modern jazz on the banjo, in a Focus album. He sounds like a man doing the twist in a waistcoat and spats.) The Red Norvo Trio of the '50s included such outstanding guitarists as Jimmy Raney, Tal Farlow and Jimmy Wyble.

In 1962, bossa nova lent a badly-needed impetus to the guitar in jazz. Almost abandoned by the few remaining big bands, and out of place in the hard-driving neo-bop and avant-garde combos, the guitar was a logical means of expression for this delicate, melodic music. The Brazilians helped to revive the unamplified Spanish concert guitar, often played "finger style" (without a plectrum). Jazz guitarists whose sounds had been standardized now found it permissible to emerge from behind the electric mask and play an occasional solo on a "real" guitar.

Most of the bossa nova guitarists (Joao Gilberto, Luis Bonfa and Antonio Carlos Jobim) were not basically jazz-oriented; but at least one, Bola Sete, showed equal facility in every medium—electric and unamplified, Brazilian and modern jazz and every stop along the way. His collaborations with pianist Vince Guaraldi, and his unaccompanied performances, confirmed that Bola Sete is the most gifted and versatile Brazilian guitarist.

Prominent also in bossa nova were Charlie Byrd (ex-Woody Herman, 1959), a classical and jazz guitarist from Washington, D.C. whose technique, taste and adaptability are as remarkable as Bola Sete's; and Laurindo Almeida, a Californian since 1947 but a native of Sao Paolo, Brazil. Almeida was teamed with Bud Shank on some records in the early 1950s that foreshadowed the cultural alliance later represented by bossa nova. A superb finger-style concert guitarist, Almeida has worked successfully with many U.S. jazzmen to produce pop-jazz works.

Several countries besides Brazil have recently enriched the guitar heritage of jazz: notably Belgium (Jean "Toots" Thielemans and René Thomas), Hungary (Gabor Szabo and Attila Zoller) and Switzerland (Pierre Cavalli).

Since 1956 the guitar has found an important new *locus operandi* in Hammond organ combos. Records featuring organ, guitar and drums have offered solo space to Grant Green, Kenny Burrell and Les Spann in New York; Joe Diorio in Chicago; Ray Crawford and Howard Roberts in Los Angeles.

Four outstanding guitarists gained acceptance in the late 1950s or early 1960. Bill Harris of Washington, D.C. showed an impressive range of amplified and Spanish styles in his Mercury albums. Jim Hall's keen rhythmic and harmonic sensitivity were heard in fruitful collaborations with such hornmen as Jimmy Giuffre, Sonny Rollins and Art Farmer. Joe Pass, in the Gerald Wilson band and the Shearing Quintet, showed a stunning technique and a phenomenal capacity for swinging. Wes Montgomery is a self-taught performer of whom George Barnes said, "He uses his thumb as if it were a pick." His admirable technique is often deployed in grass-roots re-examinations of the blues.

CHAPTER 14

THE BASS

The role of the bass in jazz has been constantly undervalued and misunderstood. To the layman, or the economy-conscious night club proprietor, it seems incredible that this instrument, so seldom heard in solo flights and even then so hard to hear, can possibly be a necessity in every group from trio to symphony. The jazz unit can no more dispense with a bass than a house with its foundation or a ship with its hull. Since the motivating element in both written and improvised jazz is the harmonic structure by the composition, it devolves upon the bass to provide a constant guide to this structure, most often by playing the root of the incumbent chord, or its fifth, and by linking these notes together with other notes of the chord or with passing notes. At the same time, through the depth and penetration of its tonal quality, the bass provides the fundamental rhythmic beat. The pianist and guitarist may "comp" (fill in with rhythmic punctuations and syncopation); the drummer may invest in a variety of complex counter-rhythms, but through it all the bass provides the deep, rich four-to-the-bar sine qua non that gives the band, literally, its lowest common denominator.

Brass bass instruments, such as the tuba or sousaphone, alternated with string basses in the early years of jazz. During the past decade the tuba has made a tentative return, though usually supplementing rather than replacing the string bass and functioning as much melodically as rhythmically. The string bass (also known as bass fiddle, bass violin, etc.) gradually ousted the brass bass from jazz orchestras during the 1920s, though until

the early 1930s most of the leading bass players were required
to double on tuba.

The bass strings are tuned upwards in fourths (E, A, D, G),
starting an octave and a sixth below middle C; in rhythm section
work these strings are usually "walked"; that is, played continuously, four notes to the bar. The pizzicato (plucked) use of
the bass strings in the rhythm section "came up with the boys
from San Francisco," according to Eubie Blake; other sources
credit it, in what is doubtless an apocryphal story, to an incident
that occurred around 1911 when Bill Johnson, playing with his
Original Creole Band, one night forgot to bring his bow and was
constrained to spend the evening plucking the strings. Many jazzmen feel that the use of the string bass in this manner antedates
the turn of the century. At all events, it was commonplace by
the time recording began; several of the original records by Negro
jazz orchestras use string basses. The earliest exponents included
Ed Garland, with Kid Ory; Bob Escudero, with Fletcher Henderson; George "Pops" Foster, the New Orleans pioneer who played
with Bunk Johnson, Luis Russell and Louis Armstrong; and Well-
man Braud (Ellington, 1926-35); Walter Page with Benny Moten
and Count Basie.

During the 1930s a few recorded bass solos achieved some
prominence: *Blues of Israel* by Israel Crosby with Gene Krupa,
and *The Big Noise from Winnetka,* a Bob Crosby band novelty
in which Ray Bauduc played his drumsticks on the strings of
Bob Haggart's bass. But by 1938, when John Kirby was established as the first bassist-leader of a successful jazz group, most
bass work was still limited to strings of quarter notes or sometimes at slow tempi, dotted eighths and sixteenths.

There is a curious parallel between the history of the guitar
and the bass in jazz. Each underwent a sudden and radical
change at the hands of one musician who revolutionized the concept of the instrument's capabilities. In both cases the year was
1939; in both the innovators were young men destined to die
within three years, victims of tuberculosis. What Charlie Christian did for jazz guitar, and for modern jazz itself, Jimmy Blanton
did for the hitherto almost unexploited bass violin.

Blanton joined the Duke Ellington orchestra in October 1939.

The following month he recorded two bass-piano duos with Ellington: *Blues* and *Plucked Again*. During the next year he was a central participant in arrangements played by the full band, notably *Jack the Bear*, and was heard in four more duo performances: *Pitter Panther Patter, Sophisticated Lady, Body and Soul* and *Mr. J. B. Blues*, in which he was heard in both arco (bowed) and pizzicato solos.

Blanton's amazing technique enabled him to improvise melodically, in horn-like style. Even his ensemble work revealed a crispness of timbre that gave the bass a new dimension.

During the 1940s there were great advances. The logical successor to Blanton, also featured with Ellington (from 1945-8) was Oscar Pettiford (1922-1960). The advent of bop, with its intricate harmonic-melodic demands and its frequent fast tempi, brought to light such newcomers as Ray Brown, introduced by Dizzy Gillespie in the mid-1940s; Nelson Boyd, Percy Heath and Al McKibbon, also early Gillespie alumni; Tommy Potter, with Charlie Parker; Ed Safranski, who as Stan Kenton's bassist (1945-8) enjoyed poll-winning popularity; Milt Hinton (Cab Calloway, 1940-51); and Chubby Jackson, of the first Woody Herman Herd, who for a while experimented with a five-stringed bass (tuned E-A-D-G-C).

The most-recorded bassist in jazz in the mid-1940s was "Slam" Stewart, inventor of a novel humorous technique: he bowed his solos and hummed them simultaneously in octave unison. The idea has been used in recent years by Major Holley.

Starting with Harry Babasin in 1947 in Los Angeles, bassists began to experiment with pizzicato ad lib cello. This was developed effectively by Oscar Pettifford in 1950, later by Ray Brown, Sam Jones and El Dee Young.

Several leading bassists acquired an enduring reputation in the 1950s less as virtuosi than as dependable, rhythmically supple rhythm section members. They included George Duvivier, Ben Tucker, Art Davis, Bill Crow, Wendell Marshall, Jymie Merritt and the late Doug Watkins in New York; Leroy Vinnegar, Red Mitchell, Jimmy Bond, Monty Budwig, Ralph Pena

and the late Curtis Counce in Hollywood. Two greatly underrated Chicago-born bassists are Gene Wright, a mainstay of the
Dave Brubeck Quartet from 1958, and Wilbur Ware, ex-Monk-
and-Blakey.

Of the school stemming directly from Blanton and Pettiford,
the most important in the further emancipation of the bass was
Paul Chambers, heard from 1955 with Miles Davis. Like many
of his generation, Chambers (born in 1935) emerged as a mature solo voice in both pizzicato and arco solos.

The first bassist since John Kirby to establish himself as an
over-all force in jazz was Charles Mingus, who soon after becoming a leader around 1955 was hailed as one of the great
masters of the bass. Capable of huge-toned, melodically startling lines, he used every device from whole notes to 32nds,
glissandi, slaps and whatever else aided the mood of creative
surprise.

The experiments of Mingus foreshadowed a development that
took place around 1960. A new school of young bassists began
to ignore the laws of timekeeping, tonality, cycles of fifths, ton-
ics and dominants, and all the other guideposts of the bop-era
bassists. Fulfilling a virtual solo function even while theoretically background members, they would delete, delay or anticipate
notes during ensemble choruses. They had keener ears than their
predecessors and refused to limit themselves to the traditional
role of the bassist as beat-purveyor.

The unofficial founder of this school was Scott La Faro, of
the first Bill Evans Trio. Born in 1936 and killed in an accident in 1961, La Faro inspired such brilliant newcomers as
Chuck Israels (who succeeded him with Evans); Charlie Haden,
who came to prominence with Ornette Coleman; Gary Peacock,
heard with various avant-garde groups; and Steve Swallow of
the Jimmy Giuffre combo.

Bass standards are so high today that I can only offer a token
list of other first-rate players: Chuck Andrus, Keter Betts, Ron
Carter, Richard Davis, Jimmy Garrison, Henry Grimes, George
Tucker, Butch Warren.

The resurgence of the tuba has produced such talents as Bill Barber, of the 1949-50 Miles Davis nonet; and Red Callender, the bassist who has doubled as a tuba player on countless Hollywood studio dates.

CHAPTER 15

THE DRUMS

In any analysis of the role of the drummer in the development of jazz it should be borne in mind that an essential difference exists on several levels—dynamically, tonally, empirically, pragmatically—between the terms "drums" and "percussion." The drum specifically, in one form or another, has been an ancestor of jazz as far back as Dr. Marshall Stearns was able to trace its genealogy.[1] A set of three drums at West African tribal ceremonies may have produced, two or three hundred years ago, a complex of rhythms such as 4/4, 6/8 and 3/4 simultaneously, without regard for bar lines. Drums of various sizes were pummeled by the fingers, fists and feet of performers in New Orleans' Congo Square in the late nineteenth century.

Percussion, taken in the broad sense to embrace all instruments that must be struck to produce a sound, and in the special sense applied to it by jazzmen to denote the variety of equipment at the disposal of the jazz drummer, is a more comprehensive art than drumming in that its products are not limited to a few specific tone colors produced by drums. Drumming is predominantly rhythmic in nature; percussion involves, at times, both melody and harmony. The completely equipped percussionist can double on bells, chimes, xylophone and related mallet-struck instruments. Tuned tympani and tonal effects on the snare drum have also been used effectively by many jazz drummers.

The history of jazz percussion, in direct relationship to the barlines, syncopations and compositional forms of the earliest jazz, is of comparatively recent origin. Washboards and other primitive media were the recourse of the folk blues artists, while large bass and snare drums hit with mallets and sticks played a bombastic role in the brass bands. As the blues, ragtime and the brass bands fused into the earliest jazz, the function of the drummer became clear. Unchanged in essence since the beginning of jazz as we know it, it was succinctly assessed by George Wettling: "It's not a question of two beats or four. It's a matter of feeding the band with rhythm and underlining what they're doing—that's what you call shading. And the secret of that is simply listening to the other fellows."

The adolescent jazz fan who clamors for louder and longer drum solos at every concert, every dance, every night club performance, is either unaware of this simple truth or reluctant to concern himself with it. Jazz is a fusion of three interdependent units: melody, harmony and rhythm. The drum solo, dispensing with the first two, divorces itself from the essence of the music. Zutty Singleton recalls that except for occasional novelty effects the drum solo was a rarity in the early days of jazz. The drummer played a subsidiary role: "We just kept the rhythm going and hardly ever took a solo. But when we did, the drummers had all kinds of different sound effects; a bucket gimmick that almost sounded like a lion's roar; skillets, ratchets, bells, everything. I remember when I used to play in the Lyric Theatre in New Orleans with John Robicheaux, they'd wait until the end of the tune and then put the spotlight on the drummer and he'd start hitting *everything*."

"Everything" in those days, four decades ago, did not quite have the significance that could be attached to the word today. Aside from the gimmick sound effects the drummer's task had to be accomplished on the snare drum, small Chinese tom-tom ("we used to have four of 'em, with different tones," Zutty recalls), and a Chinese cymbal with a morgue-like tone. Zutty believes that the tension drums, tuned with keys or thumb screws, came into general use around 1915. When asked "Was there much rhythmic variation, much syncopation, any concentration on the drummer's role in the band?" he answered, "Very, very little. All you had to do was keep good time and keep the sticks going. It was drumsticks generally, though mallets were used in the brass band, of course, and on the tympani, and for special build-up effects in finales on the cymbal."

The use of wire brushes in place of drumsticks enabled the drummer to achieve a softer, smoother, more legato sound that was especially effective on ballads. The date of origin of the brushes is in doubt, though white musicians certainly used them during World War I. "The first pair of brushes I ever had," says Zutty, "were sent from Chicago by Manuel Perez to Louis 'Old Man' Cotrelle, the drummer with Piron. I studied his work a lot in the early days. But Cotrelle didn't care about them and gave them to me, and those were the first wire brushes I ever saw in my life, around 1921. Before that, you had to get your soft effects just by controlling your touch with the sticks."

Tony Sbarboro (Spargo), who reached New York with the Original Dixieland Jazz Band in February 1917, attests that he had never seen a pair of wire brushes before this time. In earlier years, in New Orleans, the function of the drummer was simpler though his responsibility was greater. Spargo recalls: "At the average dances that we'd play, the picnics, there was no such thing as a piano. We would work with guitars and string bass. You had to keep going, keep filling in as much as possible, and you never thought of a drum solo. You used the sticks because you needed that punch to make up for the missing piano. Because it fell to the drummer to keep the rhythm going, there was no such thing as individuality or distinctive styles among the drummers, and no difference between the work of the white and the Negro musicians." Nevertheless, there was a considerable difference between the accomplishments of the percussionists. "In April 1919," Spargo continues, "while we were in England, they had a six-piece band with two drummers. They'd never heard of one fellow playing two drums. But we had a guy in New Orleans, Emile Stein, who was the greatest and most ferocious of them all, and who played so many things that he worked from a piano stool, swiveling around on that stool from the tympani to the bells and the snare and everything. He was the first I saw to do that. He could play jazz with the best of them and turn around and play high-class cabaret work."

Both Spargo and Singleton recall that Paul Detroit, who later became- a successful MGM studio drummer in California, was one of New Orleans' foremost early percussion artists, and that a musician known simply as "Battleaxe," who played with Jim Europe's Army band in World War I, was among the first Negro jazz drummers. In the East there was no shortage of percussive excitement: Willie The Lion Smith singles out for tribute Arthur "Traps" McIntyre. "That guy was so fast, the only drummer today who could come near holding a candle to him would be Jo Jones," roars The Lion.

The sound of jazz has changed with the decades not only in the nature of the music, but in the rapid evolution of its physical raw materials. A comparison between the early percussionist and the highly skilled and well accoutered percussionist of today must take into account not only the extent of the latter's studies and their application to an advanced technique but also the immeasurable advance in the quality and quantity of his equipment.

George Wettling points out that much of the early drummer's kit was used more for novelty and comedy effects than for real integration into the performance: "The tom toms originally were all Chinese and made of thick pigskin; they featured painted dragons and all kinds of art work, and no two were alike. They were there as much to be seen as heard. And those corny temple blocks—they had sets of those, of different pitch, used for tonal effects. Vic Berton deserves a lot of credit for making the drummer's job easier and more varied. I think he started the foot-cymbals back around 1925, and way back around that same time he was using a pair of tuned tympani with an octave range— from low F to B Flat and from B Flat up to F."

New timbres were at the drummer's disposal constantly during the next decade. The crude Chinese cymbal gave way to the sonorous, majestic Zildjian. Originally made in Turkey and now the product of U.S.-domiciled Turks, their diameter may be as much as 22 inches. The insistent tone of the Zildjian has assumed an increasingly important part in contributing to the beat of the rhythm section. The foot-cymbal gave way, soon after 1930, to the "high hat cymbal," two cymbals facing each other and made to meet through pedal control.

Wettling credits Warren "Baby" Dodds, whom he heard in

Chicago with King Oliver 35 years ago, as the first to extract the full potential from the bass drum. Like the string bass, it became part of the foundation of every jazz group, furnishing a pulsating rhythmic undercurrent that had to flow evenly through every performance.

The first important white drummers of the 1920s were Ben Pollack, the Chicagoan heard with the New Orleans Rhythm Kings and from 1925 with his own band; Ray Bauduc, from New Orleans, who took over the drums· in Pollack's orchestra when the latter devoted himself to conducting; and Chauncey Morehouse, heard on most of the Bix and Trumbauer records and one of the first to use the high-hat cymbal to distinctive effect. There is regrettably little recorded evidence of the actual performances of these drummers, since the early recording systems were limited in the frequency range they could handle and the use of the bass drum was forbidden at record sessions. A mild sensation was created upon the release, early in 1928, of four titles by McKenzie and Condon's Chicagoans in which Gene Krupa set a precedent by including a bass drum in his equipment.

Krupa, Dave Tough and George Wettling, all about the same age, had roughly parallel careers, playing in Chicago during the 1920s and later settling in New York. Wettling most clearly reflected the influence of Baby Dodds; Tough, a diminutive figure who looked scarcely strong enough to lift a pair of mallets, was credited with the most dynamic and sensitive use of cymbals and evolved from a career in small combos to a decade of great distinction with many name bands before his death in 1948.

Gene Krupa, who in the mid-1950s was Cozy Cole's partner in a drum school, and who in his early days spent endless hours in the informal tuition offered by Chicago's Negro drummers, recently said: "Any idea that I knew anything about skins had to go out the window once I started hitting those South Side joints. For one thing, I had no idea of the wide range of effect you could get from a set of drums. I picked up from Zutty Singleton and Baby Dodds the difference between starting a roll or sequence of beats with the left or right hand and how the tone and inflection changed entirely when you shifted hands. Those Negro drummers did it nonchalantly as though it were a game.

"Taking my cue from what I heard, I next went to work on the tom-toms trying to get them in tune and knowing when to use 'em. I punched holes in them with an icepick, as Zutty told me, until they were just pitched right. Another trick I got from Baby Dodds was how to keep the bass and the snare drum in tune and how to get cymbals that rang in tune and were pitched in certain keys. Then came the cowbell and the woodblock. You see, most white musicians of that day thought drums were something you used to beat the hell out of. The monotonous pattern made you feel weary after listening to it for a while. Few of them realized that drums have a broad range of tonal variations so they can be played to fit into a harmonic pattern as well as a rhythmic one."[1]

Krupa, a master technician, was as flexible as Wettling and as dynamic as Tough. His beat was steady and relentless, his knowledge of the history and nature of percussion constantly increasing through an unquenchable thirst for information. Though Krupa made his most important contribution as a member of the metronomic rhythm section in the Benny Goodman 1935 band, it was his lengthy solo on the Goodman performance of *Sing, Sing, Sing*, recorded in 1937, that led directly to the acceptance of the jazz drummer as a much-used solo voice in the orchestra.

Several other drummers came to the forefront during the 1930s, mainly for their contributions to the rhythm section rather than for their exhibitionistic potentialities. Chick Webb, almost a fixture at the Savoy Ballroom during the middle 1930s, had a superb control of bass drum, snare and cymbals and was Krupa's perennial idol. Big Sid Catlett, playing in the bands of Benny Carter, Fletcher Henderson and Don Redman, developed a beat of rock-like steadiness, perhaps less obtrusively than any of his contemporaries, as did Cozy Cole, who showed himself as adaptable to the big band work he did with Benny Carter and Willie Bryant, as to the small combo requirements of the Stuff Smith Quintet, with which he earned first prominence along 52nd Street in 1936. Catlett and Cole were essentially functional drummers, men who knew that their primary task was that of integrating their rhythmic contribution into the work of the entire group. (Lionel Hampton, a master of the whole percussion family, had no such reservation about his role: he preferred to be heard, and was eventually to develop a fantastically showmanlike style in which visual effects tended to take precedence over a sense of rhythmic responsibility.)

All these drummers were adaptable enough to blend into a setting of any size, shape or style. The theory that there are a two-beat and a four-beat school of drumming is largely a fantasy dreamed up by writers; even men closely associated with the so-called "Dixieland" two-beat school, such as Ray Bauduc with the Bob Crosby band and Ray McKinley, the popular vocalist-drummer heard in many Dixieland arrangements with the Dorsey Brothers in the mid-30s, never limited themselves to any specific beat but preferred to adjust each performance to the particular requirements of the arrangement.

Modern drumming may be said to have made its first long step toward maturity when Jo Jones, arriving in New York with the Count Basie band in 1936, became the new musicians' idol. Jones' top-cymbal beat outswung that of every predecessor; more important, he was able, through rhythmic effects on the bass drum and snares, to underline and punctuate the various accents in each arrangement to an extent never heard before in swing music. Jones soon took his place alongside Krupa as a reigning favorite, a master of subtlety and elegance, with a clean, individual high-hat technique. His superlative coördination earned him the respect of musicians of every school; he has worked with Dixieland, swing and modern musicians and has been named by many musicians as one of the founding fathers of modern jazz drumming.

The next major step forward took place with the development of bop. As early as 1939-40, in the Teddy Hill band, Kenny Clarke began to experiment with the idea of transferring the essence of the rhythmic beat from the bass drum to the top cymbal, in an effort to escape from the heavy pounding of an obviously stated four-to-the-bar rhythm. Clarke was the major influence on Max Roach, who brought this style to a high degree of finesse—and to an eager national audience—when he began to record with Hawkins, Gillespie and other combo leaders in 1944-5. By this time several other drummers, tired of limping heavily on the bass drum pedal twice or four times in every measure, had taken up the new technique. Notable among them were Stan Levey; the volatile and brilliant Art Blakey; the late but unforgotten Dave Tough; Shelly Manne, a Kenton and Herman alumnus who became the West Coast's most popular and flexible percussion artist; and the influential Tiny Kahn, who died at 29 in 1953.

Less influenced by bop than by the swing tradition were two Tommy Dorsey band alumni: Buddy Rich, a man of commanding energy and formidable speed, and Louis Bellson, who during the two years when he galvanized the Ellington band (1951-2) demonstrated his phenomenal footwork through the novel device of using two bass drums.

Afro-Cuban and Latin rhythm began to change the sound of jazz drumming substantially in 1947-8, when maracas, bongos and conga drums were heard in the bands of Stan Kenton and Dizzy Gillespie. Chano Pozo (1915-1948) brought to the Gillespie band of 1948 a dramatic transfusion of West African rhythms he had heard as a youth in Cuba. Candido Camero and Armando Peraza, both from Havana, were inspired by Pozo; the latter, after a decade with George Shearing, was heard in Cal Tjader's Latin-oriented combo in the 1960s.

In the late 1950s jazz drumming made great progress. Many leading drummers formed their own groups: the explosively brilliant Art Blakey, the more conservative but quietly skillful Chico Hamilton, as well as Roach, Rich, Manne and others. *Orgy In Rhythm* on Blue Note featured Art Blakey with eight other men playing drums, tympani, bongo, timbales, congas, cencerro and tree log. *Drum Suite* (with Osie Johnson, Gus Johnson, Ted Sommer and Don Lamond) and *Son of Drum Suite* (with Lamond, Mel Lewis, Louis Hayes, Jimmy Cobb, Charlie Persip), were heard on RCA Victor; and Duke Ellington's *Malletoba Spank* and *Tymperturbably Blue* (Columbia) included nine symphony percussionists.

The drummer, once considered the musical ignoramus of the band, by 1960 was an articulate, literate student of musical history (Ed Thigpen, Oscar Peterson's alumnus, is an encyclopedia of jazz drumming) who could fit into any musical context, and who often was a composer-arranger with a working knowledge of two or three other instruments.

So broad was the variety of tonal effects and over-all nuances, the drums began to fill what was, in effect, a melodic function. Philly Joe Jones, a favorite hard bopper of the mid-1950s and father of this new school, became an essential part of the whole sound rather than a subsidiary factor in the rhythm section. This concept was carried forward in the 1960s by Elvin Jones, younger brother of Hank and Thad Jones, whose thermodynamics often amounted to near-total command of the John Coltrane Quartet.

Among the less patently extrovert drummers to emerge in the 1955-65 period were Joe Morello and Connie Kay of the Dave Brubeck and Modern Jazz Quartets. Marian McPartland, Morello's 1952-6 employer, wrote of his rare combination of "technique, ideas, ability to play unusual time signatures, humor and unflagging zest for playing . . . he may have several rhythms going at one time, tossing them to and fro with the studied casualness of a juggler. Yet through it all, the inexorable beat of the bass drum (not loud—felt more than heard) holds everything together. He moves gracefully, with a minimum of fuss, but with a sparkling diamond-sharp attack, reminiscent of the late Sid Catlett."

Connie Kay recalled a similar influence, as Whitney Balliett commented: "He shifted constantly between his four exquisitely pitched ride cymbals . . . He used finger cymbals, his hands, and the metal loops on his wire brushes in place of sticks. He was never obtrusive, never retiring. In short, he provided the sort of infectious, steadily expanding beat that his model, Sidney Catlett, is still celebrated for."

A list of the most brilliant drummers of the 1960s must include Jake Hanna (Woody Herman, 1963-4), Roy Haynes, a modernist with Lester Young in 1947 and a superb all-around artist today; Ed Blackwell, Alan Dawson, Pete LaRoca and Danny Richmond.

Among earlier performers who were brought up in the dance band tradition there has been a strong reaction against over-dominant drumming. "The modernists, who were not trained as dance drummers," says Gene Krupa, "do almost anything that comes to mind, and they get away with it, because the people who follow it have stopped dancing, or never learned how. These young drummers, and there are some outstanding ones among them, try to do too much. They try to play everything in an eight-bar break. If I beat out my wildest solo and the people couldn't dance to it, I'd be really shocked; for I learned years ago that you just can't break time."[1]

Typical of the "outstanding ones among them" to whom Krupa refers is Tony Williams. Born in 1947, he joined Miles Davis at the age of 17 and astonished jazzmen three and four times his age.

Don De Micheal wrote in *Down Beat*: "When Williams is at his best . . . he creates a screen of rhythmic sounds—tinkled cymbals, crashes, ticks of sticks on wood, sudden splashes as he flicks off his high-hat, blurred open rolls, series of off-beat accents that create the illusion of a different tempo and become so intense that the tension from the building sound feels as if it will break your head before he lets the stretched time snap back into position."

Significantly, Williams has also worked with Coltrane and Cecil Taylor. In his first album as a leader, he chose a group of musicians from the avant-garde. As he pointed out, the role of the drummer changes with each new style in music, and the drummer in the avant-garde has ideas that are as different from those of Roach and Blakey as theirs from Krupa's and Webb's.

Because there were neither records nor historiography to document it, we cannot tell where and how the history of twentieth-century percussion began; nor can Tony Williams show us where it will end. But certainly his astonishing technique and creativity, while he was still in his teens, portrayed as clearly as anything we are likely to hear in this decade the future shape and evolution of the uniquely intricate art of jazz drumming.

CHAPTER 16

THE VIBRAPHONE

The work of the painter who employs his fingers instead of a paintbrush tends at first to arouse a skeptical curiosity, but ultimately it is the quality of his work, rather than the tool employed, that becomes the yardstick of appraisal. In jazz the media of expression have encompassed almost everything capable of producing sound, from washboard and kazoo to harmonica and one-string fiddle. Because the end invariably justifies the means in any art, many instruments strange to classical music have arrived, after a transitional period of doubt, at a state of serious consideration and ultimate acceptance in jazz. Not the least of these are the mallet family, of which the precocious and successful cadet was the electrically controlled vibraphone or vibraharp.*

Mallet instruments were a novel accouterment of percussionists in the 1920s, used mainly for novelty side effects in dance band music, stage acts and brass bands. Not until the advent of Red Norvo was any of them considered as a possible outlet for jazz expression. Norvo's instrument was the xylophone, a sort of dehydrated vibraphone. Its keys were wood instead of metal; there was little resonance, and the only way to give the impression of sustaining a note was to use a half-tone tremolo or hit the same note repeatedly. The sounds resembled nothing more than the dripping of a leaky water faucet; yet Norvo, who had begun to play it in 1920 and had gone through the vaudeville phase, playing *Poet and Peasant* and doing a tap dance, began to ex-

* The term "vibraharp," a trade name, is synonymous with vibraphone.

ploit the xylophone as a jazz instrument as early as 1930. His first record was *Moon Country* with Hoagy Carmichael. In 1933 he recorded two jazz solos on xylophone and two on marimba (a fuller-sounding variant in the xylophone family, fitted with resonance tubes beneath each key) From 1934-6 he led several all-star jazz combos; from 1936 he had his own superb 12-piece band with vocals by his wife, Mildred Bailey.

During these crucial years Norvo became a musicians' idol. Nobody else even sought this particular sound and medium; and nobody, it was felt among his contemporaries, could have competed with his delicacy and finesse, the subtlety of his phrasing, the dancing grace of his rhythmic beat. Norvo was a master of a new jazz sound, bringing a new sense of insinuating understatement that had a charm unheard in any jazz produced until his day. Norvo continued to play the xylophone until 1943, when he made a switch to the vibraphone; even then he remained unique, using the instrument without the motor, thus avoiding the artificial vibrato of the electric current, retaining all the Norvo traits while gaining the ability to sustain notes.

The vibraphone, like the xylophone, was an instrument long associated with novelty music. It has the advantages of a sustaining pedal, resonating tubes under the keys, and small rotating fans, placed beneath the keys and operated electrically, to give the notes a synthetic vibrato. Usually its range runs upward two-and-a-half to three octaves from middle C.

Lionel Hampton, then a 17-year-old drummer with the Les Hite band that was backing Louis Armstrong, took up the vibraphone more or less by chance. There was a vibraphone in the studio the day he recorded *Confessin'* with Louis in July 1930; he used it for a brief ad lib introduction. Hampton remained in obscurity until Benny Goodman found him leading a band in a Los Angeles ballroom in 1936, used him on some records, then persuaded him to give up his band and make the Goodman Quartet a permanent entity.

Hampton was not the first jazz musician associated with the vibes. Adrian Rollini, known earlier as a bass saxophonist, had been concentrating on vibes since the early 1930s but played so blandly and with such a minimal beat that his efforts went almost unnoticed. Hampton, personally and musically, was a dynamo, infusing power and magnetism into his own work and all that surrounded him. The sparks generated by his pinwheel solos on fast tempi contrasted strikingly with the reflective yet fast-thinking extemporizations on ballads. Hampton and Norvo, from 1936 to 1943, remained unique, each with his own instrument, his own concept of dynamics and swing, his own choice of a suitable background. While Norvo recorded with the emancipated swing arrangements of Eddie Sauter as a gentle backdrop, Hampton from time to time assembled all-star sessions to record with men from the Goodman, Basie, Ellington and Calloway bands.

By 1943-4 Norvo was going through a transitional phase both as a bandleader and instrumentalist; Hampton, leading his own big band, was starting down the firecracker-strewn path that led to quasi-rhythm-and-blues and ever-reduced moments of the old vibes-virtuoso magic. The time had come for a challenger. He arrived in 1945 when Dizzy Gillespie brought Milt Jackson to New York. For several years, playing with Gillespie and various bop units, Jackson's accomplishment appeared simply to be the transference to his instrument of the characteristics of bebop. Not until the early 1950s, when the experiments began with John Lewis that led to the foundation of the Modern Jazz Quartet, did his musical id emerge from the bop superego—a laconic, apparently slow-thinking approach, in which the slackening of pace actually derived not from his cerebration but from the use of a reduced speed on the fans of the vibraphone motor. The effect was a langorous, meditative quality that made the listener more aware of the vibrato's presence where normally it was only sensed subconsciously.

Not long after "Bags" Jackson established himself on the scene there was a sharp detonation along 52nd Street announcing the arrival of Terry Gibbs. With this newcomer, two years Jackson's junior, came the bop era's Lionel Hampton: a tremendously vital figure symbolized by an ineluctable beat, flying mallets, and an unerringly swift ear for chord changes. Gibbs' supremely extrovert personality, born of innate enthusiasm rather than conscious showmanship, earned him national prominence earlier than Jackson. From 1950-54 it was Gibbs who won the annual jazz plebiscites; then Jackson moved into the top spot. These fluctuations had no bearing on their relative merits; both remained, and still are, the most valuable exponents of modern jazz on the vibraphone.

Meanwhile Hampton has continued, when recording with smaller groups, to play first class jazz with a few new flourishes, clearly the result of his early acceptance of and enthusiasm for bop. The gentle Norvo style was heard with various trios in the 1950s and quintets in the '60s. Tyree Glenn, a trombonist who doubled, was one of the few newcomers to be added to the slim ranks of jazz vibraphonists during the swing era, and incidentally the only vibraphonist ever featured with Duke Ellington's orchestra (1947-52).

From 1949, when the George Shearing Quintet was formed, with vibes (Margie Hyams) as a major voice, the number of vibes players in jazz multiplied rapidly. Shearing introduced a series of others: Don Elliott, Joe Roland, Cal Tjader (later a successful leader himself specializing in both jazz and Afro-Cuban music), Emil Richards and Hagood Hardy, among others.

Teddy Charles, putting his extensive studies with composer Hall Overton to provocative use, was a premature avant-gardist of the vibes, recording some precursive albums as composer and leader in 1952-6.

Two of the best new vibes men of the '50s were killed in accidents. Lem Winchester, a patrolman, discovered by this writer and presented at the Newport Jazz Festival in 1958, was a fleet, supple Jackson-derived soloist. He left the police force to concentrate on music, but died in 1961 after playing Russian roulette. Eddie Costa, heard at Newport in 1957, played in a bristling, confident style. He died in an automobile crash in 1962.

Victor Feldman, like Costa, was with Woody Herman for a while and, also like Costa, doubles on piano. He is among the most imaginative and best-equipped of contemporary vibes players. Greatly underrated was Miss Terry Pollard, heard as pianist-vibist with Terry Gibbs (1953-7) but in Detroit, almost forgotten, in later years.

In 1956 several West Coast pianists experimented with an attachment (the "vibories") that enabled the soloist to substitute fingers for mallets and thus play up to ten notes simultaneously. The initiative was never followed up, since the inventor did not put this potentially valuable instrument on the market.

Several new vibraphonists gained public attention in or around 1960. They included Tubby Hayes, a British saxophonist whose vibes work showed great promise; Buddy Montgomery (brother of guitarist Wes); Mike Mainieri, an unusually fast and sometimes exciting performer in the Gibbs tradition; Walt Dickerson, a fine instrumentalist and arranger influenced, it would seem, more by Stravinsky than by the blues; Dave Pike, an ex-member of Paul Bley's entourage; and Roy Ayers, an extremely agile young Jackson admirer on the West Coast.

The mid-1960s brought another wave of gifted young artists to the foreground. Bobby Hutcherson, heard on records with Grachan Moncur and Tony Williams, sounds like a Dolphy of the vibes. Gary Burton, with Shearing and Getz, has revealed an astonishing facility in his handling of three or four mallets for unusual and complex harmonic innovations. A teen-ager when first heard on records in the early 1960s, Burton, like Hutcherson, indicates the general direction in which jazz vibes seems to be heading.

Gary McFarland, heard with his own combo in 1965, is a capable vibraphonist but is chiefly important as an arranger.

Others who have shown promise in recent years include Donald Best, Vera Auer, Tommy Vig; Johnny Lytle, a hard swinger influenced by Hampton and Jackson; and such West Coast musicians as Larry Bunker, better known as a drummer, and Lynn Blessing, with the Paul Horn Quintet. The European scene has produced such talents as Bill Le Sage, Fats Sadi and Wolfgang Schluter.

CHAPTER 17

THE OTHER INSTRUMENTS

The search for new horizons in jazz has led to a slow and inevitable broadening of its tonal scope. Though the main instruments now in use are no different from those employed a quarter-century ago, there has been a perceptible upsurge in the use of those instruments normally classified among jazzmen as "miscellaneous".

That the violin still belongs in this category can be ascribed, as with the clarinet, to the technical difficulties in mastering the instrument; another cause may have been the shortage of job opportunities, especially for Negro jazz musicians. Despite these problems, the violin played a more important role in jazz during the ragtime decades than it has in the forty years since the official arrival of the jazz band. In many areas the violinist was considered the logical choice for the role of leader. Long before the days of Venuti and Lang, fiddlers and guitarists with little technical knowledge but much to say in the language of syncopation teamed to produce music that may have marked a no-man's land between American folk music in general and early ragtime in particular. There is more than a trace of jazz in the fiddle music played today by performers of "country and western" or hillbilly music; conversely the western sound was occasionally discernible in the jazz improvisations of Eddie South.

South is probably the greatest violinist ever to have devoted himself to jazz. A complete musician, he brought to the instrument a technically masterful approach never mitigated by condescension. His assets were (and still are) a crystal tone, impeccable intonation and a superlative jazz beat. Possibly because some of his extensive studies were undertaken in Budapest there is a gypsy strain running through some of his jazz; not surprisingly, his best recordings were those he made in France with Django Reinhardt in 1937. It is a major tragedy of jazz history that South, now in his fifties, has spent much of his life in obscure second-rate night clubs while he was perfectly equipped to enter the concert field, in which he could have offered programs ranging from jazz and tzigane melodies to classical concert works. South gave the jazz world too much too soon; in his prime he had to face the twin stone walls of Jim Crow and the complete lack of concert openings for jazzmen.

Joe Venuti, almost exactly South's age, had a far more successful career, recording incessantly in the late 1920s and making frequent radio appearances with Paul Whiteman and the other big white bands of the day. Venuti possesses most of the same qualities as South, without the gypsy traits, and where South's jazz melodic lines sometimes had a tendency to merge into country and western music, Venuti's have always been unmistakably jazz and have never been outswung. Though the golden age ended for him with the death of his guitarist partner Eddie Lang in 1933, Venuti has retained the elements that first brought him to prominence. Three decades have neither dimmed his vitality nor dated his style. An innovation created by Venuti but never followed up in jazz was a technique that involved tying the bow around the body of the violin so that the gut would strike all four strings simultaneously, enabling him to improvise passages in four-part chords. Some of the most attractive of the Venuti solos were created in this manner.

The joker in the violin deck is Stuff Smith. Discarding all the rule books, scraping away with a hacksaw tone at an amplified violin from which concert musicians shielded their eyes and ears in agony, Stuff took 52nd Street by storm in 1935, singing, clowning, and always playing with humor and a jaggedly propulsive beat. Stuff proved that barrelhouse jazz could be coaxed from a violin, in contrast with the swinging but conservative rule-observances of South and Venuti. To some degree his precepts were followed by Ray Nance, the Ellington trumpeter who, doubling now and then on violin, showed signs of blending some of the more desirable attributes of all three forebears.

Combining the academic knowledge of Venuti with the earthy swing of Stuff Smith, an amazing young Dane, Svend Asmussen, has earned warm endorsements from visiting American jazzmen for the last twenty years, among them Fats Waller and Benny Goodman. Because Asmussen has refused offers of lucrative work in the United States, it is unlikely that his name will earn the place it deserves in jazz annals. An attempt to find evidence of his full jazz potential on the many recordings he has made is a task comparable to looking for Shakespearean drama in a burlesque theater, since Asmussen has always led a novelty combo and has kept his genuine jazz solos at a minimum.

Gifted violinists often neglected by jazz critics include Al Duffy, a contemporary of Venuti; Ginger Smock, who for 20 years has displayed her musicianship in California, to little avail; the late Ray Perry, of Lionel Hampton's 1940 band; Emilio Caceres, brother of saxophonist Ernie; John Frigo, a Chicago bassist who doubles quite effectively; and Stéphane Grappelly, a South-like guiding spirit of the Hot Club de France quintet in the 1930s, still a unique virtuoso in the 1960s. Some critics have hailed Jean Luc Ponty, of Paris, as the new violin hope, perhaps the best to come along since Stuff Smith.

The post-1940 developments in jazz have been effectively captured by Dick Wetmore, who may in due course gain acceptance as the first bop violinst; and by Harry Lookofsky, best known for some multi-track records on which he played several string parts. Ornette Coleman played violin occasionally in 1965.

The use of the violin section per se in jazz has long been an anomaly. A few violinists, including Sam Kaplan, who worked in the "Charlie Parker with Strings" group on several occasions, have contrived to whip into adequate jazz shape a group of string performers not accustomed to working in this field; generally, though, both in writing and performance, the level of string section work in jazz has been low.

The Hammond organ has been a welcome but reluctant guest at the jazz table since the late 1930s, when records by Milt Herth and Glenn Hardman, because they were accompanied by jazz soloists, gave them a brighter jazz aura than their somewhat corny styles deserved. The Hammond organ (and, on some very early records, the pipe organ) made an ideal medium for Fats Waller, who in the last three years of his life employed it for several swingingly tranquil solos on original instrumentals and, perhaps even more effectively, on ballads.

Count Basie, who studied organ informally with Waller, has used it occasionally on records since 1939, generally for slow blues and always to pleasingly moody effect. Former jazz pianists who have enjoyed a vogue in the rhythm and blues field through the employment of a hard-driving, voluminous approach to the electric organ include "Wild Bill" Davis, who started this trend in 1950, Bill Doggett, whose records sold at least a million in 1956-7, Jackie Davis, and Milt Buckner. Among the more modern-oriented pianists who have occasionally indulged in manual and pedal experimentation at the organ are Hank Jones, Oscar Peterson and Mary Lou Williams. Hammond organs are standard equipment in providing the alternating romantic and jazz atmosphere at Harlem bars such as Count Basie's on Seventh Avenue, where another ex-pianist, Marlowe Morris, has revealed considerable proficiency.

The first attempt to bring the Hammond organ into the orbit of contemporary jazz was undertaken by Jimmy Smith. An extraordinary musician who makes fuller use than the other jazz organists of the variety of stops at his disposal, Smith plays fast-tempo jazz improvisations in a style that would have blended perfectly with Charlie Parker's combo had Smith risen to prominence during Parker's lifetime. Smith's rise to vast popular success in the 1960s led to a rash of organ trios and of pianists taking up organ. The best newcomers were Shirley Scott, Clare Fischer, Jack McDuff, Richard "Groove" Holmes, Freddie Roach, and singer Ray Charles; also John Patton, a winner in the 1965 *Down Beat* critics' poll.

Dick Hyman, when not restricted to commercial-style LPs, extracts first-rate swinging sounds from a Lowrey organ, an intriguing invention capable of producing glissandi.

The flute has been obliged virtually to gate-crash its way

into jazz acceptance. Though many saxophonists began to double on flute during the 1940s it was not until late 1956, when the jazz flutists outnumbered clarinetists, that the *Down Beat* readers' poll started a flute category. The pioneer records of Wayman Carver (Benny Carter, Spike Hughes, 1933; Chick Webb, 1937) were shrugged off as novelties. The next solo flute on records was by Harry Klee on *Caravan* with Ray Linn in 1944. Full-scale use of jazz flute began in 1953-4 with Frank Wess in Basie's band, Herbie Mann with Mat Mathews' combo and Bud Shank with Howard Rumsey. The first combo to put flute to full use was Chico Hamilton's, with Buddy Collette (later Paul Horn).

Herbie Mann, playing jazz and ethnic music on a variety of flutes, became the first successful flutist-leader in jazz in 1959. By now many leading saxophonists had taken to doubling on flute (also, in some cases, the warmly sonorous bass flute). Among the most colorful were Yusef Lateef and Roland Kirk, both of whom sometimes use their voices while playing; Leo Wright and James Moody of the Gillespie combos; Buddy Collette, who made the first jazz album featuring a whole flute section; the late Eric Dolphy, first avant-gardist to use flute; Jerome Richardson, Gigi Gryce, Sam Most, Moe Koffman, Les Spann, and such intense, vibrant newcomers as Charles Lloyd and Prince Lasha. Another youngster worth watching is the strongly blues-oriented Hubert Laws. Eric Dixon, with the Count Basie band, has doubled effectively on flute in recent years.

The oboe and English horn still remained almost complete strangers to jazz, though there have been commendable solo attempts on the former by Bob Cooper in California and Yusef Lateef in New York. The bassoon, played by Frankie Trumbauer in 1929 on a Joe Venuti record, apparently thereafter embarked on a thirty-year war against participation in jazz.

The French horn, an instrument that seems clumsily incapable of lending itself to technically perfect improvisations, was tackled with some success by John Graas (1924-62), a symphony and jazz musician, and by Julius Watkins, of whom critic Joachim-Ernst Berendt said: "He exploits all the festive solemnity (and the peaceful romantic mood that belongs with it) inherent in the horn." The mellophone, akin to French horn in sound and appearance, was played now and then by the late Hot Lips Page, and often by vibraphonist Don Elliott.

The late Adrian Rollini invented the goofus and the hot fountain pen, both heard on some of his records in the '20s and more notably for comedy value than for adding to the scope of jazz. The harmonica has earned two kinds of devotees: the folk blues singers such as Blind Sonny Terry, and Jesse Fuller, who use it in earthy blues solos; and modernists like Eddie Shu and Jean "Toots" Thielemans. The latter is better known as a former Shearing guitarist, and as composer of *Bluesette*.

The asthmatic dynamics of the accordion have kept it out of jazz with such rare exceptions as Leon Sash, in Chicago; Mat Mathews, an immigrant from Holland who blended his button-key accordion with flute and guitar for some of the most compelling and colorful small-combo jazz of the early 1950s; and Tommy Gumina, a phenomenally fast but rarely soulful soloist, teamed for several years with Buddy De Franco. George Shearing, a first-rate accordionist, has seldom played the instrument in public. Pete Jolly, the West Coast pianist, has recorded from time to time on accordion.

The harp has played a negligible role in jazz. Used on occasional big band recordings, mainly to play foppish arpeggios, it has been employed effectively as a solo medium by two musicians: Dorothy Ashby, in Detroit, who showed that the possibilities existed; and Corky Hale, who decided she would rather stop exploring them and gave it up in 1958 to concentrate on the piano.

Virtually a whole miscellaneous category in himself is Roland Kirk. First recorded in 1960, this blind musician from Columbus, Ohio found a couple of his most popular instruments in a shop; the manzello, which sounds roughly like a soprano saxophone but has a big flat, odd-looking bell; and the strich, which looks like a big soprano but sounds like an alto. In addition to these reed mavericks, Kirk has played the siren (used for climactic whistle effects at the end of a solo), the clavietta (also known as the melodica), which is blown through a mouthpiece but has a miniature two-octave piano keyboard; and the nose flute, played just as its name suggests. Though Kirk has achieved commercial success through such gimmicks as the playing of three horns at once, his music is a valid blend of vitality, sophistication, humor, surprise and, once in a while, a harmonic touch of the avant-garde. He has even acquired an imitator, a saxophonist named George Braith who plays the strich in a more primitive, funky-blues fashion.

The growing interest among jazz musicians in exotic sounds has led to their production from a variety of unfamiliar sources. Yusef Lateef has recorded on the argol, a kind of Indian reed flute, and sidemen on his LPs have played the earthboard, Chinese gong, a one-stringed instrument called the rabat, and such simple percussion media as Turkish finger cymbals and a soft drink bottle. Ahmed Abdul-Malik, the bassist, has played the oud, an Arabic instrument with five double strings. With the intense interest shown by jazz musicians in the work of such Indian musicians as Ravi Shankar, who plays the sitar, and Tak Shindo, a virtuoso of the koto, the entry of these instruments into the orbit of jazz became only a matter of time.

There has even been a public attempt to play jazz on the bagpipes. As this and other such experiments will eventually make clear even to the most reactionary opponent of fresh sounds in jazz, the question of how far this music will extend its instrument palette is one that will not be decided by the evolution of the music itself, but simply by the availability of equipment. As a means of melodic expression jazz is limitless in its adaptability. Improvisations of classic stature can be created on any horn, any keyboard, any suitably tuned set of beer bottles, provided they can be arranged in conformity with the chromatic scale (and even this may be expendable before long).

For several decades, ninety per cent of the most important and effective jazz was played on only eight instruments: trumpet, trombone, saxophone, clarinet, piano, banjo (or guitar), drums and bass. The jazz of today has multiplied this scope many times; certainly, then, tomorrow's jazz will be played on an even greater variety of instruments: on the theremin, possibly, or on an electronic gadget that creates synthetic sounds manufactured by scientists, or on tape recorders played backward. In short, jazz will be created through any medium available to the artist and designed within the frequency range open to that most adaptable and receptive of vessels, the human ear.

CHAPTER 18

THE BLUES AND THE HUMAN VOICE

The use of the human voice, though theoretically as much a part of jazz as of all music, has always been an anomaly. Jazz, to most of its students and performers, involves completely free improvisation; singing, on the other hand, implies adherence to a predetermined set of lyrics.

When and how, then, can jazz and singing be equated? The answer lies in two other postulates of the qualities of jazz. Individual tonal qualities have always been a part of the essential personality of the improvising musician; it is not merely the style but the personal sound of Pee-Wee Russell's clarinet, Bill Harris' trombone, Armstrong's or Gillespie's trumpet, that qualifies their performances as jazz. Similarly the vocal timbres that we accept as part of the jazz heritage have had an edge, a distinctive personality that has rendered their possessors instantly distinguishable from the conventional singers of popular songs. Bessie Smith, Louis Armstrong or Billie Holiday singing the national anthem would still sound like jazz to many ears, because of their unique tone quality and because of the second postulate: that phrasing, as much as improvisation, separates the jazz wheat from the "pop" chaff. Leonard Bernstein provided a cogent demonstration of the point by contrasting *Empty Bed Blues* as sung by Bessie Smith with an operatic soprano's treatment of the same melody. The notation in the latter is still that of the blues, the form identical, yet the results are ludicrous.[1]

The earliest jazz-related singing had both sacred and secular roots. The use in the jazz sense of the flatted third and seventh was common to the vagrant blues moaners and the singers in Negro churches all over America in the late nineteenth century.

The first singers who, unconscious of their role, set a pattern for vocal interpretation in jazz, were a thousand faceless blues callers in the South. Of them, the earliest to reach records and survive in the memories of jazz critics are Blind Lemon Jefferson and Ma Rainey. As Orrin Keepnews points out, "Lemon, who was singing for years before they ever got him to a recording studio, symbolizes all the anonymous people who may have been his contemporaries or predecessors."

Bending notes, leaning heavily on blue thirds and sevenths, limiting themselves most often to the 12-measure blues, these early singers had as much in common with the Sarah Vaughans of today as a mud hut with a Hollywood hacienda; they were neither able nor called upon to read music, and the stories they told, generally self-composed or improvised, reflected the poverty, squalor and deprivation of the Jim Crow lives they led. They sang the *Jail House Blues, Graveyard Blues, Cemetery Blues, Boll Weevil Blues, House Rent Blues, Sing Sing Prison Blues.* The men often accompanied themselves on battered guitars, unleashing a repeated strain set to the pattern of the three-line stanza that became the core of the blues.

As Jimmy Rushing has said, the blues "came from way back in slavery days, from the time when those people weren't treated right. A man would have a plantation with as many as 200 working for him—150 of them would be singing spirituals, and the other 50 would be singing he or she songs, or songs about other private affairs.

"And some would be singing about the time when they wouldn't be doing that hard work any more. 'The sun will shine in your backyard some day.'

"The blues came out of that—the spirituals, the he-and-she songs, and work songs, too. Today as it was then, the blues comes right back to a person's feelings, to his daily activities in life. But rich people don't know nothing about the blues, please believe me."

A complete understanding of every nuance of the word "blues" is a prerequisite of any study of the vocal history of jazz. The term has often wrongly been assumed to denote a branch of the jazz tree alongside Dixieland, swing music, etc. To the general public it has often connoted merely a mood, or a word employed in song lyrics to express that mood.

To musicians, the blues has a more special meaning. Correctly used in the singular (a jazz musician may say "the blues *is*", rather than "the blues *are*"), it denotes a particular musical formula on which melodies and improvisations have been based since the earliest days of jazz. Indeed, as has been shown through the example of *Frankie and Johnny*, it has its roots in antecedents that predate jazz by many decades and are part of American folklore.

The significance of the word "blues" to musicians can be expressed quite easily in technical terms. Paradoxical as it may seem, the blues does not have to sound blue any more than a French window has to be imported from France. Nor does the blues have to be played slowly; it is adaptable to any tempo. To the layman a tune like *Limehouse Blues* or *Jazz Me Blues* may seem to justify its title; actually the only relationship here is that the lyrics express an unhappy or blue state of mind. The tunes do not follow the authentic blues pattern.

The blues, in its simplest form, has a distinctive lyrical pattern as well as a traditional musical pattern. Most often it expresses the thought in the first line, which occupies the first four bars of the music, then repeats this line, perhaps with slight variations, for the next four bars, and finally expresses a concluding thought with a different line in the last four bars of the blues' 12-measure chorus. For example:

If you don't b'lieve I'm sinkin', look what a hole I'm in
Say, if you don't b'lieve I'm sinkin', look what a hole I'm in
If you don't b'lieve I love you, look what a fool I've been.

Many musicians recall hearing these and other blues lyrics sung more than forty years ago. Zutty Singleton, one of the best known drummers from New Orleans, recalls one classic occasion when he heard Ma Rainey, the pioneer blues singer, chanting this particular strain one night in a tent show at Louisiana Avenue and Howard in New Orleans, around 1914. Just as she came to the words "look what a hole I'm in," the stage collapsed. According to Zutty, the blues was something with which he grew up, something he heard from the cradle. In a band led by an uncle of his, Willie Bontemps, there was a fiddler named Lou Lewis who played splendid blues. "The blues had the same sort of melody that's still used," Zutty says. "And it was most always in B Flat then, just as it is today. And for the lyrics, everybody had their own special sets of verses. Often folks would sit around at parties, taking turns to sing their own blues lyrics for hours on end."

The blues was originally sung to the accompaniment of, or played as a solo on, whatever instruments were available to the economically blighted people who gave birth to it. Crude banjos, guitars or violins, one-stringed contraptions and honky-tonk pianos, first conveyed the blues to the world. Later, these were supplemented by the regular brass band. Ferdinand "Jelly Roll" Morton, of the original New Orleans ragtime school, was one of the first to exploit blues as well as rags. In an album of recordings entitled *New Orleans Memories*, he sang *Mamie's Blues*, which he describes as the first blues he ever heard, dating as far back as 1890. (This was also recorded by Louis Armstrong under the title *2:19 Blues*.)

Drummer Paul Barbarin, another veteran of New Orleans, recollects that Bunk Johnson used to play the blues in Economy Hall, New Orleans, around 1911. Henry "Red" Allen, from Algiers, Louisiana, remembers such early trumpet players as Punch Miller and Chris Kelly playing the same tunes. Kelly, he recalls, muted his trumpet and played the blues with breaks, and accompanying tremolo effects, on the first and third bar—a special blues device still used today. "When Chris got to the fourth bar and fell back into the regular rhythm on the fifth bar," Allen says, "everybody would holler and stomp, just the way they do today when you play breaks on the blues."

For a long time the blues was mainly the property of these pioneer instrumentalists, and of singers such as Lizzie Miles, Bessie Smith, Ma Rainey and their contemporaries. But W. C. Handy, the first musician to document and notate the blues, started this form on the road to worldwide recognition. One of the themes of *Mr. Crump* by W. C. Handy, a campaign song written for an election candidate by that name, was in the 12-bar form. This number later became famous, with new lyrics, as *Memphis Blues*.

In describing the origin of this song, Handy pointed out: "The melody of *Mr. Crump* was mine throughout. On the other hand, the 12-bar, three-line form of the first and last strains, with its three-chord basic harmonic structure (tonic, subdominant, dominant seventh), was that already used by Negro roustabouts, honky-tonk piano players, wanderers and others of the under-privileged but undaunted class from Missouri to the Gulf, and had become a common medium through which any such individual might express his personal feelings in a sort of musical soliloquy. My part in their history was to introduce this, the 'blues' form, to the general public, as the medium for my own feelings and my own musical ideas."

After *Memphis Blues* in 1912 came the more famous *St. Louis Blues,* in 1914. This contained a first and last strain both of which were based on the blues, and a middle strain which was based on an eight-bar phrase in a minor key and was not blues. However, it is with the opening twelve measures, unmistakably a blues melody, that the composition is most closely identified, and there is no doubt that the *St. Louis Blues* helped to consolidate the actual musical pattern for which this word stood, as well as establishing the word itself among a wide public.

The use of the 12-bar blues formula probably goes back as far among white instrumentalists as among Negroes. Certainly the earliest groups associated with the word "jazz" created their own variations, and with the Original Dixieland Jazz Band the pattern reached phonograph records for the first time in their *Livery Stable Blues, Bluin' the Blues* and others.

The blues has never left jazz, and it is to be hoped that it never will. Its 12-bar structure is as much a reflex to the jazz musician as the bell was to one of Pavlov's dogs. Whenever any group of musicians assembles that has never met before, it is the pattern most likely to provide the immediate and compatible meeting ground. Throughout the decades of its use as a jazz base, the blues has changed only in the sense that it has

become far more complex in many interpretations, but the fundamental tonic-subdominant-dominant-tonic pattern remains (the
technical aspects of the blues will be seen later in the examples
of improvised instrumental solos.)

Clearly, much of the credit for the documentation of the blues
must go to W. C. Handy. The esthetic credit properly belongs,
as is the case with jazz as a whole, to performers in every
populated area of the United States; yet in countless popular
songs, as well as in the reminiscenses of jazz musicians and in
the writings of historians, the belief has been sedulously culti-
vated that the blues was born in New Orleans—another mani-
festation of a tendency to localize and specialize that has long
been an obstacle to a true understanding of the origins of jazz,
and is demonstrably unfair to the talented artists, both in and
out of New Orleans, who are concerned with a truthful rather
than a wishful presentation of the facts.

Jimmy Rushing, a professional blues singer for more than
thirty years, affirms that New Orleans provided comparatively
few outstanding blues singers. "It seems to me," says Rushing,
"that the blues didn't come out of New Orleans, but out of
Texas, Oklahoma, Kansas City. An uncle of mine, Wesley Man-
ning, was playing the piano and singing in sporting houses
around Oklahoma City forty years ago. Then there was Funny
Bagby, a great blues man who was also a wonderful tenor
player; he was well known around the Southwest.

"My father and my uncle used to tell me about blues singers
that went way back before my time, and I know I heard blues
singing in the after hours spots, which were known as road-
houses in those days, way back before I ever heard of any New
Orleans blues."

Almost all the early blues singers, Rushing attests, were
Negroes. "The only ofay singer I knew was a boy named Jimmy,
in California—can't remember his last name—he had been raised
in Texas with colored people and he sang good blues."

Certainly the most influential of all the early blues singers,
originally a protegée of Ma Rainey, was the indomitable Bessie
Smith, from Chattanooga, Tennessee. Her career as a recording
artist began early in 1923; within a year or two there were

stampedes at the shops where her records were sold every time a new coupling was released. Bessie's medium was almost exclusively the blues—usually blues material written for her by others, but tailored to her own life and background. Compared with the other important blues singers of her day, many of whom were namesakes but not relatives (Mamie Smith, Clara Smith and Trixie Smith), Bessie Smith was a giant among midgets. Tall and handsome, possessed of a majestic, compelling timbre, she had a hypnotic effect on her audience. Notwithstanding the disparity between the vocal fields of blues and spirituals, Danny Barker observed that there was something of a religious quality in her performances: "If you had any church background, like people who came from the South as I did, you would recognize the similarity between what she was doing and what those preachers and evangelists from there did, and how they moved people . . . Bessie did the same thing on the stage. She, in a sense, was like people like Billy Graham are today."[2]

Bessie Smith was not the only blues singer capable of casting this kind of a spell on her listeners. Huddie "Leadbelly" Ledbetter, a singer and guitarist, told his blues stories with the same violence of conviction that marked his personal life; during the years of Bessie's initial impact he was in jail for murder. Many years later, during another prison sentence for attempted homicide, he was granted a pardon by the governor of Louisiana, supposedly after the governor had listened to his singing. Leadbelly, who played a 12-string guitar, had a repertoire made up of work songs and blues.

A male counterpart of Bessie Smith, though the years of his greatest impact came almost a decade later, was "Big Bill" Broonzy, the singer and guitarist. Broonzy's rough-edged, gracefully phrased blues works, many of them his own compositions, were dominant in the race record market through the 1930s. He died in 1958, by which time a primitive-blues renaissance had created young audiences for such folk or country blues artists as Son House, Sonny Terry & Brownie McGhee, Muddy Waters, Little Brother Montgomery, John Lee Hooker, Sleepy John Estes. The first sign of an extension of vocal jazz beyond the blues forms came with the early work of Louis Armstrong's Hot Five. Though Armstrong sang the blues frequently, he was given also to verbalizations of ad lib passages similar to those he had been expressing through his horn. *Heebie Jeebies* augured the new approach, as did *Save It, Pretty Mama, No One Else But You,* and *Monday Date.* It was not until 1929 that Armstrong turned to Tin Pan Alley for source material with his passionate sublimation of *I Can't Give You Anything But Love.* By the next year the new pattern was set; as the era of Satchmo as a blues specialist ended, popular ballads and novelties crowded the Armstrong band book.

Armstrong symbolized what were then, and to some degree still remain, the essential qualities that constituted the jazz singer. The parched, guttural tone had something akin to the sounds musicians then identified as jazz timbres; the lyrics, completely losing their importance to the song, became a mere vehicle on which to transport the melody. In later years, jazz voices by the dozen echoed the Armstrong technique, which was no technique at all but that of singing each song as if he were in the process of personal creation, as if he were blowing the lyrics through his trumpet. Perhaps not by coincidence, many of those who followed Armstrong were also trumpet players whom nature had presented with guttural voices that seemed to speak and sing the language of jazz: Louis Prima, Wingy Manone, Roy Eldridge, Sharkey Bonano clearly were able to turn this natural gift to similar advantage.

If Armstrong was the first male blues vocalist to demonstrate that jazz singing was adaptable to the popular song, his feminine counterpart may have been Ethel Waters. Billed in her early years as "Sweet Mama Stringbean, direct from St. Louis and Singing *St. Louis Blues,*" Miss Waters in fact was from Chester, Pennsylvania and had made her early appearances in Philadelphia and Baltimore before establishing herself in New York directly after World War I. In introducing and popularizing the song *Dinah,* she rephrased it, using syncopation and rubato extensively, adding a synthetic "hot" touch through the use of occasional growling tones, and paved the way for the use of Tin Pan Alley material by every jazz vocalist in later years.

Miss Waters was a great favorite among jazz musicians. Jimmy McPartland has recalled: "Bix Beiderbecke made a point of taking me to hear Ethel Waters . . . We liked Bessie Smith very much, too, but Waters had more polish. . . . She phrased so wonderfully, the natural quality of her voice was so fine, and she sang the way she felt."[3]

Jazz singing until the late 1920s was largely confined to the Negro artists, and, despite occasional exceptions such as Armstrong and Waters, was limited in substance to the form of the blues. The break on both levels may have been said to be completed with the advent of Mildred Bailey. Where earlier white singers with pretensions to a jazz identification had captured only the surface qualities of the Negro styles (Al Jolson and Sophie Tucker had all the vintage, aged-in-the-wood qualities of prohibition bathtub gin) Mildred contrived to invest her thin, high-pitched voice with a vibrato, an easy sense of jazz phrasing, that might almost have been Bessie Smith's overtones.

Some of the early Mildred Bailey repertoire had a blues flavor *(Rockin' Chair, Lazy Bones)*, some a pseudo-spiritual touch *(Shoutin' in the Amen Corner, Is That Religion?)*, but by and large her lodestone was the popular song of the day *(You Call It Madness, Wrap Your Troubles in Dreams)*. It was the effortless blend of this material with the warmth and vitality of the great blues singers that started a new chapter in jazz singing. Mildred made her record debut in 1929; the next year, Jack Teagarden's first vocal side was cut. Teagarden, too, was to lend a rich jazz timbre to songs of minor intrinsic merit, though his earliest hits were either genuine blues *(Beale Street)* or closely related forms *(Basin Street)*. But from his debut *(After You've Gone* with Red Nichols) Teagarden provided a burred, slurred, Texas-tinged sound that gave jazz a new vocal aspect, a parallel for the throaty croaks and completely unacademic plaints of Louis Armstrong.

After Mildred Bailey and Jack Teagarden, no important new voices in jazz were to be heard for several years. Though she made one record with Benny Goodman in 1933, it was not until two years later that Billie Holiday, through her long series of discs with Teddy Wilson's recording orchestra, gained national acceptance among musicians and jazz fans. It was in 1935 too that Ella Fitzgerald, then a 17-year-old singer with Chick Webb's band, embarked on her maiden voyage as a recording artist.

These were the two voices of the 1930s: Billie, the rugged and rasping "Lady Day", whose tone and Armstrong-influenced phrasing made even the tenderest love song sound caustic and thankless, whose personal bitterness toward the world led to narcotics, a ruined career and a gradually deteriorating voice of which a few magnificent shreds remained until the end; and Ella, who was the voice of light as Billie was that of darkness, swinging in insouciant and bell-clear tones an endless parade of trivial songs, dominating and conquering the material in a gaily rhythmic challenge. The consistency of honey was as compatible with Ella's voice as was the aroma of vinegar with Billie's. Both were peerless artists; neither was a blues singer, though occasionally both tried their hand (Billie's *Fine and Mellow*, Ella's *Gulf Coast Blues* and *Ella Hums the Blues);* both were throat and shoulders above the conventional treatments applied to the same popular songs of the day by singers with the swing bands of Benny Goodman, the Dorseys and Bob Crosby. Ella, in sharp contrast with Billie, expanded in scope through the years, took up the use of wordless vocalese to fit the bop craze when it arrived, broadened her vocal range to a full two octaves and finally, in 1956, began to find her material in superior show tunes and other songs congruent with her personality; this widened her audience tremendously.

Another school of jazz singers began in 1941, the year Anita O'Day joined the Gene Krupa band. Though she had more in common with Lady Day than with Ella, Anita's voice had a lighter texture, appended a trailer-like tail to long-held notes, and found a way of bending an occasional tone in such a manner that the combined effect was astringently rhythmic and unmistakably jazz. The O'Day style was popularized still further by June Christy in her alliance with the Kenton orchestra in 1945. A similar style was attempted, with occasional success, by Chris Connor, heard as a Kenton vocalist in 1953.

The voice of the new jazz era, a contribution that matched the instrumental discoveries of Gillespie and Parker, was Sarah

Vaughan, who worked with the latter pair in the Earl Hines band in 1943. Here the jazz qualities were subtler, more oblique; one had to be a musician to realize that she was herself musically literate, capable of implying changes in the harmonic form of the song through slight changes in the melody. The qualities that have earned Sarah the admiration of musicians are not all jazz qualities: they are the gentle fluency of her phrasing, the cool-water soprano sound, the ability suddenly to reach out for high notes and hit them with stunning accuracy. At times Sarah Vaughan is a jazz singer; more often, today, she is a superior popular singer of commercial songs. Her journeys between these adjacent areas can be observed as her musical setting changes, or her material, or even her mood. The Vaughan soprano, and this may be significant, has never been more gloriously presented than in her recording of *The Lord's Prayer*.

Sarah Vaughan's impact was a prelude to the advent of a succession of borderline pop-jazz vocalists. Nat King Cole, a jazz singer by any yardstick when he recorded trio accompaniment in the early 1940s, was strictly a pop singer with faint traces of jazz when he died in 1965. In a similar fringe zone are Frank Sinatra, Mel Torme, Barbra Streisand and dozens of others who have been mildly influenced by real jazz singers. There is a significant common denominator: these artists, though beyond reproach as performers, have little or no deep feeling for the blues. A few have shown real jazz qualities; Peggy Lee and Helen Merrill, for example, both have a warmth of timbre, an acute sense of phrasing and a soulful quality that gives their best work a beauty comparable with Billie Holiday's.

Most of the important new jazz singers of the 1940s and '50s were products of the Negro Baptist church or of the social milieu close to it. The most persuasive new blues sound of the World War II years was that of Dinah Washington (1924-1963). Her tart, chip-on-shoulder quality, firmly steeped in the blues, ranged from bitterness to cynical humor in her assault on pop songs, but reached back into the world of Bessie Smith when she sardonically evaluated the ordeals of the blues. Dinah

Washington's counterpart in the 1960s was a young Detroit girl, the church-trained Aretha Franklin, discovered by John Hammond.

The urbanized blues tradition, brought into swing music by Rushing with the Basie band between 1935 and 1950, was carried forward by Joe Turner and trumpeter Hot Lips Page (1908-1954), both of whom sang in Kansas City in the '30s and in New York in the '40s. Deep-dish blues of a comparable nature was still being sung in the mid-1960s by Jimmy Witherspoon, a former Baptist choir singer from Arkansas with a sly, caustically evil blues sound.

In the gap between Turner and Witherspoon, the research and encouragement of folklorists had brought many of the more primitive blues singers off the streets and placed them before enthusiastic, mainly white audiences who, while unable to identify with the roots, somehow sensed the message. The most memorable of these rediscoveries was Sam "Lightnin'" Hopkins, a singer, guitarist and pianist from Houston whom the blues expert Sam Charters called "the last singer in the grand style." Hopkins' social and sexual materials draw on the vast and (for most of his audiences) unexplored channels of his itinerant life; his sound is searingly strong and confident, yet supple and intimate, whirling unpredictably from a profound mournfulness to a mood of buoyant elation.

Folk singing, surprisingly, expanded into popular acceptance while jazz singing at the other end of the spectrum took a new step forward in terms of sophistication and artifice, through the new medium of jazz-vocalese.

Eddie Jefferson, a former dancer, was the pioneer in this field. In 1940 he observed that any improvised jazz solo, no matter how intricate, consisted of notes to which words could be fitted. After many unpublished efforts, he scored a hit with his adaptation of a saxophone solo by James Moody, based on *I'm In The Mood For Love*. King Pleasure extended the idea, setting words to solos by Moody, Getz, Young and Parker.

A British born singer, Annie Ross, set lyrics in 1952 to two

Wardell Gray solos, *Twisted* and *Farmer's Market*. They were
the wittiest and best-constructed efforts in this field; moreover,
her vocal range, equipment and beat were extraordinary. In
1958 Miss Ross teamed up with John Hendricks, an ex-drummer
and singer who shared her penchant for turning instrumental
choruses into lyrically interesting stories, and Dave Lambert, a
vocal group arranger who had recorded with Charlie Parker.
Together they formed Lambert, Hendricks & Ross; their innovations, written mainly by Hendricks, established them as the
most valid vocal group in modern jazz, supplanting such pop-
oriented quartets as the Hi Los and the Four Freshmen. The
trio recorded many Basie and Ellington tunes, and other jazz
classics to which words had never before been set. After a few
years, the novelty wore off. In 1962 Miss Ross was replaced by
a Ceylonese singer, Yolande Bavan. The trio disbanded in 1964.
The Double Six of Paris (six voices doubled by trick recording)
taped a few successful albums for which Mimi Perrin functioned as key solo voice and writer of the French lyrics.

Contemporaneous with the vocalese development was the
modernization of scat singing. Leo Watson (1898-1950), who sang
in meaningless syllables with occasional recourse to English, had
a dream-world, stream-of-consciousness sound; he was the James
Joyce of jazz, with a wild patina of comedy. A similar style was
tried by Joe Carroll, in the Gillespie and Herman bands, and by
Gillespie himself. Around 1948-9 the light-textured, sophisticated
duo composed of Jackie Cain and her husband, Roy Kral, enjoyed a vogue singing unison bop lines, using lyrics as well as
the scat medium.

A 1963 curiosity was the formation in Paris of the Swingle
Singers, an octet that gave the illusion of turning Bach works
into jazz merely by singing them as written but adding a swinging background of bass and drums.

The realms of blues and folk blues, of scat singing and vocalese, rarely had much bearing on vocal development in the big
bands. The first pop singer to add stature to a great jazz band

was Ivie Anderson, whose trim phrasing and gentle vibrato graced the Ellington bandstand for ten years. Helen Humes (with Count Basie, 1938-42) sang in a light, high, ingratiating voice akin to Mildred Bailey's. The bands of the 1940s produced a few important pop-jazz singers: Joya Sherrill with Ellington; Mary Ann McCall with Woody Herman, and Betty Roché, whose superb blues and ballad work with Ellington in 1943 unfortunately took place during a recording ban. Carmen McRae, an alumna of the Benny Carter, Basie and Mercer Ellington bands, brought the pop-jazz vocal art to a peak of artistry in the 1950s with an affirmative, dig-in-and-swing manner on rhythm songs and a tender lyrical sense on ballads.

The 1950s produced many singers who started out with the blues but who later were motivated commercially to switch to pop songs. Most important was Ray Charles, the blind pianist from Georgia whose influences were Guitar Slim, a blues singer from the bayou country; Charles Brown, the rhythm-and-blues favorite, and Nat Cole. Charles at first was a passionate link to the poverty and terror as well as the basic vocal grit of the Negro South. Success led him to Tin Pan Alley songs backed by string sections, but much of the bittersweet beauty lingered on.

Among the more serious, artistically inclined singers of popular songs, a few have succeeded in stretching their material beyond its normal borders: Jeanne Lee, Sheila Jordan and the exceptionally gifted English vocalist Cleo Laine. Abbey Lincoln brought a jazz touch to songs about racial discrimination. Mose Allison, a Southern white pianist, sang in a down-home style that suggested a hipper, more blues-aware Hoagy Carmichael.

The best of today's pop-jazz singers include Joe Williams (Count Basie, 1954-60), LaVern Baker, Ruth Brown, Ernestine Anderson, Lorez Alexandria, Bill Henderson, Woody Herman, Jackie Paris, Gloria Lynn, Lou Rawls and the top jazz-derived pop star of the mid-1960s, Nancy Wilson.

Despite their occasional association with jazz settings, such artists as Billy Eckstine, Al Hibbler, Nina Simone and Della Reese should not be classified as jazz singers. Nor, despite common roots with their jazz cousins, should such inspiring Negro religious groups as the Staple Singers, who were probably as surprised as their more devout followers when they won a *Down Beat* critics' poll.

CHAPTER 19

THE SMALL COMBOS

The term "combo," in common use for the past thirty years among jazz musicians, is usually employed to distinguish between the small group, ranging generally from trio to octet size, and the full orchestra. In the early decades of jazz no such distinction was required, for as we have seen, the typical brass bands, and the ragtime bands that stemmed directly from them, rarely comprised more than seven musicians. The earliest combo jazz of which we have any first-hand evidence, in the form of phonograph records, is the Original Dixieland Jazz Band, a grandchild of the bands Jack "Papa" Laine had led in New Orleans. A group known originally as Brown's Dixieland Band, led by a trombonist named Tom Brown and featuring mainly men who had worked with Laine in New Orleans, came to Chicago and, legend has it, was smeared by local musicians who tried to brand it as a "jass" band. Since the word at that time had sexual connotations as a verb, local musicians' union officials attempted to remove this word from the billing; but it was not long before "jazz," no matter which way it was spelled, had an important and commercially valuable meaning as an adjective and noun.

Nick LaRocca, a cornetist, followed Brown to Chicago in 1916. With him were Henry Ragas, a pianist; trombonist Eddie "Daddy" Edwards, and Alcide "Yellow" Nunez, who played clarinet. Later LaRocca moved to New York, trading Nunez for Larry Shields, the clarinetist in Brown's band. Early in 1917 LaRocca, Shields, Edwards, Ragas and a nineteen-year-old drummer named Tony Sbarbaro opened at Reisenweber's Cafe on West 58th Street in New York City as the Original Dixieland Jazz Band.(Sbarbaro, under the name of Tony Spargo, was still active in New York in the 1960s.)

The Dixieland Band made its first records February 24, 1917 for Victor. *Dixie Jass Band One-Step* and *Livery Stable Blues* reveal remarkably little difference between the basic approach, the material and the interpretation in that era and the performances by groups of this type today. Certain phrases, inevitably, became clichés and have been discarded; the level of musicianship has benefited from the broader opportunities offered to musicians, but basically the pattern is strikingly familiar.

Some critics tend to discount the contributions of the Original Dixieland Band and of all early white jazz groups. Others point to the Friars' Society Orchestra, later known as the New Orleans Rhythm Kings. This group, they claim, evidenced a warmer and more inspired approach, not so much from the work of the leader, trumpeter Paul Mares, as from the contributions of two of the sidemen, Leon Rappolo, clarinetist, and George Brunis, the trombonist.

While the white groups gained a foothold in recorded small-band jazz, the Negro orchestra, though largely ignored by the record companies until 1923, had been developing in several major centers. King Oliver opened at the Lincoln Gardens in Chicago in 1917, with Jimmy Noone on clarinet; Louis Armstrong, who took Oliver's place in the Kid Ory band in New Orleans, later joined Oliver as second cornetist while Ory moved to California. As far as can be determined, the first recordings released by a Negro jazz band were *Ory's Creole Trombone* and *Society Blues* by Ory's Sunshine Orchestra recorded in 1921 in Los Angeles, and *Mabel's Dream, Southern Stomp* and *Riverside Blues* recorded by King Oliver's Jazz Band in Chicago in March 1923 (around the same time Fletcher Henderson began recording in New York; he will be discussed in the chapter on big bands).

Despite the overall similarities in the nature of the music, the records of the Original Dixieland Band and the New Orleans Rhythm Kings both show one important structural difference from later recordings of this type: there is a constant stress on collective improvisation. Solos are usually restricted to an occasional two- or four-bar break. The sound of a trumpet- or cornet-led ensemble from start to finish, with all three horns ad libbing at once, produced results that may sound chaotic to most present-day listeners. A corollary result was the inability of the soloists to establish any firm identity: thus a comparison of *Livery Stable Blues* played by the Original Dixieland Jazz Band on Victor and the New Orleans Rhythm Kings on Riverside reveals little substantial difference, though the latter, if only on the strength of Rappolo's presence, had slightly more to offer.

There are several distinguishing features to be found in both groups. The harmonic structure is extremely limited. Most chords remain unchanged for at least a full measure, and in most instances there is little or no use of minor sevenths. The choruses of most tunes played by these bands begin and end with two full bars on the tonic. Rhythmically, there is surprisingly little syncopation; the use of dynamics for rhythmic contrasts also is very limited. Melodically, the improvisations are circumscribed by these harmonic and rhythmic limitations: there is an inclination on the part of all the musicians to resort to such obvious devices as a sustained note in the upper register to establish dramatic tension.

A tendency apparently common to many bands when "jass" was a brand new novelty was the use of jungle effects, in both the music and the titles. Both versions of *Livery Stable Blues* contain breaks that suggest animal-like sounds, presumably a sop to the public's concept of jazz as a primitive and slightly comical affair. Other titles of the day were *Barnyard Blues, Tiger Rag, Ostrich Walk*. There was also a leaning toward the naively exotic with tunes like *Oriental, Sphinx, Sudan*.

The King Oliver band, its early records disclose, was hardly less concerned with multiple improvisation but tended to offer a little more solo prominence to a few of the men. The Oliver band records began in 1923 (six years after the Original Dixieland Band but contemporaneous with the New Orleans Rhythm Kings). They show at least a hesitant move toward structural concepts, and have a stronger and more syncopated horn leading the ensemble, but fundamentally the music, generally known now as New Orleans Jazz, is no different technically from what was being played by the white groups, whose performances have been pigeonholed as Dixieland Jazz.

In effect, the nature of combo jazz changed very little during the next few years. It was not until there were more substantial attempts at orchestration that the differences between the white and Negro brands of jazz became more apparent.

Two groups that helped improvisation along the road from its polyphonic origins to a status that gave freer rein to individual solos were the Original Memphis Five and the Wolverines. The former group, recording under a bewildering variety of names from 1922 until the late '20s, usually had as its principal protaganists Phil Napoleon, trumpeter; Miff Mole, the first important jazz solo trombonist; Jimmy Lytell on clarinet and Frank Signorelli on piano. More dynamic and less stinted, in general, was the work of the Wolverines, whose personnel at first included Bix Beiderbecke and later Jimmy McPartland. In Chicago, a combo led by a gentle-toned clarinetist named Jimmy Noone earned a loyal following at the Nest, but it was the leader rather than any inherent value in the group as such that was responsible for its success. In fact, there were very few small combos in the 1920s that had any lasting importance as groups in the sense that they changed the basic nature of small-band jazz performances. From the standpoint of the frequency and impact of their recordings the most significant were the Louis Armstrong Hot Five and Seven, Red Nichols' Five Pennies, and the various units led by two famous informal partnerships: Joe Venuti and Eddie Lang, Frankie Trumbauer and Bix Beiderbecke. Almost all of these groups were assembled specially for record sessions rather than organized units.

The Armstrong records vary greatly from session to session. Many were reissued in a series of LPs, *The Louis Armstrong Story*, on Columbia. On the earliest dates Armstrong stands head and shoulders above his companions, who in 1925-7 were usually Johnny Dodds, clarinet; Kid Ory, trombone; Lillian Hardin Armstrong, piano; John St. Cyr, banjo. The real Armstrong combo classics, much more assimilable to the listener of a later generation, were all recorded in 1928 with a group that generally included Earl Hines at the piano, Zutty Singleton on drums, and sometimes Don Redman as alto saxophonist and arranger. In addition to the advantages of electric recording (many of the earlier sides, apart from their musical shortcomings, sound as though they were recorded acoustically), the pairing of Armstrong with Hines produced a team of inspired soloists who were years ahead of their time; there are occasional attempts to use as accented notes, in the exposition of a theme, what might only have been acceptable earlier as passing notes; Earl Hines' solo on *It's Tight Like That* holds an E for two beats against a D Minor chord. Both Earl and Louis indulge in rhythmic escapades that are, by the standards of earlier combo records, masterpieces of intricacy and subtly swinging jazz. Except for Redman's buoyant alto the occasional solos by the others are of minor interest; the group, in effect, is a framework for the virtuosity of Armstrong and Hines.

Less valuable in terms of solo talent but far more experimental in their attempts to extend the boundaries of combo jazz are the remarkable recordings begun December 1926 under the name of Red Nichols and His Five Pennies. When the first of these, *That's No Bargain,* was released, it caused a stir among jazz musicians comparable with the excitement aroused thirty years later by the Modern Jazz Quartet's first LP.

Among the group's innovations were the fuller integration of the drummer into the arrangement (Vic Berton made use of tympani for melodic percussion effects): the employment of the guitar for solo passages instead of the harsh and metallic banjo; the use of contrasts in dynamics in a field where, too often, the only previous level had been forte or fortissimo; and the more advanced sense of construction in the arrangements, by such means as the employment of two or three different harmonic sequences, changes of key, etc. There was also an element of humor clearly more mature than the animal sound effects, such as the drums' repetition of the closing phrase as a final tag in *That's No Bargain*. With the help of Fud Livingston and other arrangers, Nichols added new tone colors and ideas, new musicians, gradually expanding the group in scope and size until the so-called "Five Pennies" by 1930 were a dozen strong. It was in its days as a small combo that the Nichols group was musically most influential and successful; some of its experiments can be heard on Brunswick BL 54008.

Occasional contributors to the Nichols annals were Joe Venuti, the first important jazz violinist, and Eddie Lang, who filled a comparable role for the guitar in jazz history. Venuti and Lang were more important for the records made by their own groups, such as the duos *Stringing the Blues* and *Black and Blue Bottom* in September 1926. In a series of 1927 sides a piano and sometimes a saxophone augmented the group; from then until Lang's death in 1933, the creations of Joe Venuti's Blue Four and Blue Five made a gentle yet firm and ineradicable mark on jazz. The violin and guitar solos, their interplay and the velvet carpet of their arrangements brought jazz to a new pinnacle of inspiration accentuated by the finesse and swing of every performance.

Venuti and Lang took part in many other sessions, but the Blue Four sides were by far the most effective. Among the visitors in the group were Jimmy Dorsey, Lennie Hayton, Adrian Rollini and Frankie Trumbauer. Trumbauer's relationship to the Venuti school of jazz was peripheral, but in another area his contributions were to earn him his own niche alongside the cornet of Leon "Bix" Beiderbecke. The collaborations of "Bix and Tram," as they were called, were as sporadic and variable as those of Venuti and Lang; like the latter pair they were members of the Paul Whiteman band of the late 1920s and were heard in solos with Whiteman when the top-heavy arrangements gave them leeway, but in 1927-8, taking refuge from Whiteman's all-enveloping shadow, they found solace in a series of record dates under Trumbauer's name. The material mixed Dixieland standards with popular songs; the arrangements were brisk, cleanly played and to the point. The point, inevitably, was to demonstrate the solo talents of Bix and Tram. Though the earlier sessions were freer in ad lib ensemble spirit, the later dates furnished a framework for the two stars just as the Hot Five showcased Armstrong and Hines; some were played by a larger group with a saxophone section and do not properly call for consideration as combo performances.

In sharp contrast with the bright, clear patterns of the Beider-becke-Trumbauer groups was the contribution, in the middle and late 1920s, of a loosely associated group of musicians variously known as the Austin High School Gang, the Chicago School, or simply the McKenzie and Condon bunch. Theirs was a breathlessly staccato brand of improvisation, usually involving long passages of climactic, collective ad libbing toward the end of each performance. The style somehow achieved a somber and at times almost an hysterical quality. Among the unofficial ring-leaders of this sect of white Chicagoans was Red McKenzie, an ex-jockey who acted mainly as a catalyst, though he performed as a jazz-oriented singer and often took comb-and-paper solos to lend a kazoo-like sound to some of the records which were credited to McKenzie and Condon's Chicagoans or the Mound City Blue Blowers. The two men whose solos were the main *raison d'être* of the best Chicagoan records were cornetist Muggsy Spanier and clarinetist Frank Teschemacher. Others included Bud Freeman, tenor sax; Eddie Condon, then in his banjo phase; pianist Joe Sullivan and a teen-aged Gene Krupa. This school produced no one combo of firm duration, but its recordings between 1927 and 1931, in Chicago and New York, can be grouped together as representative of one fairly clear-cut type of combo jazz. *The Sound of Chicago* (1923-40) on Columbia **C3L 32** contains priceless relics of all styles of Chicago jazz.

Another series of combos assembled for recording dates in the 1920s was Jelly Roll Morton's Red Hot Peppers, heard with various personnels on Victor between 1926 and 1930. Though the general value of both solos and arrangements falls far below the level of the Armstrong groups and others mentioned above, these sessions were described by traditionalist critics as "the finest of all recorded traditional jazz."[1]

Combo jazz, as such, was neither amplified nor reshaped in any significant manner until the birth of the Benny Goodman Trio in 1935. This unit was born informally in July 1935 at a party in the home of the late Mildred Bailey. The singer's guests included Benny Goodman, Teddy Wilson and a drummer. Their improvisations were so mutually stimulating that soon after, with Gene Krupa at the drums, they recorded a trio session for Victor, and some months later Goodman broke down the color line by taking the Negro pianist on the road as a regular part of his show, using the trio as an adjunct of the band.

Goodman's trio, in a sense, brought new life to "chamber music jazz," a term previously applicable to the Venuti-Lang works of the late 1920s. The music was, of course, very different, contrasting on the fast numbers the fluent mastery of Goodman's clarinet with·the swinging serenity of Wilson's piano, adding an occasional Krupa solo for audience excitement. On the slower tunes Goodman offered an early reminder, provided a year or two before by Coleman Hawkins, that the best of Tin Pan Alley's ballad material could be sublimated by exposure to the light of jazz.

The idea of drawing a small combo from a larger orchestra did not originate with Goodman. He himself had been a member of a group known as "Ben's Bad Boys" which functioned both in person and on records as an offshoot of the Ben Pollack orchestra in the 1920s.

The Goodman Trio became a quartet in 1936 when Lionel Hampton's vibraphone was added, and a sextet or septet in 1939-41 when Benny began experimenting with a variety of combo formats, the most compelling of which was one that included Cootie Williams, Georgie Auld and Charlie Christian.

Goodman's "band-within-a-band" novelty was soon seized on by rival pied pipers of the swing years. In December 1935, Tommy Dorsey began recording with a Dixieland contingent out of his band, the "Clambake Seven"; a year later Duke Ellington started a series of sessions with his own splinter groups, under four different leaders—Johnny Hodges, Barney Bigard, Rex Stewart and Cootie Williams. Bob Crosby, whose big band was tailored to convey the effect of an enlarged Dixieland combo, complicated this system still further in November 1937 with the first session by the "Bob Cats," a small group taken from the big group that tried to sound like a small group. Count Basie's sidemen made a few dates as the Kansas City Six and Seven. Later Artie Shaw, in 1940, introduced his Gramercy 5, which achieved at least a novel tone color with the unprecedented inclusion of a jazz harpsichord.

In the groups from quintet to sextet size, except for the Dixieland combos, the general pattern marked another step away from
the polyphonic days of the '20s. Most of the arrangements were
"heads," i.e., dreamed up during the session, using little or no
manuscript paper. The usual pattern involved the establishment
of a riff (a repeated phrase) played by the horns (with piano and
guitar sometimes also included in the voicing to fill out the
harmony) for the first and last chorus. In between there might
be four-bar bridges by soloists and/or ensemble to link the improvised solo choruses. To some extent these little combos were
offering a condensed and more informal presentation of the big
bands from which they were drawn. The Ellington small groups
can hardly even be considered as combos, since in the main they
were simply the Ellington band in miniature, concentrating on a
couple of the soloists. On these sessions one found more prepared
music and fewer head arrangements. Since Ellington's band was
nearing the peak of its glory, the results more often than not
were delightful.

During this period another combo arose that went out of its
way to recast the mold. This was the John Kirby Sextet, led by
the former Fletcher Henderson bassist, and featuring, during the
period of maximum influence, the arrangements and the trumpet
of Charlie Shavers. The aim here was a frothy, amiable lightness
of tone color and a precise, compact format in which ad lib
solos were sandwiched between impeccably played ensembles.
Since the front line comprised an alto sax (Russell Procope), a
clarinet (Buster Bailey), and a trumpet that was usually muted,
the basic sound of the group was said by some critics to "lack
bottom." In terms of frequency range this was literally true, yet
the group had many endearing qualities by way of compensation.
The light timbre was unique and inimitable; the rhythm section
(Billy Kyle, piano; the late O'Neil Spencer, drums, and Kirby)
swung as gently as the horns. Scoring its first big success at the
Onyx Club on 52nd Street, the Kirby combo benefited from a
contrast with the raucous and scarcely organized sounds of most
of the small groups along that jazz-happy block. It cut a wide
swath of moods, sometimes "jazzing the classics" with *Humor-
esque* or *Anitra's Dance,* then playing a Shavers original such as

Pastel Blue or *Undecided,* or a standard popular song. Harmonically and melodically it was amazingly precocious; in fact, the first number the group ever recorded, Billy Kyle's *From A Flat to C* in October 1938, was based on the cycle of fifths, a harmonic device that came into general use a decade later when the early beboppers rediscovered it.

While the Kirby band was setting precedents on the East Coast, even landing its own regular radio show on CBS and bringing jazz to the previously undefiled Waldorf-Astoria, another combo form emerged that was to prove of lasting importance. This was the piano trio (piano, guitar and string bass), of which the archetype was the King Cole Trio. Oscar Moore's use of the electric guitar, a rarity at the time, enabled him to blend with Cole's piano in the most delicate and dexterous of voicings. The group, started in California, came to New York and was blithely ignored by the public. Returning to Hollywood the Cole Trio made its first sides for Decca in December 1940 and made several more dates the following year. Though national success did not come until Cole had recorded *Straighten Up and Fly Right,* a vocal novelty, for Capitol late in 1943, his trio had by that time established a pattern for what came to be known as "cocktail combos." Countless other groups were formed with the identical instrumentation; even Art Tatum, a solo pianist for more than a decade, started one. White groups in which the leader played piano and sang in a style akin to Cole's, such as the Page Cavanaugh Trio, achieved pleasing musical results. In the mid-1950s the tradition Cole had by now renounced was revived by the Oscar Peterson Trio, with Herb Ellis and Ray Brown. By 1958 the trend toward harder sounds led to Peterson's substitution of drums for guitar. By the 1960s the engaging piano-guitar-bass blend was all but lost to jazz.

The advent of bop involved an off-and-on partnership between its two leading instrumentalists, Dizzy Gillespie and Charlie Parker, whose appearances on small-combo records, in night clubs, and with big bands in which they were guiding forces made them the Bix and Trumbauer of the 1940s. The basic combo style here, in contrast with the simple three-part voicing of the Kirby band, usually involved a fast and rhythmically complex unison played by the horns; the harmonic departures of bop were stated directly by the pianist, but only inferentially by the horns.

Gillespie and Parker were dealt with in detail in their respective instrumental chapters. The unison bop approach to combo jazz initiated by them has endured firmly and can be heard today in the "lines" (i.e., compositions played in unison as the first and last chorus of an otherwise improvised performance) used by the Horace Silver Quintet and others of this type. The style was also extended in the late 1940s to the use of one or two horns with a human voice in unison. Charlie Ventura, the country's most popular combo leader in 1947-9, led several such units. The Gillespie-Parker Quintet format provided the inspiration for many combos in the hard bop era of the late 1950s, including Cannon Adderley's first quintet.

An offshoot of bop was the George Shearing Quintet, one of the most widely imitated groups of its kind. Organized early in 1949, it featured piano, guitar and vibraphone, playing in unison on the original instrumental numbers and in harmony on the slower-tempoed ballads. Though Shearing and the other soloists were capable bop musicians, the brand of music they offered, widely acclaimed as a jazz innovation for the first year or two, was later regarded as "commercialized bop" and appeals today mainly to popular-music audiences, having outgrown its original jazz appeal. During the mid-1950s Shearing modified the original sound with the addition of Afro-Cuban rhythms. His piano-vibes-guitar blend still has many imitators.

Initiated around the same time as the Shearing group was the series of recording combos under Miles Davis' name on Capitol records. Basically the group involved a small-band offshoot of the Claude Thornhill orchestra of that time, more by coincidence than design. Gil Evans and Gerry Mulligan, both writers for the Thornhill band (Mulligan also played in the sax section for a while) were instrumental, with Davis, in shaping the group, which included such Thornhill sidemen as Junior Collins, French horn; Bill Barber, tuba; Lee Konitz, alto sax, and Joe Shulman, bass.

Only three sessions were recorded, in 1949 and '50, and the group only appeared once in public, for an engagement at the

Royal Roost, yet its impact on jazz was inestimable. The group, nine pieces strong, was on the borderline between combo and big band jazz. Its importance lay in the incorporation of tone colors new to modern jazz. The French horn was completely unknown to a jazz context of this nature; so was the tuba, which had served a crude rhythmic function in the jazz of an earlier generation. A variety of rich timbres was created; the arrangers, while retaining the innovations of bop that had changed the basic nature of modern jazz, added a framework that gave the product a new and homogeneous texture. The soloists, at one time or another, included Kai Winding and Jay Jay Johnson, Al Haig and John Lewis; the arrangers were Mulligan, Evans, Lewis and John Carisi, a trumpet player whose composition *Israel* was perhaps the most successful of a totally impressive group of performances.

Many combos, most of them slightly smaller, have attempted to capture in their recordings the restrained sonorities of the Davis group. The fresh sound created by the Capitol sides may be said to have been the starting point of the "cool jazz" era. A slightly related application of the cool approach was the series of records made, also for Capitol in 1949, by Lennie Tristano, in which the lines, most often in unison, hinted at a departure from strict tonality. They were played by alto and tenor saxophones (Konitz and Warne Marsh); Billy Bauer's guitar was another integral element in both solo and ensemble functions.

Tristano's group, reorganized occasionally for a public appearance, is one of the comparatively few combos to have achieved a new collective sound without recourse to a radically different instrumentation. Two other combos of the 1950s, both successful within a conventional instrumental line-up, were the Red Norvo Trio (vibes, guitar, bass) and the Modern Jazz Quartet (vibes, piano, bass and drums).

The Norvo unit and the MJQ came into jazz at a period when loud, entertainment-oriented groups were a dominant force, among them those of the saxophonists Louis Jordan (a pioneer in the rhythm-and-blues field), Arnett Cobb and Illinois Jacquet. Their more cerebral appeal found a ready audience at a time when the intellectual reaction to jazz was gaining ground. Norvo's soft, paint-brush swing often used guitar in an ensemble role, leaving the rhythm burden to the bassist. Since the latter was first Charles Mingus, then Red Mitchell, the group never lacked a subdued yet pulsating drive.

John Lewis' Modern Jazz Quartet emphasized composition. In its Bach-inspired counterpoints and fugues, its fragile Lewis pieces inspired by the *commedia. dell'arte*, there is a stronger sense of form than in any combo since John Kirby's, yet with extensive freedom of creativity for the improvisers: Lewis' piano, delicate and simple yet with modified echoes of Bud Powell; Jackson's delayed-action vibes phrasing, Percy Heath's tonally and technically formidable bass, and Connie Kay with his light fusillade of rarely-used percussion instruments such as the triangle and finger cymbals.

The MJQ, as it is called, has been criticized by André Hodeir for its allusions to European classical forms. Disparaging judgments have neglected to mention that its repertoire also includes simple blues and riffs tunes to round out a unique modern musical vocabulary. Seldom submerging the personalities of its members, the quartet achieved intricate group effects of lasting value to jazz.

In 1952 Gerry Mulligan startled the jazz world by showing that a small combo could function without any chordal underbrush in its rhythm section. Normally a piano, guitar or both had supplied this harmonic element. Mulligan left the harmony implicit in the horns' solo patterns. His successful use of just bass and drums for rhythm seemed incredible; here was a man who had drunk his soup with a fork. The front line has usually consisted of Mulligan's baritone sax with a trumpet (Chet Baker or Art Farmer) or a valve trombone (Bob Brookmeyer). What seemed like an empty sound soon came to be accepted as a challenging new combo timbre and led to the formation of many other pianoless and guitarless combos.

Two important new combos of the 1950s comprised piano, saxophone, bass and drums. The resemblance ended there. In

Dave Brubeck's quartet the determining traits were the pianist-leader's classical training, heavy touch, frequent use of such odd meters as 6/4, 5/4, 9/8, 12/8, and the suave counterpoint of Paul Desmond's alto. Thelonious Monk's quartet tended toward piano-tenor unison lines by Monk and Charles Rouse; quixotic, technically imperfect yet sometimes engaging solos by the leader, and an adherence to the traditional 4/4 meter.

The mid-1950s produced a series of bland Hollywood groups led by Shorty Rogers and others that tried to emulate the innovations of the Miles Davis nonet; and a novel, short-lived (1954-6) quintet co-led by two trombonists, Kai Winding and Jay Jay Johnson. The two-horn format with its "contrast through contest" style was also put to effective use by various pairs of tenor saxophonists: Gene Ammons and Sonny Stitt, Eddie Lockjaw Davis and Johnny Griffin and, off and on for the past decade and more, Al Cohn and Zoot Sims.

Combos that stemmed from the harp bop movement included Art Blakey's Jazz Messengers and the Max Roach Quintet. The Blakey group was a valuable proving ground for soloists who later formed their own groups: Horace Silver, Benny Golson, Jackie McLean, Bobby Timmons,·Donald Byrd. In quintet form, the Messengers were mainly a driving, intense medium for solo blowing. In the 1960s, the enlargement to sextet size gave the unit a more cohesive personality determined by the advanced writing and playing of the tenor sax soloist, Wayne Shorter.

Chico Hamilton, integrating his drums into the sounds of a highly original 1955-7 combo, featured cello, flute (doubling on reeds), bass and guitar, alternating between impressionist music and gentle modern swinging. Public acceptance waned and Hamilton later had to form a more aggressive group with saxophone and trombone.

Charles Mingus was vitally important as a combo leader from 1955-65. Despite frequent personnel changes, every group was stamped with the towering personality of its leader. Its musical components, often heard elsewhere but never before in conjunction, included gospel-church-folk-blues roots, furious dissonances and collective improvisations by the horns, stomping solos by tenors and trombones, excursions into ternary meters, and through it all, the phenomenal Mingus bass.

Mingus' innovations set the stage for the avant-garde combos. Ornette Coleman, from 1960, used drums, bass and Don Cherry's "pocket" trumpet, with the leader as alto man and composer. The quartet became identified with total freedom—intermittent atonality, freak sounds and squeaks, raw emotion, unpredictable shifts in rhythm, tempo and texture. In sharp contrast, the John Coltrane quartet leaned to modes rather than atonality, and to the building and sustaining of a mood rather than its frequent interruption. Coltrane's modal view of jazz was taken up by such groups as the Paul Horn quintet.

With the exception of Coleman and Coltrane, few combos of the 1960s merit discussion in this chapter. Socio-economic developments have precluded the establishment of more than a handful of new groups. Changes of personnel or instrumentation have often made it impossible for a combo to mold itself firmly enough to make a lasting mark in jazz. This lack of direction is typified by the case of Jimmy Giuffre. Since the 1950s he has had a pioneer atonal trio; then a blues-folk-oriented combo with guitar and bass; a two-horns-plus-guitar trio; and a clarinet-piano-bass avant garde group, as well as other contexts for recordings.

The personalities of the various Miles Davis, Sonny Rollins and Art Farmer combos are in essence simply those of the leaders, despite the often expert integration between their members. This is true also of the various trios led by pianists with bass and drums, such as Bill Evans, Ramsey Lewis, Ahmad Jamal, Oscar Peterson, Gene Harris (The Three Sounds), Cecil Taylor and Denny Zeitlin.

Bossa nova has produced no combos with any stable or influential instrumentation. Hard bop survives in a tough, bristling West Coast group, the Jazz Crusaders, led by Sticks Hooper.

The avant-garde of the mid-1960s, plagued by problems of survival, had been unable to mount any fixed, lasting combo formula. The various groups led from time to time by George

Russell deserve a stability they have been unable to find, as do the temporary recording units assembled by such adventurous young experimentalists as Grachan Moncur III and Andrew Hill.

CHAPTER 20

THE BIG BANDS

There is no firm boundary line between the small combo and the big jazz band. Normally the latter term is taken to denote any group that can be broken down into sections (reeds, brass and rhythm). Using this yardstick one can state that to all intents the big jazz band began with the orchestra of Fletcher "Smack" Henderson, and that Henderson's first attempts at organization marked the earliest significant step forward in the evolution of jazz from its folk origins.

Coleman Hawkins, one of the earliest Henderson sidemen, recalls that Henderson originally recorded with a small combo and gradually enlarged it for later sessions; he had ten men at the Club Alabam as early as 1923. The larger group became a permanent entity when he found a suitable *pied-à-terre* at Roseland, the Broadway ballroom where the primary requirement was the dispensation of music for dancing. The musicians who visited the hall were even better able to appreciate what Henderson was offering than the dancers at whom his music was aimed. "When Smack's band hit town and Louis Armstrong was with him, the guys had never heard anything like it," recalled Duke Ellington. "There weren't the words coined for describing that kick."[1]

Armstrong was just one of scores of soloists who were to make the Henderson band a virtual who's who of jazz during the next twelve years. When Louis joined Fletcher for the Roseland opening in 1924, he played third trumpet; the brass section was brought to quartet size by a single trombonist. Buster Bailey, Don Redman and Coleman Hawkins played a variety of reed instruments. The rhythm section was typical of that period: piano, banjo, tuba and drums. Henderson played piano, but in later years occasionally ceded the chair to his brother Horace or to Fats Waller.

The band grew steadily in size, reputation and musicianship. By 1929 there were four saxophones, two trombones, and the modern rhythm section with guitar and shring bass replacing banjo and tuba. Surviving members of the early Henderson band are unanimous in their insistence that its records give an inadequate idea of the excitement generated by the swing-conducive arrangements and the galaxy of soloists that passed through the ranks between 1922 and 1936. The three-minute time limitation on performances for the old 78 speed records, the psychological pressures of the recording studio and the happy-go-lucky morale of the men made the production of representative discs an impossibility. (John Hammond, who supervised some of the recording sessions around 1932, recalls that on one occasion a three-hour date was scheduled to start at 10 a.m.; by 11:30 there were five musicians present, and the bassist, John Kirby, wandered in at 12:40). Despite the consequent raggedness of ensemble and lack of dynamic cohesion, the records show some of the band's catalytic qualities.

The list of Henderson band alumni is astonishingly rich. Grouped approximately in chronological order of their incumbence, the trumpeters were Louis Armstrong, Joe Smith, Bobby Stark, Rex Stewart, Red Allen, Joe Thomas, Roy Eldridge, Emmett Berry. In the same order, the trombonists included Charlie Green, Jimmy Harrison, Dickie Wells, J. C. Higginbotham; the alto saxophonists Don Redman, Benny Carter, Edgar Sampson, Hilton Jefferson, Russell Procope; the tenors Coleman Hawkins, Lester Young (briefly), Ben Webster, Chu Berry; the clarinets Buster Bailey and Jerry Blake; the banjoists or guitarists Charlie Dixon, Clarence Holiday (Billie's father), Bernard Addison; the bassists Bob Escudero, June Cole, John Kirby, Israel Crosby; the drummers Kaiser Marshall, Walter Johnson, Sid Catlett.

Henderson precariously held a band together during the late 1930s, but his main identification was as arranger for Benny Goodman, whose band he joined as pianist for a few months in

1939. The bands Henderson led intermittently during the 1940s were of minor importance.

Henderson set the classic pattern for jazz orchestral arranging, pitting reeds against brass for "call-and-response" effects, fusing them for block-voiced ensembles, and always placing a firm accent on a sense of swing, in which the use of syncopation played a dominant part.

Almost contemporaneous with Henderson was Duke Ellington, whose first orchestra in New York grew out of a group under the leadership of a banjo player, Elmer Snowden, at Barron's in Harlem. Ellington had been a leader off and on since his teen-aged debut in Washington, but a discussion of his work in the context of a survey of big-band jazz must begin around 1926, when the orchestra began to move perceptibly along the path it was to pursue as the first completely effective synthesis of arranged jazz and ad lib solos, the former ideally geared to the personalities and styles of the latter.

Ellington was responsible for many other innovations. His was the first orchestra to make frequent and effective use of form in arrangements (most of Henderson's performances consisted of a string of choruses based either on popular songs or on instrumental themes borrowed from outside sources); of the rubber plunger mute for brass color effects (played originally by Bubber Miley, trumpet, and Joseph "Tricky Sam" Nanton, trombone); of the baritone saxophone as a solo vehicle (Harry Carney joined the band in 1926 and was still a member in 1965); of ingenious variations on the blues, such as the juxtaposition of themes in two modes; of the use of the human voice with an orchestra for pseudo-instrumental effects (Adelaide Hall on *Creole Love Call* in 1927 and Baby Cox in *The Mooche* and *Hot and Bothered* in 1928 pioneered in a device still widely imitated today.

In its early years the Ellington band was given to so-called "jungle music," a survival of the Original Dixieland Jazz Band days when titles and sound effects suggesting a zoölogical background were a part of the game. Though Duke's titles sometimes could be classified as Americana (his original radio theme was *East St. Louis Toddle-O* and his early compositions included *Birmingham Breakdown*, *Washington Wobble*, *Harlem River*

Quiver) there were also such works as *Echoes of the Jungle, Jungle Nights in Harlem, Jungle Blues.* Ironically, for all its growls and pseudo-primitivism the Ellington music was further removed from the jungle than any other jazz then being performed. The unique timbre of the orchestra that helped give birth to the Ellington legend was no accident; it grew from the mating of great natural talent with skilled musicianship on the part of each instrumentalist, and from the welding of these talents into an inspired and cohesive whole through the use of orchestral voicings, melodic contours and rhythmic innovations that were the product of the Ellington genius.

Duke Ellington and his orchestra have gone through three important phases of musical creativity. The first, which lasted until the early 1930s, covered the years of instrumental experimentation on the level of new sounds, new frameworks for instrumental solos, new variations on harmonic patterns that were common to all jazz. The second, which began in 1934 with *Solitude,* was the era of Ellington the songwriter, the creator of melodies, most of them originally conceived only with his own orchestra in mind, that were to become a beloved part of America's twentieth century popular music.

The third phase was Ellington's "extended forms" era. Though he had tried several times during the 1930s to break the bonds of the three-minute record format (first with the eight-minute *Creole Rhapsody* in 1931, then with the four-part *Reminiscing in Tempo,* 1935) it was not until the world premier of *Black, Brown and Beige* at Carnegie Hall in January, 1943 that the most ambitious of his ventures was able to gain momentum. This work, 50 minutes long in its original version, combined all the traditional values of jazz, all the qualities that had developed from within, and applied them to what was nominally a programmatic work (a "tone parallel to the history of the American Negro" as the composer called it) with results that gave jazz a new dimension. From then until 1950 Ellington composed a new extended work annually for presentation at Carnegie Hall: among them were the *Deep South Suite, New World A-Comin'* (titled after a book on American Negro life by Roi Ottley), the *Liberian Suite,* commissioned by that country's government to celebrate its centennial, *Blue Belles of Harlem, Blutopia* and *The Tattooed Bride*. During the 1950s there have been a few works of a similarly expansive and experimental nature: the *Harlem Suite*, played at an Ellington concert at the Metropolitan Opera House in 1951; *Night Creature*, for which the Ellington orchestra was combined with the Symphony of the Air at Carnegie Hall in 1955; the *Newport Jazz Festival Suite*, premiered at that event in 1956; a unique, oratorio-like work, using guest singers and Ellington as narrator, *A Drum Is a Woman*, offered as an hour-long television presentation in 1957; and *Such Sweet Thunder*, comprising twelve short cameos inspired by characters from Shakespeare.

The late 1950s and the '60s saw no diminution in the potency and durability of the Ellington-Strayhorn initiative. Among the most captivating long works of recent years have been two weddings of the band's sound with the classical concert repertory (Tschaikowsky's *Nutcracker Suite* and Grieg's *Peer Gynt Suite*, both in Columbia albums); the original cast performance *My People*, presented at the Century of Negro Progress Exhibition in Chicago in 1963 and preserved in a Contact LP; and four performances for which the band was amalgamated with musicians drawn from symphony and opera orchestras in Paris, Hamburg, Stockholm and La Scala, Milan. This last album, on Reprise, includes expanded versions of two earlier works, the *Harlem* suite and *Night Creature*, as well as two new pieces, *Non-Violent Integration* and *La Scala, She Too Pretty to be Blue*.

Every Ellington work, whether a casual three-minute riff tune or a half-hour suite in four movements, has always drawn its strength from within the essential qualities of jazz itself; even the most ambitious pieces have remained essentially and fundamentally jazz. While Whiteman, Gershwin and others tried desperately to make a lady out of jazz, Ellington achieved a much worthier and more logical goal; he made a man of it.

The big bands of the 1920s, aside from those of Ellington and Henderson, offered very little of lasting orchestral value. Ben Pollack and, to a lesser extent, Jean Goldkette, gave white musicians a jazz haven while Whiteman was holding his jazz stars down to an occasional brief solo. Pollack, who organized his band in Chicago in 1925 but later enjoyed popularity in Chicago and New York, was a drummer who knew the value of such sidemen as Benny Goodman, Jimmy McPartland and Glenn Miller, all of whom were heard on his early records. The arrangements, often by Glenn Miller, drew from popular songs of the day, standard blues themes and occasional original instrumentals. Goldkette, a concert pianist who was never a jazz instrumentalist, hired such musicians as Bix Beiderbecke and Frankie Trumbauer for his band, a quasi-symphonic dance outfit with arrangements by Bill Challis. There were some records of interest in 1926-7, but their value today lies entirely in the solo passages.

Goldkette, active in the Detroit area, also participated in jazz as a businessman, organizing and booking other bands. It may be contended that the contribution he made to jazz with his own orchestra was less valuable than the role he played in booking McKinney's Cotton Pickers. Bill McKinney was an ex-drummer who lent his name to a band in which Don Redman, as alto saxophonist, arranger and musical director, played the most important role. Redman had his own orchestra from 1931 to 1940; the first Negro band ever to be part of a regularly sponsored radio series, it was known to millions through the Redman composition used as the band's theme, the smoky and sonorous *Chant of the Weed.*

The 1930s saw the rise and fall of innumerable big bands and a gradual increase in the size and scope of their' instrumentation. The saxophone section, some or all of whose members doubled on clarinets, usually numbered four, but was increased to five by Ellington in 1939; the trumpet section increased occasionally from three to four and the trombones from two to three. The rhythm section remained unchanged.

The Negro ballrooms and night clubs such as Fairyland Park in Kansas City, the Grand Terrace in Chicago and the Savoy Ballrooms in Chicago and New York provided the settings for the music of a number of hard-swinging bands during the '30s. Chick Webb, a dimunitive drummer who fought an amazingly successful battle against both Jim Crow and a natural physical deformity, led his invincible gladiators through a "Battle of the Bands" against Benny Goodman one night at Harlem's Savoy and scored a memorable victory. The Webb band's instrumental numbers followed the general pattern of the Henderson and Redman bands, with Edgar Sampson of the sax section as chief arranger; many of the biggest Sampson-Webb hits, notably *Stompin' at the Savoy, Blue Lou, If Dreams Come True* and *Don't Be That Way,* were later popularized more widely by the Goodman band.

Earl Hines, from 1928 until 1948, led a band that was important for the gifted sidemen that it produced rather than for any individual style. Best known in the '30s for its radio theme, *Deep Forest,* and for the leader's own composition, *Rosetta,* the Hines band was to evolve in the early '40s into a virtual cradle of the bop movement.

A King Oliver dynasty began when the Oliver band, gradually enlarged from combo to orchestra dimension, came to New York and Luis Russell, Oliver's pianist, led a band composed mainly of ex-Oliver sidemen. In turn, Teddy Hill, who had played tenor sax with Oliver and Russell, formed a band of his own that had some popularity in the East from 1935 to '40. The Oliver and Russell bands included Barney Bigard on clarinet and J. C. Higginbotham on trombone; among Hill's sidemen were Roy Eldridge on trumpet, Chu Berry on tenor sax, and later Dizzy Gillespie.

Benny Carter was a bandleader when economic conditions allowed it during most of the 1930s, but like many of his contemporaries he was more important for his mastery of the pen and the horn than for his control of the baton and is therefore discussed elsewhere. Cab Calloway's band, fronted by the "hi-de-ho" scat singer, offered an acceptable pastiche of popular music, pre-swing and competently arranged jazz.

In Kansas City during the late '20s and early '30s the bands of Andy Kirk, in which the piano and arrangements of Mary Lou Williams lent an incandescent touch, and of Benny and Buster Moten, with Count Basie and Jimmy Rushing often featured, adumbrated a style that was to be illuminated fully in the great Basie band that came to New York in 1936.

The Kansas City tradition was later continued by Jay McShann, the Oklahoma-born pianist. Like many bands from his area, McShann placed a heavy accent on arrangements built around the blues and boogie woogie, as did Harlan Leonard, an ex-Moten saxophonist from Kansas City, whose band achieved some slight prominence in the east in 1940.

Glen Gray's Casa Loma orchestra, an outgrowth of the Orange Blossom band, a 10-piece group that played at the Casa Loma Hotel in Toronto in 1928, was a great favorite with college audiences during the early 1930s and is credited by some as having been the first white band with a deliberate jazz policy. Nevertheless the·arrangements were as relaxed as a freshly starched shirt; many of them were built on riffs so simple that they seemed to call for nothing more than a knowledge of the member notes of a few triads and scales. This was the band whose arranger, Gene Gifford (composer of *Black Jazz, White Jazz, Maniac's Ball* and *Casa Loma Stomp)* was popular among some of the best Negro bands of the early swing years and was responsible for the stiffness in some of their performances.

More important to jazz was the Dorsey Brothers' orchestra, which leaned mostly on Glenn Miller arrangements of popular songs, novelties and some jazz items, and which enjoyed some popularity in 1934-5; still more meaningful was the Benny Goodman band, which reversed the Casa Loma-Gene Gifford procedure by implanting the styles of Negro arrangers on a white band. Fletcher Henderson was the principal arranger for the Goodman orchestra, which attempted, in effect, to bring downtown the spirit of Harlem's Savoy Ballroom. The simple, swinging antiphony of the reed and brass sections and the smooth-flowing four-four of the rhythm section gave America a new kind of music, suitable for the utilitarian purposes it had to serve in ballrooms at the onset of the era of jitterbug dancing, but no less attractive to musicians and jazz fans who found special delight in following the solo flights of Goodman and his stardom-bound apprentices—in the early years they included Bunny Berigan or Harry James on trumpet, Vido Musso on tenor sax, Jess Stacy on piano and Gene Krupa on drums.

During the first years of the Goodman gold rush, the two leading Negro orchestras of the 1930s were beginning to attract national attention: Jimmie Lunceford, whose peak years ran from 1934 to '39, and Count Basie, who began to record with his big band in 1937. The chief Lunceford memory is that of a highly trained group of well-disciplined and musically literate musicians playing in a style that involved the use of staccato phrases, suddenly soaring brass chords and sharply contrasted mellow, almost glutinous saxophone section work, interspersed with novelty vocals sung by a trio, a single instrumentalist doubling as rhythm vocalist, or a ballad singer. Lunceford, who fronted the band but played no instrument (though fully qualified on saxophones and flute) was a professional bandleader in a sense that had nothing in common with the earlier concepts of the term. Henderson worked wonders within the limitations of his own nonchalant personality; Ellington could write arrangements in a taxi on the way to the recording session and wait hours for his musicians to arrive; but Lunceford made a success out of his organization on every level. The musicians not only worked well together, but even waved the brass derbies over their horns in perfect unison. To some this meant that the band was too correct, to the point of stiffness; yet the Lunceford band in person was as exciting a sound and sight as can be observed on any bandstand today.

Sy Oliver, who played trumpet in the band and took an occasional puckish vocal, wrote most of the great arrangements; others were the work of Edwin Wilcox, the band's pianist. *Dream of You*, written by Oliver in 1934, is still being copied, while the routines and orchestrations established on *Margie, For Dancers Only* and dozens of others have survived through the pseudo-Lunceford bands of later years. The influence of the Lunceford style, carried directly to the Tommy Dorsey band when Sy Oliver joined the latter as staff arranger late in 1939, has been observed no less distinctly in the orchestras of Billy May, Georgie Auld and George Williams, and in occasional excursions along similar lines by Ray Anthony and others.

In contrast with the brittle and shrill Lunceford approach to big band jazz, the Count Basie orchestra offered more informality and longer solo opportunities in a looser setting than any other band of the '30s. The free-flowing rhythm section, with Freddie Greene's guitar, Walter Page's bass, Jo Jones' drums and the leader's piano, was the key to the rhythmic miracle achieved by Basie.

The whole band played as if it were one vast rhythm section. Most of the best numbers were founded simply on the 12-bar blues, or on easily digested 32-bar patterns, including occasionally a popular song of the day. Basie's band later acquired a girl singer (the sedately swinging Helen Humes) and a retinue of arrangers, among them Jimmy Mundy, Buster Harding and Don Redman, but the accouterments of fame and fortune did little to increase the emotional value of the original, genuine article. The trigger-fingered, elliptical piano style of the Count (occasionally expanded into a Fats Waller "stride" technique) was but one of the band's many solo virtues; the others, in the old band, were Buck Clayton and Harry "Sweets" Edison on trumpets, Dickie Wells and Benny Morton on trombones, Lester Young and Herschel Evans on tenor saxes.

During the late 1930s Ellington, Lunceford and Basie contested for recognition as the country's foremost Negro jazz orchestra. Ellington had arrived first and was firmly set as the master composer-conductor-songwriter, already an international legend; Lunceford achieved new heights of commercial recognition on the strength of his superb showmanship; Basie was the surprise contender from left field. Meanwhile, on the white side of what was still an almost completely segregated jazz world, a chain reaction had begun. What Goodman and his men were to Harlem swing, Bob Crosby and his band became to old-time Dixieland jazz as Bing's younger brother was made nominal leader and vocalist with what was mainly a resurrection of a band that had been led until 1934 by Ben Pollack.

The arrangements featured by the Crosby band resembled a Brobdingnagian counterpart of the music that had been played a decade earlier by the New Orleans Rhythm Kings and other pioneer white bands, with a few important added elements, noticeably the voicing of clarinets and tenor saxophones. The band had a joyous ensemble spirit and a succession of capable soloists, most of whom were later to abandon their lives as touring jazzmen and settle down in Hollywood and New York as high-priced studio musicians. They included Matty Matlock, clarinet; Eddie Miller, tenor sax; Yank Lawson, trumpet; Bob Haggart, bass. The musical direction of the band was in the hands of one of the saxophonists, Gil Rodin. Crosby's orchestra, which lent a unique tone color to the annals of the swing era, lasted from 1935 to 1942 and has been revived periodically.

The Crosby band was less directly competitive with Benny Goodman's orchestra than several other bands that rose to prominence in the late 1930s, all of them led by instrumental soloists. The freshest and most adventurous was an ensemble organized in 1936 by Artie Shaw. During its all-too-brief career his orchestra comprised two trumpets, a trombone, one sax (Tony Pastor, tenor), a string quartet, and the conventional piano-guitar-bass-drums rhythm section. Though Shaw's clarinet lacked the emotional variety and warmth of the Goodman style, the unprecedented setting of a string quartet, successfully integrated into a jazz group, was an augury of the instrumental expansion jazz was to undergo many years later. Too far ahead of his time, Shaw ran into financial difficulties and had to disband the group and form a more conventional orchestra, with an instrumentation similar to Goodman's, less than a year later.

Glenn Miller, whose often ingenious arrangements had enlivened many a jazz record date as well as the libraries of such pioneer orchestras as Ben Pollack's, Red Nichols' and the Dorsey Brothers', was a late starter in the swing field. After a couple of unsuccessful years on the road he scored a sudden and overwhelming success in 1939. The Miller band's contribution, however, was a minor one from the jazz standpoint, despite the band's popularity among swing fans. Neither in the orchestration nor in the solos by such men as the tenor saxophonist Tex Beneke did the band make any but a superficial impression as a jazz unit.

The Dorsey Brothers' band, in which Miller had played a key role as chief arranger, became Jimmy Dorsey's orchestra in September, 1935 when Tommy, walking out after a disagreement with his brother, formed a new and immediately successful band of his own. Both Dorseys continued along individually popular lines through the 1940s until their reunion under the fraternal banner in 1953, when Jimmy disbanded his own orchestra to align himself with Tommy's band. Neither Dorsey orchestra was primarily a jazz group, though both featured many jazz soloists and occasional instrumental arrangements. Jimmy's success stemmed principally from the popularity of his singers. Tommy, while even more successful as a discoverer of vocal talent (Frank Sinatra, Jo Stafford, the Pied Pipers, etc.) developed a series of techniques for his instrumental numbers, first by adapting classical compositions *(Song of India, Liebestraum,* Mendelssohn's *Spring Song)* and later through the adoption of a strutting, Lunceford-like swing style for which the authentic arrangements were provided by Sy Oliver.

A gently rhythmic and delightfully subtle orchestra of the swing years was formed by Red Norvo in 1936, with the leader's xylophone, vocals by his wife, Mildred Bailey, and arrangements by Eddie Sauter that were, at the time, exceptionally colorful and venturesome. Norvo retained the big band format until 1942, by which time the imprint of the Eddie Sauter personality had been transferred to a rejuvenated Benny Goodman band.

Charlie Barnet, a saxophonist who had been active around New York since his late teens, made his first big hit when he recorded *Cherokee* in 1939. Barnet played an explosive style of tenor sax, an occasional Hodges-oriented solo on alto, and sometimes led his reed section most effectively on soprano sax. In the band he led between 1939 and '43, the arrangements by Barnet, Billy May, Andy Gibson and others often bore the unmistakable imprint of the Ellington band and at one point Barnet was publicized as "the white Duke." His had been the first white band ever to play at the Apollo Theater in Harlem in 1933, and during its peak years the band had a great deal of the driving enthusiasm, if not the originality, of the Ellington and Basie bands.

Of all the orchestras generated by the swing era, Woody Herman must be credited with the most evolutionary variety of styles. The original Herman band was founded in 1936 with a nucleus of the disbanded dance orchestra of Isham Jones, in which Herman had worked for two years. Using a slogan, "The Band That Plays The Blues," Herman built up a repertoire of pops, blues and instrumentals. His first big hit was *Woodchoppers' Ball,* a fast blues, in 1939. Herman played Hodges-like alto, climactic clarinet, and sang pleasant quasi-blues and ballads.

During the 1940s Herman's popularity remained at a fairly steady level despite several changes in style. For a while the semi-Dixieland ensemble style gave way to a series of arrangements, many of them written by Dave Matthews, that drew heavily on Ellington for their source material. In 1943-4 the band took on a modernist tinge and became the first white orchestra conspicuously influenced by bebop. Neal Hefti and Ralph Burns played and arranged in the band at this time; Bill Harris and Flip Phillips were featured soloists, and the rhythm section, one of the happiest teams of its kind in modern jazz history, included Billy Bauer, guitar; Chubby Jackson, bass; Dave Tough and later Don Lamond on drums. For a couple of years, between 1945 and '47, Herman enjoyed the kind of recognition among jazz fans that was later to be accorded Stan Kenton. The original band broke up in December 1946. Since 1947 Herman has led a big band intermittently; his orchestras frequently have been the grammar school for rising jazz stars. The 1947-9 ensemble came to be known as the "Four Brothers" band because of the unique reed section blend achieved by the tenor saxophones of Stan Getz, Zoot Sims and Al Cohn and the baritone of Serge Chaloff.

The Herman band's most important contribution to jazz was the team spirit engendered by the 1944-6 personnel, in which there was a parallel for the Basie orchestra of a decade earlier, in that the "head" arrangements and the general atmosphere of spontaneity seemed pragmatically more important than anything found on the manuscript paper.

A similar atmosphere seemed to pervade the Lionel Hampton band when the vibraphonist left Benny Goodman and resumed his bandleading career in 1940. For a few years the band managed to maintain a policy of euphoria without hysteria; the latter quality took over almost exclusively in later years as Hampton tended more and more toward a policy of erotic excitement that had much in common with rock and roll. Hampton displayed an uncanny knack for discovering great new jazz soloists, but many of them complained on leaving the band that they had had little or no opportunity to display their talents properly in this chaotic setting. Nevertheless, the Hampton band has shown enough of the pioneer Savoy Ballroom spirit on occasion to supply some valid mainstream music.

More important by far, in that it was the first big band to reflect the tremendous impact of bebop, was the Billy Eckstine orchestra. Formed by the singer in 1944, the band lasted for three years and during that time featured arrangements by Tadd Dameron, Budd Johnson and Gerald Valentine, vocals by Eckstine and Sarah Vaughan, solos by Dizzy Gillespie, Miles Davis, Fats Navarro, Charlie Parker, Gene Ammons, Dexter Gordon and Art Blakey. Like the Fletcher Henderson band, Eckstine's team had to be seen to be remembered in its true perspective, for the few records it made were inadequate both in performance and recording.

More effective and longer lasting in the translation of bop into big band terms was the contribution of Dizzy Gillespie, whose first full orchestra toured in the summer of 1945. The following year he reorganized a big band, retaining it, with numerous personnel changes, until 1950. He resumed the orchestral format in 1956. Gillespie's band combined the innovations of bop with the élan and spark of the leader's personality, the brilliance of the arrangements by Gillespie, Tadd Dameron and John Lewis, the new element provided by the Afro-Cuban drums of Chano Pozo in 1947, and the contributions of Milt Jackson, Kenny Clarke and other key sidemen. Since 1958 Gillespie has been forced by economic conditions to work with a quintet.

Before the episodes with Eckstine and his own bands, Gillespie had worked briefly with an orchestra led by Boyd Raeburn, a saxophonist and arranger whose contribution to big band jazz has been overlooked by fans who came along too late to be aware of its impact. Raeburn, between 1944 and '47, made use of harmonically ambitious arrangements by George Handy, Ed Finckel and Johnny Richards. His band indicated a path that was to prove popular among avant-gardists of the '50s, by its inclusion of modern soloists in a somewhat more cerebral orchestral framework.

Several other orchestras, during the late '30s, the '40s and the early '50s, played big band jazz but served mainly as dance bands and made no significant contribution in terms of jazz styles.

Among them were those of Les Brown, whose smooth and popular orchestra has been operating partly on a jazz level ever since its inception more than two decades ago; Elliot Lawrence, a pianist and arranger in whose band Gerry Mulligan wrote some of his early arrangements; and Claude Thornhill, also a pianist-arranger, whose dance orchestra was the first to be enriched by the timbre of French horns, and several of whose sidemen, as was pointed out in the combo chapter, played an important role in the founding of the Miles Davis orchestral style.

The Savoy Ballroom tradition was carried on by a series of capable dance bands, none of any earth-shaking importance from the jazz standpoint, but all capable of stirring up the kind of excitement associated with the old Henderson band. Among the leaders of these groups were trumpeter Erskine Hawkins, a band-leader since 1935, whose hit record of *Tuxedo Junction* in 1939 became his theme; and the pianist, Buddy Johnson, a great favorite with rhythm-and-blues followers in the 1940s.

Though we owe to Duke Ellington an incalculable debt for the work he and Billy Strayhorn contributed to make the Ellington orchestra the most successful and esthetically valuable of the 1940s, the greatest excitement among young jazz fans during those years was caused by the advent of a California-grounded orchestra led by Stan Kenton, a pianist and arranger who started his group at Balboa Beach in 1940 and had gone into high gear with the release of *Artistry in Rhythm*, the band's theme, recorded in 1943. The Kenton orchestra went through four main phases. During the first, Kenton himself and Ralph Yaw wrote the arrangements. The predominant style was the staccato phrasing of the saxophones. Keystones of the second phase of Kenton were a series of "artistry" motifs (*Artistry in Bolero, Artistry Jumps, Artistry in Bass,* etc.) and a number of attempts to crash the popular market through vocals by June Christy and others. In this period, from 1945-9, the band rose to become the most popular with American jazz fans, winning its first *Down Beat* poll in 1947 and making great use during the next year or two of the slogan "Progressive Jazz." Pete Rugolo was the chief arranger.

Kenton's third phase, after he had spent most of 1949 in retirement, was the "Innovations in Modern Music" band, which used a large string section and mixed atonal concert arrangements, sometimes reminiscent of Bartok, with works that had a tangential relationship to jazz. During the next few years, though he dropped the strings, Kenton continued to record occasional experimental arrangements by Bob Graettinger and others that appeared to have very little jazz validity. Overlapping with this stage of the band's evolution was the fourth phase, in which jazz returned through the arrangements of Shorty Rogers, Bill Holman and Gerry Mulligan. The bands organized by Kenton from 1954 on were mainly dedicated to this kind of music and bore a closer resemblance to the Woody Herman orchestra of the late 1940s than to any previous Kenton organization.

It is difficult to gain a clear perspective of the more ambitious works introduced by the Kenton orchestra. At this stage it can only be said that considerable doubt has been expressed by musicians and critics concerning its place in jazz. Kenton has been important, however, as the jazz world's foremost barker. Whatever the sideshow he introduced, be it the sword-swallowing attempt of an arranger to incorporate the steel of Hindemith into the body of Hampton or the two-headed man who could talk simultaneously in the languages of Tanglewood and Birdland, he has never failed to draw attention to jazz, no matter how indirectly, and it would be unfair to Kenton to classify him as the 1950s' parallel to Paul Whiteman. Kenton's musical course never has been a straight line, but in zig-zagging its way through the past twenty-five years it has blazed a trail that can neither be dismissed nor eradicated.

Mainly because the economics of the music business have made it unprofitable to invest in the formation of a big band, there have been very few new orchestras of lasting importance in recent years. Eddie Sauter and Bill Finegan, who had worked frequently as arrangers for Benny Goodman and Tommy Dorsey respectively, pooled their talents to organize the Sauter-Finegan band in 1952. The novel tonal effects and clever orchestrations gained them a wide audience. The value of the music varied greatly, since the main objectives seemed to be novelty for its own sake and the greatest possible variety of tone colors, obtained through the use of odd instruments, miscellaneous percussion effects, etc. Here too, as with Kenton, there were attempts to straddle the fence with works borrowed from the classics, semi-jazz works showing strong classical influences, and occasional ventures of an extremely pretentious nature, most notable of which was the recording of the *Concerto for Jazz Band and Symphony Orchestra*, written by Rolf Liebermann and played by the Sauter-Finegan orchestra combined with the Chicago Symphony orchestra conducted by Fritz Reiner.

In its best moments the Sauter-Finegan orchestra showed an admirable sense of humor and provided vehicles for interesting solos by vibraphonist-percussionist Joe Venuto, trumpeter Nick Travis and others.

On the periphery of jazz since the early 1950s have been the bands specializing in mambo music, Afro-Cuban rhythms and related forms. The sidemen in some of these orchestras often include former members of jazz bands. Machito, whose orchestra has been heard at Birdland, used such jazzmen as Flip Phillips and Howard McGhee as guest soloists and was teamed on records with Charlie Parker. Tito Puente, a vibraphonist whose band also became popular in such jazz clubs as Birdland, occasionally reflected the influence of Kenton, Herman and Basie. Among the other orchestras popular in Latin-American circles have been those of Noro Morales and Tito Rodriguez.

For the record, brief mention should be made of a number of musicians who at some time in the past quarter-century have organized and toured with big bands. Some of the leaders were major jazzmen, but none led a band of enduring stature or individuality, though a couple (notably those of Coleman Hawkins and Teddy Wilson in 1940) were greatly underrated and regrettably short-lived. The list includes Will Bradley, Sonny Burke, Sam Donahue (fronting a Tommy Dorsey "ghost band" in the 1960s), Les Hite, Claude Hopkins, George Hudson, Jeter-Pillars, Gene Krupa, Hal McIntyre, Ray McKinley (with a Glenn Miller ghost band), Jan Savitt, Freddie Slack, Muggsy Spanier (an excellent big Dixieland-oriented group along Bob Crosby lines), Jack Teagarden, Cootie Williams.

By the middle 1950s, with the advent of rock 'n' roll, one of the main sources of income for the big bands was eliminated. The small combos with the big, crude beat now supplied music for dancing. This and a variety of other factors made it almost impossible to maintain a big band.

Maynard Ferguson led a 13-piece band from 1957 until 1964, featuring some excellent arrangements by Willie Maiden and Slide Hampton, but with a tendency toward the shrill triple-fortissimo. The band achieved some of its most relaxed moments when the leader put down his trumpet to play valve trombone.

Harry James, a bandleader since 1939, and still capable of fluently convincing solo moments, has fronted a superior, swing-oriented band in the past decade, emulating the Basie ensemble and using some of the same arrangers (Neal Hefti, Ernie Wilkins, Thad Jones).

Gerry Mulligan has led a 13-piece band from time to time since 1960. Sounding sometimes like an extension of the quartet, sometimes like a slightly more modern Basie group, it has made a series of rewarding albums.

Quincy Jones formed a superlative band, involving a number of former Gillespie sidemen, for an onstage part in a jazz opera seen in Europe in 1959-60. The show was not successful; neither was Jones in keeping the band together in the U.S. His arrangements showed how far the tonal palette of the big band in the reeds-brass-and-rhythm tradition could be extended by the subtle incorporation of the flute into the section and block voicings. He has reorganized a big band from time to time.

Gil Evans has made a few short-lived attempts to keep a band together. On the strength of his records, and of those he made in collaboration with Miles Davis, he would seem capable of organizing what could be the most important large orchestra since Ellington's. Gerald Wilson, on the West Coast, has used his off-and-on band to display his richly textured, often Spanish-and-Mexican-tinged arrangements.

Ray Charles has had a big band for some years, but its ensemble is ragged and the group serves mainly as a backdrop for the leader.

Most of the other musicians who have led big bands (usually only for an occasional record date or concert) will be dealt with in the next chapter, since all are composer-arrangers.

CHAPTER 21

THE COMPOSERS AND ARRANGERS

"It all starts with the soloist. What he plays today the arranger writes tomorrow."
—Tony Scott

Once the premise is accepted that jazz can be composed and arranged, a postulate once rejected by experts but now accepted by most, it becomes necessary to assess the similarities and distinctions between composition and arrangement. These are two of the most misunderstood terms in jazz; the layman is aware of the first and vaguely conscious of the second, while even the musician at times tends to confuse the terms.

The composer (etymologically, *together-putter*) assembles a group of notes horizontally on the manuscript paper, or interprets them with voice or instrument, to form a melodic line pleasing to the ear. The arranger's task clearly is more complex, since he is charged with the orchestration (scoring) of a composition in such a manner that the voicing of the instruments, vertically, is no less attractive than the melodic line; in many instances the arranger himself devises the melody and orchestrates it more or less simultaneously. Even when he is scoring a melody created by another writer, he may invest it with all the qualities of harmonic and rhythmic subtlety, of variations on the theme, that lead to the creation of a successful jazz performance. Thus, in effect, whether he wrote the original line or not, the arranger always is also a composer. The converse is not true. Some writers of melodies have no knowledge of orchestration or, even if they do, prefer not to concern themselves with it. Even some of the most talented of jazz composers have never written orchestrations (Lennie Tristano, Charlie Parker and Thelonious Monk are outstanding cases in point).

The listener, uninformed concerning these nuances, may praise a composition when in fact its only merit lies in the attractive orchestral setting given it by the arranger; or he may condemn the composer in an instance when a fine composition has been ruined by an incompetent, unfeeling arrangement.

In arranging, the manner of orchestration often determines the degree to which a performance may be classified as jazz. In composition the jazz element often is secondary or completely immaterial, and the line that usually separates jazz from popular music disappears completely. Duke Ellington is the greatest arranger (i.e., composer for orchestra) jazz has known; yet the melody of his *Solitude* could just as easily have been written by Irving Berlin. It is built from notes of the diatonic scale and is of little or no melodic interest; only the manner in which he voiced it in its first performance by the Ellington band led to its acceptance as a "standard." Ellington the songwriter operates on the same level as Richard Rodgers, Cole Porter and Jimmy McHugh; Ellington the arranger, a far more vital figure, must be viewed as a contemporary of John Lewis, Gil Evans, Quincy Jones.

This does not imply any disparagement of the songwriter, or of the non-orchestrating jazz composer. The mere fact of the general acceptance by many jazz soloists and writers of a tune such as Victor Young's *Stella By Starlight* in recent years is a reflection of their justifiable admiration for its melodic content and harmonic basis; on the other hand the same composer's *Sweet Sue*, which came to jazz acceptance in an era of harmonic simplicity, has no intrinsic value whatever, either as a popular song or as a jazz vehicle.

Since musical literacy in the first couple of decades of jazz was at a level that did not encompass any knowledge of orchestration, the value of every performance lay in the merit of the melody line and in its susceptibility to syncopation. The main source materials came from a blend of marches (some of Creole, French and Spanish origin), spirituals (the ragtime played on the way home from the funeral might include *Ain't Gonna Study War No More* or *When the Saints Go Marching In*), blues (most of which were passed along by word of mouth, to be documented later by W. C. Handy and others), and ragtime (usually a little more complex than the others, involving two or three themes linked by interludes, etc.). It was not until the early 1930s, when such pioneers as Coleman Hawkins and Benny Goodman showed how the treasury of jazz could be enriched by the incorporation of Tin Pan Alley's better products as media for jazz treatment, that composition per se made an appreciable step forward. Meanwhile, however, for almost a decade, the art of writing for jazz had been given a new dimension as the pioneer arrangers went to work.

The first jazz arranger of influence and importance was Don Redman. Because he was a saxophonist in Fletcher Henderson's orchestra, and because Henderson subsequently earned independent acceptance as one of the great jazz arrangers, the true proportion of Redman's contribution has been virtually ignored. Trained in conservatories in Boston and Detroit, a child prodigy and instrumentalist from the age of three, he made his first tentative efforts at composing and arranging as early as 1915.

Redman told it in his own words: "When I was 14 or 15 I used to write things for theater groups—those nickelodeons where they had real bad shows—they would come through maybe once a month. We had seven pieces; this was in West Virginia, and we played for an all-white show. I used to write a lot of things for the shows and a song that I did for one of them a little later on eventually became popular; but being a country boy, I didn't know what to do about copyrighting it, so I lost it. It was called *Prohibition Blues*.

"I first came to New York with a band from Pittsburgh called the Broadway Syncopators. They didn't last long here, but we got a lot of comments on the arrangements. I was with them in 1922; the following year I joined Fletcher Henderson's band and did just about all the arrangements. When we started out there were just two saxophones—Coleman Hawkins and I—and three brass. Hawk and I were definitely the first to start playing riffs behind the solos. This was at the Club Alabam; later on, when we came to Roseland, we decided to put on another saxophone and we got Buster Bailey.

"Shortly after Louis Armstrong joined the band, King Oliver sent him a little notebook with lines drawn on it. Together they had written a lot of things. Louis gave it to me and said, 'Pick out anything you want and make it up for future use.' They had things like *Cornet Chop Suey* and *Dippermouth Blues*, which later became known as *Sugar Foot Stomp*. I made up *Dippermouth* for Fletcher's band and we recorded it in 1925. Later on, Fletcher copied the arrangement for Benny Goodman, but I made the original, and that's the record that made Fletcher Henderson. All those early numbers like *Whatcha Call 'Em Blues*, *Stampede* and *Snag it*—those were my arrangements.

"Fletcher came much later as a writer. He didn't really start arranging for the band until after I had left to join McKinney's Cotton Pickers; then, a year after I left, Benny Carter joined the band, and he took over a lot of the writing."

The earliest Redman works, of which the recording of the Armstrong-Oliver *Sugar Foot Stomp* is a prototype, showed that he had captured what was then the first essential of jazz arrangement: to express in sectional and ensemble terms the same nuances of phrasing and melodic construction that gave jazz improvisation its character. There were passages scored in simple harmony for three clarinets, or three saxophones, or for the brass section; there were rhythm breaks and background riffs behind the ad libbing soloists. Three-part harmony prevailed. The most advanced idea in the entire arrangement of *Sugar Foot Stomp* is the use of a major seventh in the penultimate chord, played by unaccompanied saxophones in the coda and leading to a "blue seventh" ending. Though the Redman arrangements of that period sound comically crude when compared with his own later work, they were able to move jazz along the road to maturity and were certainly ahead of their time.

The first white composer and arranger to document jazz was Elmer Schoebel. Though he created arrangements for the Friars' Society Orchestra and the Midway Dance Band in the early 1920s, at first they were dictated rather than written, since some of the musicians could not read. Schoebel's specialty was the transcribing to print of Dixieland arrangements. In 1922 some of his most durable compositions first appeared in print, among them *Farewell Blues* and *Bugle Call Rag*. "Three-part harmony was only featured in the large orchestras at that time," Schoebel recalls. "As far as the real Dixieland arrangements were concerned, this was done very much in the same way that you hear them now—very flexible and not too fixed, with many spots completely ad libbed.

"In addition to introducing the first real Dixieland · arrangements in print, I transcribed all of Jelly Roll Morton and Joe Oliver's tunes from the early '20s on."

Concerning the contrast between white and Negro styles in the early years he comments: "There wasn't any particular interchange of ideas as there simply weren't enough arrangers. However, they mixed plenty and played together when they had a chance."

The use of jazz arrangements took a more ambitious step forward in 1926-8, when Don Redman provided a series of orchestrations for some of the first white groups that were then experimenting with large-scale jazz, among them the Paul Whiteman and Ben Pollack orchestras. Meanwhile Fletcher Henderson, after Redman had quit the band, began to contribute more actively to his orchestra's library.

Henderson Stomp and *King Porter Stomp* were in essence embryonic treatments of fuller voiced arrangements that were later to earn him a belated reputation with the general American public through his work for the Benny Goodman orchestra.

Henderson, before forming his band, had worked as a house pianist and writer with companies that published music or phonograph records; it was not a lack of capability, but the laissez-faire streak in his disposition, that prevented him from assuming a larger share of the writing responsibilities with his orchestra. Henderson's work had a great deal in common with Redman's; he made superlative use of the comparatively limited instrumentation at his disposal.

The catalytic efforts of Henderson and Redman stand out in sharper relief when contrasted with the contemporaneous works of other composer-arrangers attempting to present jazz in orchestral forms. An examination of Jelly Roll Morton's *Cannon Ball Blues* and *Someday Sweetheart* reveals that both the writer and the men written for had less to work with. Despite occasional lapses of sectional accuracy in the Henderson performances, they are models of precision and swing when compared with the stiff, unimaginative phrasing of the Morton group. *Someday Sweetheart* opens with a violin solo, playing strict melody in a completely non-jazz style, with background effects based either on sustained notes or on syncopated phrases invariably played too staccato to swing; on the second chorus a bass clarinet takes over the solo role, also playing straight melody with little beat. Morton's following piano solo is a model of non-swing; his left hand limps along, playing single notes and triads while the right produces trite variations on the melody. Only in the final sixteen measures played by the ensemble does the band swing collectively and in obviously improvised style; evidently whatever arrangement had been written for the close, if any, proved unsuitable for use, or else Morton realized that collective ad libbing gave this band its only chance for inspired jazz expression.

Cannon Ball Blues, recorded at the same time (December 1926), reveals that even when working in the familiar framework of the traditional blues Morton's men had either too much (the last measure of the trumpet break) or too little to say, and that the framework he offered them in which to say it was no less limited. His own wobbly piano solo is backed by shakily held "organ harmony" by the horns, all played directly on the beat; again the final chorus, played ad lib, is the only part that swings, and the four-bar coda could be the twin of a passage from one of Billy May's 1957 satires on Dixieland jazz, so obviously and "cornily" does it state its arhythmic message.

Twelve days before Morton recorded these numbers, Duke Ellington had opened at New York's Cotton Club with a band that already had to its credit two years of recording experience, the second year having been dedicated entirely to music born within the Ellington band and arranged by Duke himself. Ellington had already found the path toward a more enlightened concept of the blues, interweaving major and minor themes, finding colorful new voicings even within the limitations of an instrumentation only ten men strong. Already on record were his hauntingly exotic theme, *East St. Louis Toddle-O;* his "jungle-style" variation on the blues, *Black and Tan Fantasy,* and the beautiful simplicity of *Creole Love Call,* in which Adelaide Hall's voice was blended wordlessly with the instruments.

Ellington's concern was with form, an area in which he had shown himself a master from the start; with timbres, which grew in color and scope as his orchestra and his knowledge expanded through the decades; and with personalities. From the beginning his work was inextricably a part of the musical make-up of its exponents; more and more he conceived his themes in terms of their potential use as a framework for the uniquely gifted soloists at his beck and call.

The voicing of an Ellington arrangement invariably bore the unmistakable imprint of his own feeling for tone combinations. An Ellington score, whether devoted to jungle-style effects with the brass using plunger mutes or to the joyously abandoned spirit of a stomp, was inseparable from the sounds and styles of the men who played it; yet, giants though they were, it was Ellington's greatest triumph that the overall band effect was even greater than the considerable sum of its parts.

For at least ten years after his ascent to the jazz Olympus Ellington was unchallenged as a completely original force in jazz writing. For the most part, arranging during the 1930s continued to consist of the relatively innocuous art of ranging brass and reed sections against each other, or sometimes with each other in block voicing, and of using occasional variations such as a combination of clarinets and tenor saxes (much used by the enlarged Dixieland bands, heard in the arrangements of Deane Kincaide for Bob Crosby) or a trumpet voiced with saxophones (a device employed effectively in Mary Lou Williams' charts for the old Andy Kirk band).

Glenn Miller earned stature as an arranger for jazz groups of every size in the late 1920s and throughout the '30s. Though some of his later big band scores for the Dorsey Brothers and for his own band seemed stiff and unemotional in conception and execution, his contributions in the days of Ben Pollack and Red Nichols had a stamp of jazz authenticity that was lacking in most of the more pretentious offerings of Paul Whiteman, the self-styled "King of Jazz," or of Gene Gifford, arranger for the popular Casa Loma orchestra during its years of peak acceptance by the college students of the early 1930s. Gifford's scores, built on interminable repetitions, symmetrical and plain as a brick wall, had the subtlety, inspiration and shading of a West Point drill; yet much of this type of writing passed for jazz while the contributions of the arrangers who worked on a broader melodic and harmonic canvas went almost unobserved.

In the latter group were Benny Carter and Edgar Sampson, two saxophonists (Carter with his own band and Sampson with Chick Webb's) who, though both contributed to the library of the Benny Goodman band, remained virtually in obscurity throughout the swing pandemonium. Both were equipped to lend form and substance to a ballad, and to blend an attractive melody with a swing-conscious beat on faster instrumental numbers. Carter was most admired for his scoring for saxophone sections: a passage in his recording of his own composition *Lonesome Nights* in 1933, recorded again the following year by Benny Goodman under the title *Take My Word,* can be offered today as an undated and completely charming example of voicing for four saxophones. Sampson was more closely identified with up-tempo instrumentals, in which reeds and brass were employed in chant-and-response fashion along Henderson lines. *Stompin' at the Savoy* and *Don't Be That Way* illustrated his gift for investing melodically simple themes with a sweep and lift in which even the repetitions never became trite.

Certainly the arranger of that period whose impact was the firmest and longest of duration was Sy Oliver, key writer for the Lunceford band during its optimum years (1934-9) and later for Tommy Dorsey. Oliver's technique was a brittle, brusque one in which sharp-edge staccato brass passages would give away unexpectedly to an interval by low, mellow reeds, rhythm section pauses would punctuate the theme for humorous effects and the whole score would convey the sense of a tightly-knit unit, often building to a tense and compelling climax. The Oliver style, the determining factor in the Lunceford band's personality, was in sharp contrast with the loose, informal riffing that gave the Count Basie band its less precise but more relaxed brand of swing.

In the Basie band the arrangements were comparatively unimportant; in fact, most of the earliest successful Basie records were a conglomeration of "heads," routines created spontaneously, or worked out by the men without recourse to manuscript paper, forming a gradual and extemporaneous accretion of riffs and counter riffs, sometimes combined with scraps of previous performances of diverse and obscure origin. *One O'Clock Jump,* said to have sprung from an early blues by Buster Smith, was a case in point.

Eddie Sauter, who had studied at Juilliard and was better equipped academically than almost any other jazz arranger of the 1930s, also struck out into new territories, first with a series of arrangements for the Red Norvo band that made silk purses out of the ears of corn provided by Tin Pan Alley and then, more significantly, with such originals as *Superman* and *Benny Rides Again* for the Goodman orchestra in 1940, in which the 32-bar structure, the saxes-battling-brass and other traditions were subordinated to the search for ingenious new frameworks for the soloist and startling new tonal blends in the scores. Sauter reached his peak as a jazz writer at this time; later he became so deeply concerned with novelty of sound for its own effect (as with the Sauter-Finegan band, 1952-7) that the very qualities once so relevant to his value as a jazz writer became a detriment. Along with Bill Finegan, a capable writer who had worked for Glenn Miller and Tommy Dorsey, he declared himself disinterested in improvisation; soon, as might have been expected, both his own arrangements and Finegan's swung less and trained their sights on the popular-music market.

As the arranger sought a means of escape from the restrictions of the reeds-versus-brass concept, jazz writing began to acquire new tone colors, new instrumental combinations and a greatly expanded sense of form. Once again Ellington led the way, writing a series of miniature concertos, each built around a particular soloist in the band (a procedure strange to jazz in 1936, though now a daily occurrence) and making the first jazz explorations into extended forms (*Reminiscing in Tempo* in 1935 was spread over four 78 r.p.m. sides, in a precedent-setting circumvention of the phonograph record's restrictions before the advent of the LP).

Some of the best arrangements written during the final years of the swing craze were accomplished within the narrow, confining framework of one trumpet, alto sax, clarinet, piano, bass and drums. The arranger was Charlie Shavers and the John Kirby band his medium. Shavers' voicing of the three horns, the variety of tonal textures and orchestral ideas he was able to extract from this unit (in which his own trumpet, usually muted, was the principal voice) lent a new dimension to small-combo arranging.

With the close of the swing era came the advent of a new crop of arrangers, all of whom made new and important contributions without departing radically from established patterns. Billy Strayhorn, with the Ellington band from 1939, had absorbed the Ellington techniques with a sensitivity that transcended the merely photographic; to them he added, in some of his mood pieces *(Chelsea Bridge)* a harmonic flavor that recalled Ravel. As short in stature and broad in scope as Strayhorn, young Ralph Burns was to the Woody Herman band from 1944 what Billy was to the Duke. Around the same time, Dizzy Gillespie was translating the new language of bop into terms of both big band orchestration and simple unison quintet arrangement, while Neal Hefti, also writing for the Herman band, was among the first to bring bop's innovations downtown from Minton's.

As the war decade progressed, a new school of jazz writers emerged, and for the first time it became abundantly evident that the jazz arranger of the new generation would be a man of considerable training, with a reservoir of knowledge extending deep into the older and newer classical forms. Pete Rugolo, who had studied with Darius Milhaud, applied such a background to his scores for the Kenton band from 1945; two years later John Lewis, a former music student at the University of New Mexico, wrote *Toccata for Trumpet and Orchestra*, premiered by the Gillespie band at Carnegie Hall. Bill Russo, who had studied with Lennie Tristano and reinforced his knowledge with extensive research into music literature, began to apply his extra-jazz ideas to an experimental group in Chicago and joined the Kenton staff in

1950. The works of George Handy and Johnny Richards were performed by the adventurous Boyd Raeburn band of the mid-1940s as musicians began to detect evidence of a Stravinsky influence on jazz writing. Stravinsky himself was commissioned to write a work for the Herman band, but most critics both in jazz and concert music circles found the result (*Ebony Concerto*) a curiously dissatisfying hybrid.

Also during the war years there emerged another branch of modern jazz writing, that of the men who were important mainly as composers. The spare, moody lines of Thelonious Monk's compositions (*'Round Midnight* and *Ruby My Dear* are typical) were an X-ray view of the man's eccentric, probing mind. Of the more prototypical boppers Bud Powell, Charlie Parker and Dizzy Gillespie all created original "lines" (i.e., themes mainly horizontal in concept and most often played by horns in unison) that proved to be of lasting value; Gillespie, in addition, composed the exotic melody of *Night In Tunisia* and revealed himself, through his work for his own and other name bands, as an orchestrator of exceptional skill.

Lennie Tristano and his disciples were composers, too, of "lines" that followed contours identical with those of their improvisations. Tristano preferred, even more frequently than the bop musicians, to base his themes on the chord outline of a standard tune, though the departures were the product of a mind so fertile and original that the original point of embarkation became unimportant.

The policy of using old harmonic structures as a foundation for new melodic ideas became widespread among jazz composers of the late 1940s. Charlie Parker's *Ornithology* soon was as celebrated as its source, *How High the Moon*. Dizzy Gillespie's original treatment of the Tin Pan Alley warhorse *Whispering* started it on a new life as *Groovin' High*. There have been hundreds of such transformations. The practice seems likely to continue indefinitely, since there is no legal means of copyrighting a chord sequence and the latter is usually far less important musically than what the jazzmen build on it.

Since 1950 jazz composing and arranging has moved in two general directions. One is represented by the avant-gardists who have drawn heavily from European music and from twentieth-century classical forms and devices, including polytonality, atonality and the twelve-tone system. The second direction has grown from within the natural resources of jazz, with frequent reference (in wider voicings and with greater harmonic instrumental scope) to the basic swing-era writing of Fletcher Henderson, Jimmy Mundy and their contemporaries.

In reading the following observations the reader should bear in mind that most of today's jazz writers are not limited to either of these directions. Oliver Nelson, though identified chiefly with the big swinging band background he has written for Jimmy Smith and others, has written works for string quartet, contralto and piano; Jimmy Giuffre has been associated with almost every school of composition extant; Charles Mingus is well known for his gospel-blues-inspired combo work but has also recorded an ambitious third stream composition. In the comments below I have attempted to concentrate on that aspect of the writers' work with which they are primarily associated in the public ear.

Among the swing-derived arrangers, the youngest and most protean is Quincy Jones. Born in 1933, he has a background of big band experience, with Lionel Hampton's Orchestra, Dizzy Gillespie's, and his own band. Much of his orchestration reflects this background, though the reeds-vs.-brass concept of yesteryear was greatly modified by the skillful incorporation of one or two flutes into the texture, by a less sectionalized approach, and by a variety of influences that include swing, bop, the modern blues forces (Ray Charles) and the classical impressionists.

The Stan Kenton band of the mid-1950s featured the work of Bill Holman, Shorty Rogers and Gerry Mulligan. They were writers who hewed closely to the fundamental swing band spirit, while using intricate contrapuntal effects for additional spice.

The Count Basie band of the 1950s provided a showcase for a series of other gifted writers in a comparable idiom. They included Neal Hefti and Johnny Mandel, both of whom later went into the motion picture writing field; Manny Albam and Ernie Wilkins, still active in jazz; and more recently Quincy Jones' most distinguished alumnus and emulator, Billy Byers.

The most effective popularizer of the basic big band style of jazz writing is Henry Mancini. A highly successful writer for television in the late 1950s, originally through the *Peter Gunn* series, he moved on to even greater commercial success with a series of award-winning motion picture scores. Quincy Jones feels that Mancini's role has been of vast importance, since his writing opened up these fields for other big-band-trained, jazz-oriented writers to whom they were previously closed. Though geared to a mass audience, Mancini's writing retains a jazz flavor much of the time and has produced some thematically enduring material.

Turning to the more ambitious modern jazz writers, one finds a vast diversification among those who have brought classical influences to bear on jazz. Some have a background of formal conservatory training and may be comparatively new to the jazz environment; others may have reached the new ground with a long history of experience in jazz. All have attained a new hybrid of music sometimes referred to as "the third stream."

The term is a misnomer. In putting diamonds and rubies together on one bracelet, the jeweler does not create a third precious tone; the confluence of two musical streams does not create a third. A better definition is "classical jazz."

The many processes of amalgamation of jazz and classical music can be studied in a comprehensive two-record album on Columbia, *Outstanding Jazz Compositions of the 20th Century.* Two of the composers whose works are included, John Lewis and Gunther Schuller, were in effect co-founders of the third stream movement. In 1955 they organized the Jazz and Classical Music Society to bring together musicians in both fields. In a concert at Town Hall they achieved a new chamber music through the combination of the Modern Jazz Quarter with a harp and woodwinds. The following year they recorded three works for a small brass ensemble: J. J. Johnson's highly contrapuntal *Jazz Suite for Brass,* John Lewis' dynamically wide-ranged yet sometimes simple and blues-based *Three Little Feelings,* and Jimmy Giuffre's ceremoniously colorful *Pharaoh*. All three are included in the Columbia LP, along with ten other works, six of which (by Schuller, Giuffre, George Russell, Harold Shapero, Charles Mingus and Milton Babbitt) were commissioned by the 1957 Brandeis University Festival of the Arts. Compositions by Duke Ellington, Teo Macero, Teddy Charles and Bob Prince complete this indispensable LP.

Some of the works in this album are structurally and thematically indistinguishable from contemporary classical music and might better be classified as such; others, to varying degrees, include passages in tempo with bass and drums rhythmic pulse, and improvisation, sometimes in the traditional jazz manner, sometimes (as in Shapero's *On Green Mountain*, subtitled *Chaconne After Monteverdi*) based on classical thematic and harmonic material.

Schuller's work, *Transformation*, is a highly instructive illustration of the process of amalgamation. The opening section, as he points out, is "indistinguishable from any of my other non-jazz compositions; it makes free use of the passacaglia idea . . . ever so gradually, however, against this background, tiny embryonic fragments of jazz material are introduced. These fragments grow in size and frequency until they predominate and the music has transformed itself into jazz . . . Notice how beautifully Bill Evans manages the transition from my written background . . . to his own improvised solo. Most listeners will be unable to tell where one ends and the other begins. This, incidentally, is one of the central problems in jazz today: the integration of improvisation into increasingly complex compositional contexts."

Perhaps the most successful example of this integration was accomplished by Gil Evans in his series of orchestral works for Miles Davis. Such albums as *Miles Ahead, Porgy and Bess* and *Sketches of Spain* show in full fruition the value of a musical background as wide and eclectic as Evans'. Almost entirely self-taught, Evans has studied chiefly through listening and reading. Before writing *Sketches of Spain* in 1959 he read a number of volumes on Spanish music and the life of the Spanish gypsy, and borrowed a number of recordings and folk and primitive music. The results, based partly on the original material and partly on folk melodies, demonstrate as vividly as any album in modern jazz history the extent to which musicians identified with jazz have reached out beyond its prescribed borders to incorporate elements from other worlds of music. What Evans wrote, and what Davis played so lyrically within this kaleidoscopic framework, cannot be classified as jazz, classical music or folk music. It draws its strength from values that are essential to all music—form, tone color, melodic inspiration—as well as from those that are associated with jazz.

Since the impact of the Evans-Davis series in the late 1950s, the quantity and quality of jazz writers and writing has continued to advance at a remarkable pace. There have been two major attempts to fuse classical and jazz elements in orchestras organized for experimental concerts. The first was Orchestra U.S.A., formed in late 1962 by John Lewis, with considerable help during its first two seasons from Schuller and Gary McFarland, as conductor and assistant music director respectively. Orchestra U.S.A. set its sights high: the intention, it was stated, was to provide a forum for the performance of any type of composed or improvised Western music, including jazz and contemporary non-jazz works as well as music from the classical and baroque periods. It included a string section, which had difficulty in swinging when there were jazz requirements; its repertoire included many enlarged versions of works previously recorded by Lewis with the Modern Jazz Quartet and other groups. By 1965, though it had not quite achieved anything memorably unique, its value as a showcase had been proved beyond dispute.

Another group along slightly less ambitious lines was the Los Angeles Neophonic Orchestra, which made its debut in 1965 under the direction of Stan Kenton. The state of third-stream composition was easily determined by the four concerts given during the orchestra's initial season. The writers included the Viennese classical-and-jazz pianist Friedrich Gulda, playing his

Music For Piano and Band; movie-oriented quasi-pop writers such as Russ Garcia, Elmer Bernstein and Nelson Riddle; and a broad selection of jazz-directed composer-arrangers, among the most impressive of whom were George Shearing, Gerald Wilson, Clare Fischer, Bill Holman, Lalo Schifrin, Marty Paich, Julian Lee, Johnny Richards and Kenton himself.

Examining the work of the writers for these two orchestras, the listener is likely to draw one important conclusion: jazz writing today is aiming in an infinity of directions. It has broken out of its socially segregated shell, is no longer living a life apart, and as often as not its practice overlaps into other musical forms to such a degree that the use of such terms as "jazz arrangement" and "classical composition" may soon be obsolescent.

Very few of the most respected writers on this borderline have managed to retain a strong jazz essence in much of their writing. Perhaps the most skilled and successful in this respect is George Russell. His repertoire both for the various small groups he has led, and for larger ensembles, reflects the range of influences that have shaped him: Evans, Mulligan, Lewis as well as Berg, Bartok, Stravinsky and Wolpe. Russell's Lydian Concept of Tonal Organization, completed in 1953 after many years of work, is a theory far too complicated for most students to grasp without very extensive study, but its value can easily be judged in the astonishingly original *All About Rosie,* one of the Brandeis-commissioned works, and in parts of *New York, N.Y.,* a Decca album in which original Russell works are mixed with his highly personal views of three standard tunes.

A survey of today's jazz writing must include mention of those who, according to the definitions outlined on page 192, are composers but not arrangers. The most important writer on this level in recent years has been John Coltrane. Many of his works, such as *The Promise* and *Afro-Blue,* mirror a blend of Indian, African and miscellaneous exotic influences. Often they are harmonically simple and deliberately limited, using scalar and modal devices instead of a variety of chords. They may be less meaningful as compositions than as points of departure for improvisation, but their importance is unquestionable, since their popular acceptance in jazz circles has changed the course of small combo jazz. Paul Horn has written a number of admirable works along Coltrane-inspired lines, some of them with the added value of unusual metrical concepts.

Other small-group composers, who have written light, melodically charming works along the lines of earlier jazz schools (mainly bop), included Nat Adderley and Horace Silver. A combo writer of great importance has been Ornette Coleman, some of whose works are surprisingly simple in their Bird-like unison lines while others are fascinatingly complicated (see earlier comments on Coleman in the alto saxophone chapter).

Bossa nova has produced a long series of charming melodies by such writers as Antonio Carlos Jobim, Luiz Bonfa and Vinicius de Moraes. They are songs of a high caliber but do not have a place in a discussion of jazz composition.

In summing up the present state of jazz writing it is necessary to take into account the possibility, sometimes pointed out by opponents of evolution, that by fusing with music from other fields jazz may be losing its identity and reaching a dead end.

Asked whether he felt that this was a real danger, Teo Macero once said: "Jazz may be losing its identity, but it's gaining something too. I think when a person gets married, it's the same thing . . . another part of your personality develops. You're still an individual, but you evolve to a new kind of person."

On the other hand the late Don Redman, the first arranger to give meaning to the term "jazz orchestration" 45 years ago, said: "I don't think real jazz and classical music will ever mix. Real jazz will remain real jazz . . . and I don't think atonal music and jazz will ever mix, either."

Exercising our uncanny powers of hindsight, we can see that the Redman statement, made in 1957, was totally wrong. Though the simpler forms of jazz writing will survive, along with tonality and improvisation, they will have to find a modus vivendi along with the wave of the future. By now it is a vast and huge tidal wave represented by the ambitious, complex, extended works of the brilliant new writers discussed above, as well as by many others who have dipped their toes at one time or another into the third stream (Dave Brubeck, Leonard Beinstein, Don Ellis). Along with jazz literacy, the level of jazz writing has made more progress since 1955 than in the previous half-century. Inevitably, more and more jazzmen will also be classical musicians and vice versa; musicians will find themselves on common ground and jazz will at last have integrated itself completely into twentieth-century musical society.

CHAPTER 22

THE ANATOMY OF IMPROVISATION

The actual documentation of jazz, in historiographic treatments of the subject, has been sketchy and in many cases based on false premises. In order to set down jazz on paper and submit it to the microscope, the critic first must be sure that every nuance of the musician's phrasing has been correctly captured, for these are the subtleties without which some jazz, on paper, might be indistinguishable from "pop music" (the songs and lush orchestras rooted in the mythical Philistine wasteland of Tin Pan Alley). Second, he must be equipped with a natural feeling for the texture of jazz improvisation and an understanding of its harmonic substructure.

Academically equipped classical musicians examining jazz have tended at times to adopt the benign attitude of a deity inspecting the human animal from a haven in Olympus. To many of them, the following example (Ex. 1) would be meaningless.

EXAMPLE 1

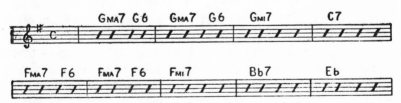

To any jazz musician the above is instantaneously recognizable. Though it does not show a single note of music and consists simply of chord symbols and diagonal strokes (each standing for

209

one beat of the bar), no literate jazzman would fail to see in it, at first glance, the first nine measures of *How High the Moon*. (By the same token it is the chord pattern for Charlie Parker's *Ornithology* and for other tunes of identical harmonic nature, though it was *How High the Moon* that created the pattern and inspired the other works.)

How, the reader may ask, can this identification be made when not one note of the tune is included? The answer is that to the jazz musician *How High the Moon* is not simply the melody in whole, half and quarter notes that can be found on the sheet music, but a harmonic ski-trail along which ten thousand musicians have traveled. The improvisational bases of jazz are not melodies, but chord structures. Thus the uninitiated listener who complains "Where's the melody?" must be instructed in following the *new* melody created by the jazzman, based not on the missing melody the listener is seeking, but on a harmonic routine identical with that of the unplayed tune.

A similar misconception, prevalent among musicians academically equipped to know better, is that jazz has its own scale. The manner in which the flatted third and flatted seventh are used in jazz (Ex. 2) certainly gives them a special status, but the

EXAMPLE 2

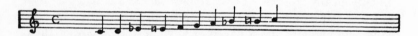

scales used in all tonal jazz are the normal major and minor diatonic scales.

The non-jazz musician, who tends to think of the flatted third and seventh as if they were part of a "jazz scale," overlooks certain basic values. The diatonic scale is, after all, merely part of the chromatic scale, bearing to it the same relationship as that of the vowels to the alphabet. *All* the notes in the diatonic and chromatic scale are fully used in jazz, as in most European music; the status of the flatted third and seventh might be compared with that of the letters W and Y, which in cer'ain areas and contexts may be considered vowel members of the alphabet.

Nor is it mandatory, as has been implied in some diagnoses of jazz, to employ quarter tones. If it were, jazz would be unplayable on the piano. The slurring of notes and the occasional existence of a borderline area between the third and flatted third do not necessarily connote the use of a quarter tone any more than a glissando emphasizes the existence of the infinite number of gradations through which it passes. Jazz, or at least jazz today, says what it means. If the jazzman hits an E Flat while improvising in the key of C, and if the rhythm section is playing an F 9th chord, there will be no social, racial or mystical implications in his playing the note halfway between E Flat and E; he will merely sound a quarter-tone sharp and the note he plays will not be consonant with the chord at hand. Quarter tone effects admittedly can be and are used in jazz, but not in the sense that they imply any uncertainty on the part of the performer as to whether, for example, the flatted seventh or the major seventh is the chord involved.

Jazz, of course, incorporates the three essential elements of all music—melody, harmony and rhythm. Three additional elements are essential to authenticity in Jazz: syncopation, improvisation and (or) composition in the spirit of improvisation.° The chords

EXAMPLE 3

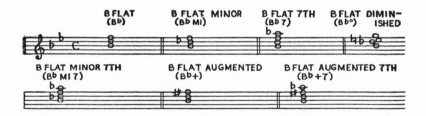

shown in Ex. 3, all arbitrarily placed in the key of B Flat, are the most important basic harmonic guideposts to improvisation. These chords are shown here only in their simplest forms, and

° In an analysis in *The New Encyclopedia of Jazz* (the chapter entitled *The Anatomy of Jazz*, p. 60), there are detailed references to these factors.

always in root position. Ex. 3a is a sample of the manner in which
the plain B Flat chord can be enriched by the addition of the
sixth (G), major seventh (A) and ninth (C); Ex. 3b shows how

EXAMPLE 3A & 3B

the B Flat 7th chord can be made fuller and more interesting by
the use of the flatted fifth (E Natural), ninth (C) and thirteenth
(G). All the other chords are subject to similar mutations.

Jazz improvisation is based on notes that sound appropriate to
the background of chords such as those in Ex. 3. Extensions and
inversions of these chords do not basically affect the nature of
the improvised solo, since their addition is voluntary and does
not change the fundamental quality of the chord. The soloist, in
addition to playing notes that fit into these chords and their extensions, plays passing notes that link the solo line together to
give the performance horizontal continuity. (The adjective "horizontal" or "linear" is applied to the flow of single notes in the
solos, which if documented would be read horizontally across the
manuscript; "vertical," the term used in discussing written music
as it is examined in an analysis of all the notes played by the
instruments at a given point, is so employed because they may
be read from top to bottom at a certain place on the score sheet
of the orchestration.)

For many years it was tacitly assumed that a binary time (any
pulse in two beats or multiples of two) signature was indigenous
and essential to all improvised jazz. Virtually all the music was
in common (4/4) time; the only variations were in the multiples
and divisions of four (Dixieland often had two main accents to
the bar, boogie-woogie generally had eight). Until the 1950s it
was impossible to persuade the jazz critics, and even most mu-

sicians, that the phrase "jazz waltz" was anything but a ridiculous contradiction in terms.

The fact is that waltz time, in order to be compatible with a jazz interpretation, required only a group of musicians equipped (as they all are) with a feeling for the 4/4 beat, plus a theme that lends itself to syncopation, and a performance with the same rhythmic and dynamic nuances heard in 4/4 solos and arrangements.

My own experience in trying to prove this point was a long drawn out and frustrating example of the problems faced by any would-be innovator in jazz. In 1936 and 1938 I produced two 3/4 blues records, respectively by Benny Carter and an all-star group of my own. Both were faintly praised or dismissed as incongruous novelties. In 1946 I tried again, recording Mary Lou Williams' *Waltz Boogie* for RCA. A couple of years later I composed *Bebop Waltz* (later released as *Waltzin' the Blues*), the first modern jazz theme of its kind. Skeptical at first, the musicians on the session (Eddie Shu, Joe Roland, Barbara Carroll, John Levy and Denzil Best) soon adjusted themselves to the "strange" meter.

The early 1950s brought a few isolated attempts to write original jazz works in 3/4 time, but by 1956 there were still barely a dozen, most notably Duke Ellington's *Lady Mac* from his *Such Sweet Thunder* suite. The following year Max Roach's album *Jazz in 3/4 Time* was released; soon the dam broke.

The history of 5/4 time involved similar obstacles. In 1955 I wrote *Blues in 5/4*, and the next year recorded it under the title *Bass Reflex* as part of my *Hi Fi Suite*. The soloists (Oscar Pettiford, Dick Hyman, Thad Jones and Frank Wess) each took 12 measures ad lib, though the job seemed horrendously difficult at the time.

The 5/4 beat remained dormant, except for a couple of experiments by Max Roach, until the release in 1960 of Dave Brubeck's *Time Out* album. This included Paul Desmond's tune *Take Five*, described in a *Down Beat* review as "like Chinese water torture . . . if this is what we have to endure with experiments in time, take me back to good old 4/4." But with the passage of a couple of years, almost all jazz musicians as well as the general public (and even critics) had accepted as commonplace the use of 3/4, 5/4 and such other meters as 9/8 and 12/8 once considered out of bounds. Today there are no meter restrictions in the performance of jazz.

The technical qualities of jazz improvisation are subject to modification effected by nuances of phrasing and dynamics. In these shadings, as much as in the adherence to the harmonic requirements, lies the potential difference between a genuine jazz solo and one that the jazzman classifies as corny; between the workmanlike performance and the *chef d'oeuvre;* between the cold granite of mathematical extemporization and the fulfilling warmth of improvisatory genius.

There are three kinds of melodic improvisation. In the first and simplest, the original written melody is respected completely; the only change lies in the lengthening or shortening of some notes, repetition of others, use of tonal variations and dynamics to bring out its values in conformity with the personality of the interpreter. In the second, the melody remains completely recognizable but its phrases are subject to slight additions and changes; here and there a note is added or subtracted and perhaps a whole phrase is transmuted, but to the layman listener the original melody remains perceptible throughout either in the actual statement or by indirection. In the third type of improvisation the soloist departs entirely from the melody; in fact, rather than using it as a point of departure, he uses instead the chord pattern of the tune. To the trained ear of the jazz musician it will still be apparent on what basis he is improvising.

This third category, which may be called full improvisation, is in turn composed of three subdivisions. There are the notes that are decided upon completely impromptu; the notes that are predetermined to the degree that they follow a natural sequence (possibly as part of an arpeggio, chromatic sequence or scalar run), and third, the notes that are played automatically, without real cerebration, because they happen to lie under the fingers and perhaps because they are part of a previously used sequence at the back of the performer's mind. Often a sequence of these notes may constitute a musical cliché; often, too, they will be a direct quotation from some other and completely irrelevant work. The cliché is not an evil per se, provided it is used occasionally, and with discretion and humor. Louis Armstrong plays countless phrases that have become clichés in his own work and in that of his imitators; Dizzy Gillespie can be recognized frequently by his use of phrases he has been playing for a decade. It has long been the belief of Duke Ellington that there is no such thing as complete improvisation, that a certain degree of predetermination governs the hands and mind of every musician. This theory is at least partly in accord with the analytic concept of the various types of improvisation as outlined above.

Another factor that controls the notes selected by the improvising jazzman is, of course, his personality and the environment and background from which it evolved. No two musicians will react alike to any given set of chords, any prearranged melodic pattern or even any group of words to be set to music. To illustrate this point, in what might be called a "Rorschach in rhythm" test, I presented three jazzmen, each of a different era, with a sample line of lyrics and asked them to interpret it spontaneously in music. The line used as the basis for this test was:

You told me that you loved me but you told me a lie

Louis Armstrong's reaction was simple and logical:

EXAMPLE 4

You told me that you   loved me but you   told me a   lie

Armstrong based the entire phrase on the major triad, the only chord implied being the tonic.

Roy Eldridge produced this interpretation:

EXAMPLE 5

You told me that you loved me   but   you told me a   lie

Curiously, Eldridge placed the accent on *you* in the second part of the phrase, instead of using *but you* as a pick-up. His main melodic thought did not differ from Armstrong's in any significant respect, but the final G Sharp clearly implied a change from the tonic chord to a C augmented 7th, leaving the way clear for a logical continuation.

John Gillespie, confronted with the same line, commented: "That sounds like the blues to me!" and played:

EXAMPLE 6

You   told me that you   loved me but you   told me a lie

Here the melody, though simple, was piquant in its use of grace notes; and instead of staying within the confines of the major triad, as had Armstrong and (but for the last note) Eldridge, he used the sixth (D) at two points and the second (G) at another.

Jazz improvisation most often constitutes a reaction to certain chord sequences (and sometimes to melodies based on those sequences) just as the above samples are a melodically free reaction to the rhythmic pattern suggested by a line of lyrics. In order more fully to illustrate the extemporaneous musical emotions that have always been the core of most jazz, I have selected examples of the work of those musicians whose instruments are among the commonest jazz solo vehicles (trumpet, trombone, clarinet, alto and tenor saxes, piano, guitar) and whose styles have been among the most influential.

To commence a survey of this nature without initial recourse to Louis Armstrong would be comparable with the omission of Bach from a primer of classical composition. The example chosen dates back to the year of his creative zenith, 1928, and to the phase marked by his partnership with Earl Hines, whose piano is a vital part of the overwhelmingly effective interaction that made *Muggles* one of the definitive jazz records of its period.

The context of this solo is important; it follows two choruses of uninspired solo work by a trombonist and clarinetist, both playing in slow tempo with a lumpy, thudding four-to-the-bar rhythm background that could as well have been created by a robot. Armstrong, unheard up to this point, steps into this dim scene and illuminates it instantaneously with a four-measure unaccom-

LOUIS ARMSTRONG / *Muggles*

panied solo in which he doubles the tempo. From Measures 5
through 20 the blues is played in "long-meter," i.e., as if it were
based on a 24- instead of a 12-measure pattern. When the slow
tempo is resumed for the last third of the chorus, the sluggish-
ness has disappeared; for the final chorus (Measures 25-36) Hines

ROY ELDRIDGE / *Trumpet Blues*

and Louis inspire not only each other but even provide artificial respiration for the drowning rhythm section.

Armstrong's opening break is a masterpiece in itself, climbing determinedly a tenth from its middle C opening, but spacing and syncopating the notes, melodically and rhythmically, so that no mere diatonic or chromatic rise is even hinted at. Having established this upbeat mood, he maintains an extraordinary tension through a constant reiteration of the tonic, almost without relief, for the next twelve measures, heightening the sense of drama by raising it an octave unexpectedly toward the end (14 and 16). Even in the rest of this chorus, and indeed throughout the whole solo, Louis remains on firm, basic harmonic ground, never straying from the blues' elementary 1-4-5 pattern, leaning heavily on "blue notes" (first beat of every measure from 25 through 30; fourth beat of 31, third of 32, second of 33, first of 34 and 35) and also (especially toward the end) on the sixth.

The endless variety of his dynamic approach and articulation is also easily observed in this solo. Many notes are tongued sharply; others, as the first note in 7, are played with a fast vibrato. Some, like the anguished blue notes that launch the closing chorus (25, 26, 27) are bent in pitch while the fingering remains unchanged; others form part of a slow, heartfelt glissando, of which the one at Measure 29 is perhaps the most moving. The last note in 29 is fluffed, though the mood has by now been so exquisitely established that it is no more jarring than a small pebble to a limousine. Lee Castle, who transcribed this solo, substituted an A for the fluffed note, though it suggests a C to this listener. An emotional high point is reached when, by happy coincidence, Armstrong comes out of the G in Measure 31 with three notes that happen to have exactly the same time values as three notes played by Earl Hines—an E Flat, C and D corresponding with Hines' A, G and A. This is one of those polyphonic miracles on which collective improvisation so often depends.

The next example shows a Roy Eldridge improvisation, at fast tempo, on the regular 12-measure blues pattern. It is heard about one minute and 55 seconds from the start of *Trumpet Blues,* immediately after 36 measures by Gillespie. Eldridge spars gingerly for the first two measures, playing the chromatic triplets (fourth through fifth) that became a jazz cliché in the swing era and were constantly used by Fats Waller and Basie. Swinging up to the flatted seventh to establish that this is, after all, a blues, he

JOHN (DIZZY) GILLESPIE / *Jessica's Day*

uses a naturally rhythmic pattern (quarter, triplet eighths and four eighths) to swoop down to the C, which also represents a phase of jazz harmonic thinking rarely encountered before the 1930s, since it is a thirteenth built on the 7th of the subdominant. Armstrong would rarely have used a thirteenth except in proceeding from the dominant (F 7) to the tonic (B Flat).

After a three-beat pause, Eldridge builds the tension again with a rising phrase, then descends with a group of syncopated notes (the C followed by two B Flats), returns to the quarter-triplet-and-eighths pattern in Measure 8, and throughout Measures 9, 10 and 11 maintains a continuous pattern of eighth notes but avoids the impression of playing a scale by hitting the E Natural instead of moving directly to the F in Measure 10, and similarly avoids the monotony of repeating the unadorned E Flat 7th sequence of notes by using the thirteenth again (C). It is interesting to observe that while Eldridge plays notes that may seem to imply an E Flat 7th pattern through bars 10 and 11, Oscar Peterson's piano accompaniment furnishes an F 7th and a B Flat. At this rapid tempo any series of fast-moving eighth notes is protected from conflict with the underlying chords; the overall horizontal patterns must conform with that of the blues, but the arbitrary passing chords of the rhythm section move too quickly to call for complete conformity.

The extraordinarily fast-changing mood pattern of which John Gillespie's imagination and technique render him capable can be discerned in the sixteen measures reproduced from *Jessica's Day*, heard in the second chorus immediately after the theme and interlude, one minute and 35 seconds from the start.

Gillespie establishes a "funky" mood by repeating the tonic and subjecting it to tonal variations through the use of the half-depressed valve effect and grace notes. After thus establishing tension during the two measure break, he offers simplicity and relaxation in Measures 3 and 4 of the chorus (though even simplicity, for him, includes what is virtually a pair of grace notes, the C and B Flat preceding the G). Then, in effect, Gillespie says "All right, you've heard what this is—it's one of those tunes with the conventional B Flat, G, C, F base, a *We Want Cantor* affair—so now we'll try to make something of it." Then comes the flurry of sixteenth notes, but given rhythm balance through the use of syncopation (third beat of Measure 5) and a triplet on the first beat of Measure 6. This serves as a warm-up for an even busier upward sweep in which the tension mounts; notice that the rise is diatonic, except that the flatted seventh (A Flat) and flatted third (C Sharp) are used. After this surge, a three beat pause for breath and thought (Measures 9-10) leads to another concept in which a buoyant mood is established, this time not by the multi-note fury of the preceding phrases but through a concept built symmetrically around a simple thought based on the three quarter notes at Measure 11, repeated at Measure 13 in the same descending pattern but with a different formation and an octave lower. Measure 15 is a superb example of the obliqueness of Gillespie's approach to a chord. The root of the F Minor 7th is preceded by notes on either side of it (E Natural and G); the ac-

JAY JAY JOHNSON / *Indiana Winter*

cent of the third beat corresponds with the dissonant E Natural and E Flat against the B Flat 7th chord before the consonant D is reached; and on the fourth beat the B Natural and A Natural are neighboring notes on either side of the B Flat that opens the next measure. The naturally swinging 16th measure (dotted quarter, eighth, two sets of triplets) leads smoothly into a series of sarcastic comments on the return to harmonic home base: Fs fingered naturally, producing the normal tone, alternate with E Naturals fingered at half-valve, with the squeezed sound, before Gillespie concedes to the inevitable and returns to the tonic.

One of the earliest and most constant criticisms leveled against bop at the time of its initial impact was the complaint that it was too complex, was characterized mainly by a flurry of notes displayed simply for the sake of technical exhibitionism. No more eloquent refutation could be found than in the sample solo by Jay Jay Johnson. This is an excerpt from *Indiana Winter,* a variation in fast tempo (62 bars per minute) on the same chord sequence as *How High the Moon.* Here one is reminded that creative improvisation is composed not merely of the notes played, the tone in which they are expressed and their relationship to the chord pattern, but also to such relevant factors as their relative dynamic values, intervallic relationship, and their exact duration (it might be said that to all intents and purposes no two quarter notes are ever exactly the same length; the path from staccato to legato is broad and flexible). Johnson's solo is brusquely emphatic, resorting frequently to the notes played directly on the beat and syncopating as a rule only toward the end of each phrase. There is a legato swing, a dynamic ebb and flow to his phrases—the notes in Measures 3-4 furnish a perfect illustration. The E Flat and D Flat in Measure 4 suggest a G Flat 13th passing chord.

The entire motive of Measures 5-12 is that of following the harmonic curves of the theme with a minimum of melodic suggestion. A three-note phrase, changed slightly in its melody each time to conform with the rhythm section's chords, is altered also in its rhythmic use (the syncopation is omitted in Measure 7, and there seems to be a slight fluff in Measure 9, which leaves in doubt the question of whether or not there would have been a syncopation here). At several junctures there is a sense of missing eighth notes, or of eighths barely suggested (in Measure 14 one may hear mentally, in place of the eighth note rest, a B that is not actually stated, and at the last eighth there is another B that is scarcely heard).

It is part of the essence of jazz improvisation that a solo sometimes may be almost as much a reflection of the instrument's nature as of the soloist's; this chorus by Johnson is a case in point. One can imagine it played by Gillespie, possibly by Parker, but in the quality and phrasing of the notes it is as purely a trombone solo as *Jessica's Day* is the creation of a trumpet player.

Just as Johnson's solo contradicts the allegations of excessive complexity in modern jazz, trombonist Jack Teagarden's example offers a fiery answer to modernists' accusations that exponents of the more traditional jazz styles are technically limited. The example from *Blue Funk* shows Teagarden's opening chorus in an 18-bar theme (16 plus a two-bar tag) built mainly around a descending chromatic stairway of ninths. Taken at a very slow tempo (24 measures per minute), it enables him to give full play to his technical mastery of the instrument and to the passionate warmth and exciting sense of continuity of which he has always been pre-eminently capable.

Here again there are some intangibles, nuances of tone and shading that are not easily documented. The same notes played by Jay Jay Johnson certainly would lack the burry intensity of the Teagarden sound, just as Johnson's notes if played by Teagarden would be cold, flat and meaningless. Teagarden is a master of the portamento; there are several striking examples in this solo (note particularly the gradual, almost imperceptible descent to the E Natural in Measure 14, dramatically followed by a jump of a tenth).

Curiously, a predominant feature of this solo is the effect it gives of "double time," a gambit normally associated with bop; frequent use is made of 16th notes, though never continually in the uninterrupted fashion found among bop soloists. Triplets, grace notes, appoggiaturas and occasional long notes and simple phrases (as in Measures 13, 15, 17) insure the retention of the earthy blues mood. Not for a moment does the listener have the

JACK TEAGARDEN / *Blue Funk*

impression that technical virtuosity has become the servant of exhibitionism.

A curious detail is the D on the third beat of Measure 1, in conflict with the rhythm section's G Flat 9th. Why does this sound consonant? Is it because, played staccato, it is too brief for the contrast to be conspicuous? Is it because the D could be interpreted as part of a G Flat Augmented 7th? Or is it simply that the G 9th feeling has hung over momentarily into the third beat?

The same problem presents itself in Measure 5, when Teagarden plays notes that suggest he is still thinking in terms of a G 9th. This is one of those instances when the ear reacts in terms of an overall harmonic pattern, of the long sweeping phrase with which the soloist leads the way from its opening chord (G 9th) to its last (E 9th) with such authority and conviction that the degree of adherence to the intermediate stepping stones becomes unimportant.

Just as Teagarden's style and instrument combine to optimum impact in a slow blues mood, the personality and instrumental vehicle of Benny Goodman lend themselves most effectively to an up tempo, in which his fluency reaches an exciting peak of improvisatory expression. The clarinet, though every artist from Barney Bigard to Jimmy Giuffre has found it ideal as a blues medium in the middle and lower registers, is an instrument that brings out more fully in its upper reaches and at faster tempi the advantages of which the technical perfectionist can avail himself.

Slipped Disc, recorded by the Goodman Sextet, in 1945, emphasizes the genius of Goodman in a perfect blend of theme, tempo, accompanying personnel and mood. Taken at 60 measures per minute, it is based on a time-tested chord sequence known since the days of *King Porter Stomp.* The excerpt shown occurs immediately after Teddy Wilson's piano solo. In the first four measures Goodman plays the same phrases twice, but with just enough variation (in the pair of opening notes) to create an effect of symmetry without redundancy. Measures 4 through 7 again show the value of repetition, this time finding variety through rhythmic instead of melodic changes—on the first statement it is the opening note (D) that is held longest, on the second statement the entire phrase is played in two beats (Measure 6, beats 2 and 3) while on the third statement the C Sharp is held unexpectedly.

Measures 8-12 form one long and incredibly ingenious phrase, dipping suddenly at the start into the nether reaches of the chalumeau (lower) register and coursing upward to the D, almost three octaves higher, in Measure 10, then continuing in eighth notes until the long sequence is broken fittingly by a syncopated phrase in 12.

BENNY GOODMAN / *Slipped Disc*

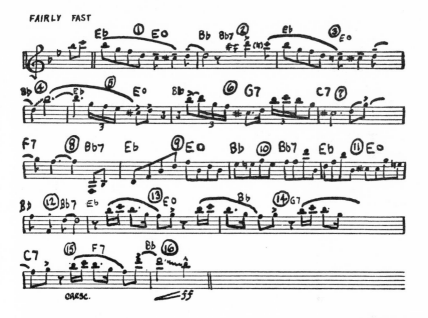

The final four measures, again using the device of repetition with rhythmic revision, give an effect of tremendous tension that is further heightened by the leap out of this phrase into the high D and then to the B Flat in Measure 16 that actually forms a link to the first phrase of the next sixteen measures.

Though speed and technique clearly are not musical virtues in themselves, part of the enjoyment of a performance such as this is derived from the facile flow of ideas at a challenging pace; the same solo at half the tempo would lose most of its meaning. This holds true of many of Goodman's most moving solos.

The peerless control that made Goodman unique has seldom been challenged in jazz. One of the few clarinetists to offer a comparable mastery of the instrument, adapted in his case to the bop idiom, is Buddy De Franco. In the example chosen, *Monogram,* De Franco exemplifies mental and muscular control brought to bear on an ad lib blues at fast tempo. This is his third ad lib chorus (following the two theme chorus), starting exactly one minute from the opening of the number.

BUDDY DE FRANCO / *Monogram*

A study of the first four measures demonstrates his consummate sense of swing and symmetry, of construction and phrasing, at a tempo that would call for considerable technical mastery merely for an unbroken improvised sequence of evenly-played eighth notes. After displaying syncopation (into Measure 1), grace notes (in 1), a perfectly timed and placed triplet in which the notes are played parenthetically (notice how on the record they almost have the effect of grace notes leading into C and A), the passage ends with a "bebop" (an eighth, on the beat, followed by a syncopated quarter note—the A and D). Next (Measure 5) comes a long sequence of eighths starting shrilly on an excited triplet the first note of which, unexpectedly, is A, the thirteenth added to the C 7th chord. To compensate for the chromatic descent that follows, the next two measures (7-8) offer rhythmic and melodic change of pace as well as the harmonic subtlety of an implied B Minor 7th and E 7th. Another "bebop" ends the phrase (Measure 9, beat 2). After a generally heated and fast-moving chorus De Franco ends with the contrasting simplicity of the unsyncopated notes of Measure 11 and a pause of several beats before he sails into another dazzling sequence.

An even.more startling visualization of the inroads of bop, and a striking contrast between solo styles of two different eras on the same instrument, can be observed in the alto saxophone examples.

In Charlie Parker syncopation (rhythmic obliqueness) and implied passing chords (harmonic obliqueness) are rife. The sample is the third ad lib chorus after the opening theme on *Bloomdido,* 58 seconds from the start of the track. The G pick-up notes leading into Measure 1 are split almost imperceptibly into two sixteenths and an eighth, creating a sputtering effect that was a specialty with Parker, a sort of epileptic grace note technique. The next phrase might have been expressed by Hodges simply as six eighth notes (C Sharp, C, A Sharp, G, A, G), though it is unlikely in the first place that Hodges would have started a chorus of blues in G with an initial accent on C Sharp. Measures 2 through 7 are one continuous thought in which resourceful originality abound; in Measure 4 alone, which fundamentally is a G 7th portion of the blues, he runs a G Augmented arpeggio for the first two beats, then on the third beat raises the implied chord half a tone (a frequently employed bop tactic) before planting his mind and fingers in the G 7th groove with the F Natural and D. All this takes place in a single second, for this is an up tempo blues at about 58 bars per minute. This amazingly swift train of harmonic thought is never expressed at the expense of rhythmic pulsation; the entire six-measure passage swings exhilaratingly, with triplets used at expedient moments to insure variety in what is mainly an eighth-note approach, and with certain notes lightly touched (the lower E in Measure 3) and others accented at totally unpredictable points.

The element of surprise never failed to enrich a Parker solo. In Measure 10, basically a D 7th passage, only the two notes on the final beat (F sharp and A) are drawn from that chord; the previous five are from the related A Minor 7th, and the G Sharp on the first beat is Parker's way of saying: "Wait; I'll get to that G Natural in a moment; this is to show you I'm on my way down." In other blues choruses at this point he has carried the idea further. by running a B Flat Minor 7th chord before making the chromatic step down to the A Minor 7th.

The most casual glance at the Johnny Hodges solo reveals immediately a musical mentality utterly opposed to Parker's. Hodges' unique alto saxophone personality illustrates the success that can be achieved through individuality of tone and smoothness of phrasing rather than for any startling rhythmic or harmonic originality. In *Confab with Rab* (the second chorus, immediately following the opening theme) he improvises on the age-old *I Got Rhythm* chord changes, used on dozens of his combo records. What emerges is a pattern of eighth note passages, separated by long pauses. He is given to syncopated accents, most often on the fourth eighth note of the measure (as in 2, 4, 9, 12, 13 and presumably in 16, though the articulation is imperfect). There is a curious uncertainty of intonation about the E Flat at the end of Measure 4 that may indicate to some an attempt to find the quarter tone between E Flat and E Natural; more probably it was intended and fingered as an E Flat. The octave jump in Measure 9 is the only dramatically unexpected effect in the entire sixteen measures, which otherwise are uneventfully but impressively characteristic of the strikingly effective use to which Hodges puts his tonal and articulative gifts.

In Hodges' solo, as in most of the other music in this chapter, the eighth notes are played evenly in terms of time, though with varying degrees of accentuation. There is no feeling of dotted eighths and sixteenths. In earlier jazz forms a great deal of music was written in dotted eighths and sixteenths though actually played in something a little closer to even eighths, or in a compromise ternary rhythm that would be more correctly notated by a triplet composed of a quarter and an eighth. It should be noted that if the many dotted eighths and sixteenths in jazz

JOHNNY HODGES / *Confab with Rab*

CHARLIE PARKER / *Bloomdido*

COLEMAN HAWKINS / *Platinum Love*

arrangements were played as written, i.e., with the first note three times as long as the second, the result would sound absurdly corny and could not possibly swing. The dotted-eighths-and-sixteenths notation system presumably was instituted because it it easier to read than the ternary division of the notes.

Hodges' style has undergone little or no fundamental change since he joined Ellington thirty years ago. Some of his contemporaries have shown a stronger tendency through the years to absorb new ideas and incorporate them into their work. In Coleman Hawkins today, for example, we hear a different personality from the volatile youngster who in the 1920s peppered his phrases with staccato notes, with long trains of dotted eighths and sixteenths, with "slap-tongue" effects on the reed. The veteran tenor saxophonist now offers a style that has mellowed in tone and acquired a far higher degree of rhythmic and harmonic finesse. *Platinum Love,* recorded in 1949, reflects the changes wrought in Hawkins during the past ten or fifteen years. A slow, melodic theme of his own, this is played at 26 measures per minute. Linking the styles of two eras, Hawkins combines traditional and modern tendencies. The rococo jazz roots can be heard in the warm tone and vibrato of the half notes held in Measures 2, 5, 7, 13, 16, in the swing-era style of the triplets in 9, the occasional retention of the dotted-eighth-and-sixteenth technique as in 11. The modern elements appear in Measure 2 (the flatted fifth used against the C Sharp 7th), in 8 (the F chord implied before the E 7th), and in 14 and 15 (the double-times sixteenth notes).

Paradoxically, though his work has undergone more modification in the direction of contemporary usages, Hawkins' style today is less appreciated and less imitated than that of Lester Young, who rose to prominence much later but whose musical character lost more than it gained in the postwar jazz cycle. The Young solo shown is a chorus from *The Opener,* a medium-fast blues (on the original Jazz at the Philharmonic concert disc it followed a trombone solo by Tommy Turk; there was one intervening 12-measure chorus of which applause covered the first four and Lester played the remaining eight measures). Lester's laconic statements find much of their impetus in the exact quality of each note—in the slight wavering of the G, the staccato D, the slight slur into the E Flat—and in the sense of carefully built tension: notice how Measures 3-4 become an extension-repetition of 1-2, leading up to the "blue seventh" (B Flat), which like the corresponding G in the original statement of the phrase is played with a suggestion of vibrato. Measure 7 is a typical Young construction—the one-beat pause erupting into a rising triplet and subsiding into a long-held note (in this instance a major seventh, an interval not conventionally found at this stage of the blues progressions before Young's time). The major seventh feeling is carried into the eighth bar, but the use of a B Flat suggests either the flatted ninth of an A 7th or the fifth of a minor seventh progression in which the patterns for Measures 8-9 would be E Mi 7, E Flat Mi 7, D Mi 7—a downward chromatic sequence

much favored by the boppers and their precursors. (It also fits a
G Diminished, which the pianist, Hank Jones, happens to hit at
that point.) The next phrase is a long one occupying the rest of
the chorus, starting with a full beat anticipation on the A and
winding gracefully into a tailspin that ends abruptly on dominant, syncopated tonic, dominant. The power of understatement
is implicit in this Young improvisàtion as it so often has been in
the solo work of his former employer, Count Basie.

By far the most difficult task in jazz documentation is the transcribing of piano solos. Even when, as in two of the three instances selected, there was no rhythm section to obscure the left
hand lines, the exact notation of the bass clef part has to be at
least partly conjectural; no less elusive, at times, are the exact
constructions of chords in the right hand. In undertaking the
hazardous job of reproducing the solos by Tatum, Wilson and
Powell, Frank Metis, the transcriber, has occasionally adhered
to the spirit rather than the letter, though in each case an examination of the manuscript along with a study of the record itself
will bring into sharp focus the ratiocination that motivates the
three styles.

The Tatum passage consists of the four-bar introduction and
the opening 12-measure chorus of the moderately slow and infi-
nitely relaxed *Blues in B Flat*. What strikes the piano student in
particular, and the jazz fan in general, is the large proportion of
the notes played by Tatum that are virtually, if not technically,
grace notes. The triplets in the third beat of Measure 1 and the
second beat of Measure 2 serve this purpose; in Measure 9 one
might consider that the only essential notes are the F Flat,
E Flat, D Flat and B Flat in the second and third beats, while
everything else is ornamentation. The difference between Tatum
playing the blues and an earth-bound jazz pianist undertaking
the same assignment is the difference between poetry and prose.
But not all of Tatum's poetic finesse is confined to the gentle
rhythmic impact of the grace notes; the harmonic approach, too,
is oblique and unpredictable, as in Measure 3 when the first right
hand chords are struck against a G Flat 9th bass, moving no less
unexpectedly to an augmented chord in Measure 4 rather than
the F 9th that might have been anticipated. Tatum's feeling for

LESTER YOUNG / *The Opener*

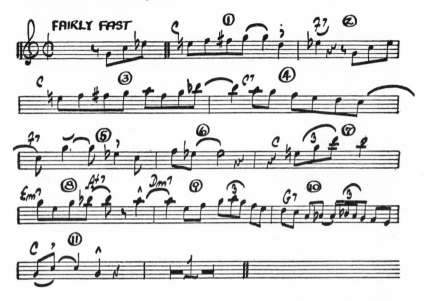

the blues involves the use, always in exquisite taste, of octave tremolos (as in 5 and 9), of adherence to the basic chords of the blues despite the added subtleties of such passing chords as the chromatic descent in Measures 12 and 13; and the incredibly swift use of straight arpeggios—notice that in Measure 11, after playing 22 notes in less than two seconds, he promptly gets back on the rhythmic rails to contrast this technical flourish with a left hand syncopation followed by an earthy blues phrase in Measure 12.

The Teddy Wilson blues, taken at around the same tempo, also comprises the four-measure introduction and opening ad lib chorus. Wilson here gives less of an impression of embellishment than of factual statement: this is the blues. There are fewer passing chords, and during some measures the underlying harmony remains unchanged throughout. Aside from the somewhat rococo lead-in, during Measure 8, to the second blues stanza that begins with the E Flat 9th chord in the following measure, there is more here than in Tatum that can be pinned down as a definite

TEDDY WILSON / *Blues for the Oldest Profession*

ART TATUM / *Blues in B♭*

BUD POWELL / *Hallucinations*

melodic line; indeed, there are none of Tatum's grace-note-like
triplets at all; Wilson means every note he plays as part of a
statement rather than as an aside. A charming and personal

placidity rather than an elaborately built intensity seems to be his keynote, though with the arrival of the two chords that link Measures 12 and 13 a peak of warmth is reached, and with the simple and general melodic phrase in Measure 14, Wilson seems to be saying, with finality, "Yes, this is really the blues."

The difference in approach represented by Bud Powell is illustrated with a passage from one of the ad lib choruses in one of his own compositions, *Hallucinations*. The solo shown starts about one minute and ten seconds from the beginning of the performance. Although the tempo is bright, there are two chord changes per measure (i.e., two per second) almost continuously. Though Powell is capable of improvisation far more complex in character, these 16 measures typify the revolution he brought about in jazz piano, since the concept is an entirely linear right hand one, while the left hand is used only for punctuations, usually directly on, or half a beat before, the first and third beats. It is interesting to note that although this solo was played without bass and drums, Powell's left hand throughout seems to be doing exactly what it would have done had a rhythm section been present.

The choice of Tatum, Wilson and Powell for a documentation in this chapter is not intended to imply that theirs were the three most influential piano styles in jazz history. So many others might as easily be considered qualified for inclusion that an entire book dedicated to some of the hundreds of great piano artists of the past and present would be mandatory for a comprehensive survey.

That jazz at times is capable of dynamic mobility with little or no syncopation can be discerned in the illustration of a guitar solo by Charlie Christian recorded in 1941. Starting 2 min. 44 sec. from the top of the track, it is based on 16 bars of the familiar chord sequence originally associated with *Honey-suckle Rose*, played at a moderate tempo (about 46 measures per minute). Christian's pattern basically is an even flow of eighth notes. Almost the only syncopation can be found in an occasional "bebop" (as on the first two beats of Measure 3, 6, 13) and in the octave-unison D Flats that constitute the final four measures. As is often the case with modern jazzmen (among whom Christian, despite his death in 1942 at 22, certainly must be numbered) there is a constant tendency to accent the highest note of each group of eighths. In Measure 1 there is a slight leaning on the three A Flats, which are spaced three eighth notes apart while the other notes descend chromatically from F to D Flat, thus combining a melodic impression of movement with the rhythmic insistence of the three repeated notes. That Christian was capable of unusually long phrases and an extraordinary degree of continuity between these phrases can be observed in Measure 4. Just when the first phrase seems to have ended on the third beat, he moves immediately to an anticipatory use of the E Flat 7th chord (G Natural and D Flat) and continues the phrase straight through into the sixth measure. The broad range of Christian's phrases also is important, as in bars 9-12, which rise with cumulative effectiveness from a low C to an E Flat more than two octaves higher. The simple repeated octave unison in 13 to 16 may be one of the ideas Christian found in the records of Django Reinhardt, with whom this was a favorite climactic effect.

The intense excitement of John Coltrane's soprano saxophone style is shown in *Greensleeves,* excerpted from *Africa/Brass* (Impulse A-6). The solo starts 90 seconds from the beginning of the track. Though there is a raised leading tone in the theme of this old English folk song, it is essentially modal and therefore an apt vehicle for Coltrane's scalar style, a typical sample of escape from the chord changes, cycles of fifths and harmonic contrasts of the bop era.

As Gerald Siddons, who transcribed the solo, points out, Coltrane relies very heavily on chord scales and in this instance restricts himself chiefly to the three types of D minor scales. For the first two and one half measures only two notes, the tonic and minor third, are employed, but the pace and melodic variation are rapidly changed. The long runs in measures 5, 9 and 15 demonstrate Coltrane's technical ability to incorporate extraordinary quantities of notes into a single measure. They are played so fast that at times it is virtually impossible to tell exactly how many and which notes are heard; Siddons has written only approximation of close to forty notes heard in measure

CHARLIE CHRISTIAN / *Up on Teddy's Hill*

15, and clearly there can be no attempt at this pace to swing (nor would this seem to be Coltrane's intention) since the notes can bear no direct or planned mathematical relationship to the beat of the bass and drums. An ostinato accompaniment (see figure at bottom) is offered by a repeated and varied bass figure. On the record, the intensity of this passage is followed by some 14 measures that are far simpler rhythmically, and are melodically limited to five notes that form a pentatonic scale (D-F-G-A-B).

JOHN COLTRANE/*Greensleeves*

Congeniality is a transcription of an Ornette Coleman solo from the album *Shape of Jazz To Come* (Atlantic S-1317). In a book of Coleman's music, Gunther Schuller, who edited the collection, offers a singularly enlightening answer to complaints of alleged incoherence in the alto saxophonist's improvisation:

There are interesting internal relationships, writes Schuller; for instance, the phrase marked *a* in measure 1 is used and varied in 3 and 5. Another phrase, *c*, occurs four times during the solo, *d* three times, the latter "probably half-consciously derived from the sequence of notes which first appears in the eighth measure of the theme."

Like Coltrane, Coleman seems often to think in modal terms; here he seldom strays from the basic B Flat, and when he does it is generally to the step above, C Minor. Schuller's analysis adds: "Excursions into other keys like D Flat and B Natural all follow more or less the same pattern. The sequence D Flat, B Natural, C Minor to B Flat occurs three times at measures 10, 56 [and 160, not shown]; surely no mere accident. Coleman, like many other jazz artists past and present, has found a way of making the tonic and one other step in the key serve for most of his solo; in this case the adherence to B Flat and C Minor, a combination (I and II) he seems to prefer above all others, probably because II includes most of the important notes of the dominant (V) and subdominant (IV). It is also obvious from the long stretches of B Flat tonic, mostly centering around the beginnings of what appear to be larger phrase structures, that Mr. Coleman is fully aware of his place in the over-all formal design at any given moment." That this structure need not consist of eight-bar units, or any particular unit length, as Schuller adds, is one of the soloist's most important departures from tradition.

One final admonition to the student: there are two prerequisites for intelligent examination of these solos. They are the ability to read music (and to play it on one instrument or another) and, most important, a basic understanding of the language of jazz. Given these tools, the reader should find above a helpful guide to the dialects of that language, its grammar,

ORNETTE COLEMAN/*Congeniality*

punctuation, declensions and conjugations, and most important of all, its esthetics; for jazz improvisation is, above all other considerations, a language of beauty

CHAPTER 23

HORIZONS: JAZZ IN 1984

The evolutionary course of any art form tends to defy crystal-gazing. Just as it would have been impossible for an art student of the nineteenth century to foresee accurately the arrival of cubism, just as no musician even in 1941 could predict the upheaval that was to be wrought by bop only three years later, the prognosis for jazz must be heavily qualified by an admission that the only predictable factor is its unpredictability.

In terms of general trends, and more specifically on such subjects as the relationship between jazz and classical music, most musicians have managed to formulate a view, no matter how amorphous, of what the future may hold. In 1957, when the first edition of *The Book of Jazz* was being prepared, the author approached a number of jazz figures in an attempt to design a perspective of jazz in 1984. Most of the musicians questioned will no longer be a part of the jazz scene by then, though the presence of many of them will still be felt indirectly. Their answers have a special interest in the light of what has transpired in the years since, for many of the predictions have become realities or are clearly well on the way to achievement.

An interview with Duke Ellington produced the following dialogue:

What do you think jazz will be like 25 years from now?

Well, for one thing, nobody's going to worry about whether it's jazz, symphony, boogie-woogie or folk music. The categories will be abolished.

To accomplish that, classical musicians are going to have to learn a lot more about developing a feeling for jazz and vice versa, don't you think?

Well, I think it's going to be a matter of becoming more and more aware of the fact that everybody is actually doing the same thing, or at least having the same aims. For instance in the classical recitals, particularly the piano recitals, somebody in the audience would pass up a theme and the pianist would take it and develop it. That's practically what jazz musicians are doing—there's a relationship to it anyway, though in jazz the developments, or the ad lib variations, are based on the harmonic structure rather than on the melody.

Do you think that classical musicians will get the feeling for phrasing of jazz correctly? I know you had trouble when you performed one of your extended works, Night Creature, *with the Symphony of the Air at Carnegie Hall.*

I think that's a matter of language in writing. If you write it the way they understand, I think the symphony men will interpret it as you want it, but I think some of the preciseness in jazz writing has been lost and some of the rhythmic nuances have been taken for granted; a jazz musician will see a certain phrase and assume that it should be played one way or another. Of course jazz is a rather personal thing, too. Say you're writing a passage for a particular sax section. If you change an accent, move it ahead a beat, it might be much more effective for one particular sax section, whereas if it were some other sax section the musicians would say "This is not the thing we do best; perhaps there should be an anticipation here." It's like tailored music, and I think when we inquire we'll find that all music is that way. I think the music the masters wrote was written for a specific great to perform it. Nobody sits down and writes just for a fiddle or saxophone—that's a little too cold. For instance, if you are going to write something for alto sax, if you just say to yourself: "This is a concerto for alto sax" and that's all you know about it, it would make a big difference—you would write it differently if you knew that Hodges were going to play it, or Benny Carter or Willie Smith.

Do you think the kind of jazz played in night clubs now by the small groups will still continue in night clubs or do you think it will move entirely into the concert field and festivals?

Well, I consider in effect that it's in the concert field already. The best night clubs in which jazz is being played now are not dance spots, and the accent actually is on listening more than drinking, dancing or anything else, so it could just as well be called a concert hall. You take a place like the Blue Note in Chicago. Frank Holzfeind operates this place with the same dignity as the Metropolitan Opera House. You come there to listen. If you don't want to listen, you offend *him.*

Do you think there will be music that will be recognized as the same kind of music that is being played today in the name of jazz regardless of whether you want to categorize it or not?

Sure there will. Jazz has been growing up all the time, you know. It's becoming more and more mature, which is the cop-out I usually employ for my own personal things. I'm often accused of not being myself, when somebody hears a record of something I wrote in 1927 and they come back in 1957 and expect me to be writing the same thing. That's ridiculous, because all children grow up, you know. If your mind stands still, you have no business writing in the first place. If you have no aims, nothing to say, then you have a stagnant mind.

That brings up another point. Do you think things like Dixieland will survive? In 1984 will they still be playing Royal Garden Blues and Muskrat Ramble?

Sure they will. You can go back farther than that: they're still playing *I Wish I Was In Dixie.* People are always looking for something to hold onto for the purposes of nostalgia; good old homespun ideas are well supported by going back 20, 50, 100 years. The old days were always the good old days—that's a cliché from way back—no matter how good it is today. I have seen guys who are living at the highest level, who'll be sitting back and sippin' out of their golden goblets and refer to the time when they were walkin' Broadway in the hot summertime without a nickel for a glass of Nedick's, and yet they'll say, "Man, those were the *good* old days!"

Do you think there'll be orchestras of the same size and

general shape as the orchestra you have today? Reeds, brass and rhythm, with the basic rhythm 4/4 all the way through?

A lot of people are trying to break away from everything nowadays. There's always that spirit, and I think it will depend upon who's going to listen to it and who's going to buy it, which you can't predict.

How about improvisation? Do you think that's going to change basically in style or will it be based on chords the way it is now?

Improvisation styling comes as the result of some one soloist who comes up with a performance that has to appeal. It's just like a guy who introduces a new flavor in ice cream and it catches on, then everybody wants to do that. When Bechet came East, everybody said, "Yes, man, that's it—let's play like Bechet." Just like all of them. Like Hodges. When he came down from Boston everybody said, "Let's play like Hodges." Like Bird— all the guys were trying to play like him. And Hawk, who I think was the greatest influence and stimulated the greatest change in saxophone style very abruptly.

Do you think there's a possibility of atonal improvisation?

This is a matter of mathematics. Improvisation as far as this particular thing is concerned has to be planned and it has to be said, "Now we start at such and such a place and I will take a theme and play at the rate of 250 light years per second and you will only cover half this amount of ground with *this* theme." They have to converge at some point and when you say do it and improvise at the same time—how many people are there going to be in the world who will be able to do this? If you're just going to have four or five independent melodies totally unrelated, which never start anywhere together and never end anywhere together, it's a matter of "Go, go, go, and when you get through, *you* stop, and when I get through, *I'll* stop." That, to me, is *not* what constitutes atonality. I think there should be a specific aim in each one of the melodies—one specific mathematical relationship. Possibly this will happen.

Do you think the blues in the sense of the 12-bar harmonic pattern will still be played 25 years from now?

Yes, I think so, because blues hasn't shown any weakness yet —that's America. People are geared up to that 12-bar form.

But the important thing is this: you know how thin the line is between jazz and other music already. Twenty-five years from now it's just going to be that much more so. Just one big music, with everybody believing exactly what I've always believed—that if it sounds good, it's good music.

Woody Herman took a somewhat less sanguine view of the outlook: "The large jazz band is on its way to extinction. Eventually everything will be concentrated in smaller groups. I rather hope that it won't be that way, but unless there's a great economic change in our country I'm afraid it will.

"I don't think there will ever be a complete wedding between classical music and jazz, but there will be more overlapping than there is now. The supposed limitations of classical musicians in their attempts to play jazz are not as important as the jazz musicians would like to have you believe. There's hardly a guy in the world who can't be taught to phrase jazz correctly unless he just doesn't feel *any* kind of rhythm.

"I think improvisation will probably stay basically pretty much the same, with maybe a return to the scene of the more flowing melodic kind of ad libbing; at least I hope so.

"As to the international aspect, the future for jazz generally speaking looks much brighter abroad than at home. A lot of people overseas have been making great strides in terms of originality, and I am inclined to think that certainly within the next 25 years there will be groups that will set up their own kind of jazz, their own styles, in many other countries.

"As for the experimental jazz of today, only time can tell. Twenty-five years from now the people who are around will know whether it had any true value or not."

Herman's views on the broadening scope in the foreign scene were shared by John (Dizzy) Gillespie and John Lewis.

"Just as jazz moved geographically through various phases in this country—New Orleans, Kansas City, Chicago and so forth—I believe it will go through a similar series of changes on an international rather than intra-national level," Lewis observed. "The influence and impact of jazz playing and writing in other countries will be felt increasingly.

"The whole approach to jazz will probably shift, though in what direction it is hard to say precisely—you just can't tell what kind of babies will be born.

"As for the merger between classical music and jazz, I don't believe in that. All that I've contributed, all my work through the years, has been deeply rooted in jazz and I see no reason to suppose that jazz is going to merge or be absorbed into anything else.

"Nor do I believe that classical musicians will necessarily acquire a greater ability to improvise jazz. The jazz musician will still have his own individual qualities.

"As for Dixieland and the other traditional forms, I suppose that if they have managed to survive this long, the chances are that they'll still be around a generation from now. Things of that kind often go in cycles, as fads.

"On the whole, though, I find it difficult to make any specific predictions; there are so many different directions in which the future may take us."

Gillespie's first observation was: "Twenty-five years from now? It'll be finished! . . . No, seriously, it'll still be around. I wish I could look in the crystal ball—I'd start working on it right now.

"It will probably be so mixed up with all these other different nationalities—Indian scales and so forth—it's getting around the world so fast now . . . their touch is going to seep into it. I believe we've gone as far with the European music as we're going to go.

"That will be true also of the writing, which comes from the improvisation anyway—nobody writes anything unless they've heard it played first anyway.

"I've actually been working along those lines myself—sometimes I've played some things that I heard in Pakistan. And a lot of musicians are going to be going over to Asia and everywhere and they're going to add to what they already know.

"Another thing," added Gillespie. "I'm sure that by 1984 the American Federation of Musicians will have abolished the system of having white and colored locals. There'll be just one big union in every city—and that includes down South, too."

Jimmy Giuffre, the composer and clarinetist-saxophonist who

has emerged as a major figure in the jazz avant-garde, gave specific answers in a letter to the author:

"Jazz 1984: The first jazz-symphony orchestra (community or society sponsored) will be forming in New York.

"The literature of jazz will be taking form. Longer compositions will be printed and played in their entirety by many top groups.

"Soloistic improvisation will continue but a more unified group improvisation will be in vogue.

"Dixieland, swing and bop will still have their players and audiences. Cool music will settle into a category (which it is establishing now). There will be a strong atonal school (both writing and improvising).

"Some of jazz is beginning to find itself. I mean: it makes contact with the old blues—thereby maintaining the jazz feeling, but is free of clichés and schools—thereby achieving a sort of timeless quality that will be lasting. Add to this, a more extensive use of forms and devices which have been used by the symphony for centuries, and you have influences or ingredients which will mold this jazz feeling into an integrated music. This will be taking place for the next 25 years, and in 1984, jazz (it might have another name by then), partly because of this integration, will have a much higher position. There will always be bigotry against everything, but there will be much less of it against jazz than there is now.

"Jazz societies will be everywhere, and they will make the small concert a practical solution for ideal jazz live performance.

"Microfilm tape and movies combined to play on your TV set will have replaced records to a large extent. The LP will bow to tape.

"There will be many jazz shows on TV.

"Degrees in jazz will be given in most colleges.

"There will be a literature of large works (with jazz feeling) for symphony orchestra. These will be played and accepted in the same fashion as non-jazz works.

"The 1984 future is good. The struggle will be between now and then."

The only non-musician included in the symposium was Willis

Conover, who since 1953 has been broadcasting jazz records
and interviews via the Voice of America. Conover wrote:

"I assume the target date has no significance besides its built-in
usefulness as a hook. Jazz 1984 is beyond Orwell's, Orson Welles',
or H. G. Wells' ability to predict. Too many roads are being
built; you can't know where they'll lead to, this far ahead.

"One answer to the question: Jazz will be what people expect
it to be.

"Let's try for a second, more specific answer. Today, we have
our happy kids playing Chicago-styled 'Dixieland'—and our
solemn ones playing Oliver-and-Morton-styled 'New Orleans.'
Other youngsters adopt 'bop' or 'cool' as the proper socio-musical
attitude. The Swing Era band-styles are saluted and recalled in
hi-fi. The British skiffle bands' repertoires include southern Negro
blues-shouting and boogie-woogie piano melodies, note for note
off the original records. And this may be good. It's not creative,
it's something else. It's preserving the material as honorable
compositions; the Yanceys, Pinetops, and Blind Lemons add their
vitality, only once-removed, to the Chaminades of Sunday evening musicale.

"Julian 'Cannonball' Adderley, misadvertised as a new Bird
but a hell of a fine musician, finding the Parker road a dead end,
goes back a few blocks along the main highway to Pete Brown
and Hodges and Carter, carrying what he can of the riches from
Parker Road, adding some of what Wilder Hobson calls 'modern
barrelhouse,' and making for himself a fresh point of departure.

"For the birdling seeking a direction, all these approved
teachers' exercises are reliable signposts. While jazz, like a tree,
extends branches and twigs, like a tree it keeps sending its roots
deeper—to both coasts, Kansas City, Chicago, New Orleans . . .

"A second answer to the question: Jazz will be partly what it
was before. And partly what it wasn't. When people use a language, it changes; it changes them, too. Jazz is a language. It is
people living in sound. Jazz is people talking, laughing, crying,
building, painting, mathematicizing, abstracting, extracting, giving to, taking from, making of. In other words, living. It's not the
only way people live, though all of life is in it, and it's as real as

any other way, and more honest than most. You can't separate the music from the people who make it.

"Yet Louis Armstrong, Duke Ellington and Charlie Parker are rooted in widely different areas of geographical, musical and personal background. Each symbolizes a different stage in jazz's development—Louis, the joyous cry; Duke, the grand manner; Bird, the sharp commentary—and each stage parallels a change in living conditions. Already the Negro American participates in the complexity of activities known by the Italian American, the Irish American, etc. As his life grows more complex, as he grows more sophisticated, so does his music. Better food, better pay, better education, better satisfaction—these must reflect in the ways a man expresses himself.

"A third answer: Jazz will be as the people who make it will be. Meanwhile we live when history is being made. The historians will tell of Louis, of Duke, of Basie and of Bird, and of the size they gave to twentieth-century America. We will be remembered by the best of their music, and by what we did about it. Bird is gone; but let's not wait till the others go before we recognize them. What Louis or Duke does away from his music is irrelevant. That music they'll write about—it's being made now, we can hear it.

"The future of jazz? It depends on how wisely we treat it today."

An interview with Louis Armstrong resulted in this colloquy:
What do you think jazz will be like 25 years from now?
It's all personal—every tub. If the cats don't take care of their health, 25 years from now they'll be dead! You've got to have health to play any kind of music. To play like we play it takes health.
I don't mean just the musicians of today, I mean music in general. For instance, do you think classical music and jazz will move any closer together?
From the symphony orchestras I've played with, all indications are that that's going to be the next trend. A cat's gotta have tone and imagination. If he doesn't have tone and imagination he's gonna be left out. There's no use coming out with these wild

fantastic ideas—like the youngsters in the last generation. A man learns his horn—knows what he's doing—that's the next trend.

Do you think jazz will move more into the concert field?

Wherever they're going to play it, they'll play it good; because the youngsters coming up now are learning their horns right. I've noticed a couple of youngsters lately with clear tones and sense of phrasing. In that last idiom there, a few years back, everybody was bee-essing. The youngsters coming up now are serious. Just recently we played 51 concerts in the South, and I talked to kids from 10 on up. You can feed 'em with rock-and-roll, pop or whatever it is, and they probably won't say nothing about it, but they know what's happening. They can appreciate it and instill it in their parents.

Do you think there will be more jazz abroad?

There'll always be good jazz overseas. The musicians over there will play better, too. Last time we went to London, we went by Humphrey Lyttleton's place and they played some good music. They played all them good numbers. There were jam sessions. James Rushing just told me he was on his way to England to work with Lyttleton and I told him he'd be in good company.

Well, Louis, I hope you'll be wailing 25 years from now.

I got 10,000 packages of Swiss Kriss to take, and there ain't no way of missing it!

Of all the musicians questioned concerning the future of jazz, the least optimistic and most guarded in his prognosis was Bill Russo, the composer-arranger and sometime trombonist. In his early years as a writer for Stan Kenton and columnist for *Down Beat*, more recently as a teacher and bandleader in England and the U.S., Russo has remained one of the most articulate and unconventional of jazz writers.

"My belief in the value of improvisation," says Russo, "has constantly diminished over the last four years. I see it as a source, as a stimulus to composition, and as elevated 'play.' It seems entirely possible to me that improvisation—as a thing in itself—will disappear or *can* disappear. If it does not disappear, it *should* go along the lines suggested by Tristano ten years ago; that is, as a form of spontaneous yet disciplined composition. In addition, I see a renascence of sectional improvisation, in which four- to 16-measure melodic phrases are exactly repeated—in other words, more formalized improvisation.

"The use of the techniques of traditional music is already extensive among some people in jazz. Sufficiently extensive, I think, that it can be said that parts of jazz have already become absorbed. At the present time, however, I can foresee nothing approaching a merger, although this is more an historical than musicological point.

"Jazz is going through a tremendous and dangerous reaction in this period. The reaction has been strong—strong enough to sweep people like Tristano with it. The reaction is dangerous because it emphasizes those characteristics of the music which we were well rid of ten years ago. It is dangerous because it is anti-formal. It is dangerous because it stresses a feeling, emotionalism, and impact, over order, sanity, and morality.

"If this reaction is not ended, the future of the music seems very bleak to me. And I don't think the reaction can be stopped.

"It is possible, though, that even if the music—as such—continued to decay, its effect on a *new* music will have been enormous and healthy."

Benny Goodman did not share Russo's gloomy feelings about the future. Asked whether he felt that classical music and jazz might move closer, he replied, "Well, that trend has been here, in a sense, for quite a long time. Musicians are developing a higher degree of proficiency, all the new conductors are influenced or 'tainted' by it—especially the American ones, at least—and this must rub off on the musicians that grow up in this country.

"All the young kids playing in symphony orchestras think so, according to my experience in talking with them recently. We'll go to a place like Birmingham, to play with the orchestra and the oboe player will start talking about Charlie Parker, or Harry James, and who did this and that, and seems to know all about it. I don't know to what extent they're influenced by it, but obviously they are well aware of it all. All the kids who listen to music nowadays, including my daughters, they play all kinds of music, and they'll listen to jazz and they listen to Elvis, and everything. I think as long as the communications are bigger and as long as business is bigger, people will continue to have broader interests."

Though it was his concert at Carnegie Hall in 1938 that set a precedent for swing music as a concert medium, Goodman is not anxious to see jazz move entirely into the concert field. "My feeling is, it should always be with the dancers; but that's personal, that's completely biased. All the tunes that have ever meant anything have always had something to do with the dance in this country, it seems to me, and my feeling is that it should remain dance music. On the other hand, I suppose you can have both.

"You want to know what the jazz of the future will actually be like? Hmm. Well, here's a good simile: what will women be like?"

The youngest respondent in this symposium was Quincy Jones, who in 1984 will be younger than are Count Basie, Duke Ellington and other jazz stars of today. Jones is the only artist of those questioned who seems likely to remain in the jazz field, should it continue to exist, for another two or three decades.

"One of our biggest problems," said Jones, "is the question of what's going to happen to the audiences. Right now there are a few cultists who support jazz and buy record albums and so forth, but I wonder how many attitudes will be changed if jazz goes just where we want it to? If backgrounds for television shows and other situations like that become what we now call 'hip' and earn acceptance by every layman—will it still be progressive music or will it then become just popular music? In other words, if jazz becomes so widely used and accepted, then isn't it likely that it will just be considered popular music and the critics will go someplace else and find something farther out, more esoteric?

"Concerning the blending of classical and jazz forms, I don't go for it too much today—this business of jazz musicians' trying to compete with Hindemith and Stravinsky. There's really no competition at all. And the 12-tone scale may be new to us, but it's quite old-fashioned to the classical composer, so what we do with it is really a joke. It sounds very amateurish to try to write atonal things without any conception of basic composition, just for the sake of trying to be far out. That's not progress. It's like a classical composer hanging out in night clubs for a couple of nights and then trying to play bebop piano. I don't think it's a sincere effort of composition; there can't be any meaning when it's done by men who have so little real craftsmanship.

"What I hope will happen, though, is that symphony musicians' training in the future will have them better informed as to what has happened in jazz, so that when the guys are making a strong attempt to bring these two things together and combine the techniques, the orchestras will be better equipped. Contemporary writers nowadays listen to jazz, and I'm sure even a kid studying violin now, and studying Bartok, can't be unaware of what's happening in jazz. Probably the string section of the future will have a different terminology, a different notation to convey the subtleties of dynamics of jazz, even though the string musicians will be just as informed as jazzmen of things that have gone before, and will understand much more than the musicians today about matters of inflection and feeling. I know that in some string things that I did with Harry Lookofsky we had some notations of our own that we used to employ to make the strings swing.

"Eventually I think the two groups will simply be musicians—like for instance in Sweden, where a guy is just as familiar with a Ravel string quartet as he is with Lunceford's *For Dancers Only*. It will be wonderful if we get to a place where all the groups are speaking one another's language.

"This is my ultimate in the future of jazz. If there has to be a fusion of classical music and jazz, I think it will come in the day when there are capable soloists inside the symphony orchestra—when they have the same backgrounds. When everybody in the symphony orchestra can sit down and build, and have the same subtlety and looseness of rhythm. But it would have to come from the roots, and everybody in the orchestra would have to have those roots. If that happened, they would satisfy just as much as Duke Ellington—and that would be my idea of the perfect future for jazz."

The total value of these predictions may be no greater than whatever might have been derived from a similar symposium conducted among members of the Original Dixieland Jass Band in 1917. All they seem to indicate in sum is that though they cannot be sure in which direction the jazz satellite will be traveling, the prophets share an anxiety to man a telescope for observation of the flight.

The writer, who has been listening to jazz avocationally since 1929, professionally since 1933, can recall only a single prediction he made during the first years of listening that was ultimately to achieve realization: that jazz would prove to be playable in ternary time. Nothing else of consequence that has happened to jazz in all these years ever became evident until it was immediately upon us. A reader glancing at these pages in 1984 will observe, it is reasonable to assume, that the quarter century between now and then turned out to be no more predictable than the events in the previous generation.

A factor that occurred only to one of the musicians questioned (Quincy Jones), and may call for some expansion here, is the paradox that jazz has been subject, during its short but chaotic life, to what might be termed a Law of Diminishing Repute. This law, of which even the musicians directly concerned are only dimly aware, tends to bring each succeeding phase of the art along a descending path from esoteric origins to ignominious endings.

Dixieland jazz, for instance, played with a degree of conviction and musicianship comparable with that of the more highly regarded figures of the late 1920s, today can be found in occasional jam session items by "square" bands like Lawrence Welk's and Freddy Martin's; in high school bands and in amateur groups whose members are insurance salesmen and Madison Avenue executives. The music of Jelly Roll Morton, held immortal in some jazz circles, provides suitably quaint, "corny" background music for silent movies on television. (No music is sacred to this medium, in which the *Blue Danube* waltz, equipped with special lyrics, now forms the basis of a commercial for dog food.) Swing arrangements indistinguishable from some of the best played in the 1930s are heard backing dance acts on TV. One of the best swing bands of 1965, almost totally ignored by critics, was Skitch Henderson's team of first-class NBC-TV studio men.

The Law of Diminishing Repute holds good among reporters and reviewers. In the late 1950s, records by artists who less than a decade earlier would have ranked indisputably as jazz performers—among them Dinah Washington, Wild Bill Davison, Sharkey Bonano, and the former Kenton arrangers Johnny Richards and Pete Rugolo—were considered unworthy of inclusion in the jazz record review section of *Down Beat* and were shunted off to be dismissed with shorter reviews in the "Popular Records" section. The music on these records remained identical in nature to what had once been considered top-drawer jazz; only the psychological conditioning of the recipients had changed. Similarly George Shearing, when the first records by his quintet appeared in 1949, was a new jazz star with a fresh style, in the view of critics who unhesitatingly categorized this as a jazz group; but by the time the tenth or twentieth release appeared and the appeal of the style had worn thin, its character was magically transmuted into "popular music." Our critical senses of values have been more capricious than capacious. It is self-evident that there can be no firm standards in any medium as long as it remains subject to so rapid a deterioration of the level of acceptance.

Part of the problem lies in the dual nature of our listening.

A bass solo by, say, Chuck Israels or any one of a hundred bassists in the mid-1960s may far exceed, both in technique ideas, the most adventurous 1940 works of Jimmy Blanton. But this is a subjective evaluation. Blanton must be judged on the basis of his place in history and the avenues he opened up for every bassist since his day. Objectively, today's soloists must be judged in terms of our awareness of the pioneer work of the past. Our standards will continue to improve; jazz in the next 25 years will continue along lines that will turn the innovation of today into the cliché of tomorrow. A similar process may be observed in the other lively arts.

A cross-breeding process will continue to take place in the seemingly independent areas of jazz styles. Just as Dixieland

effects are employed by such modern jazzmen as Gerry Mulligan
and Bob Brookmeyer, bop has invaded the supposedly "pure"
Dixieland territory of Eddie Condon's band and the New Orleans
ramparts of the Louis Armstrong combo. Traditionalists listening
to a bass solo by Leonard Gaskin with Eddie Condon apparently
failed to observe that it was played exactly as Gaskin would have
played it when he worked with Gillespie; nor did the Armstrong
fans seem to be disturbed by the unmistakable bop nature of
Arvell Shaw's solos. Bop, the death of which was gleefully and
erroneously signaled by its opponents in the early '50s, is more
alive today than ever, having become a part of the very blood-
stream of contemporary jazz. Its innovations are heard in the
performances of every young soloist. It is reasonable to assume
that a new cycle, starting in 1970, may meet with violent critical
opposition, will be proclaimed dead in 1975, will have shown a
similar tenacity and will form an indispensable part of whatever
passes for jazz in 1984. And the Law of Diminishing Repute in
due course will bring the product of this cycle to the level of
mass acceptance and employment on esthetically inconsequential
levels; the critics will begin to dismiss it as of minor importance
and not really jazz at all; by 1990 it will be classified under
"Popular Music."

The prospects for 1990, along with a review of the forecasts
quoted in the preceding pages, were discussed in 1965 by Don
Ellis, the young composer and trumpeter who is among the most
lucidly articulate spokesmen for the "cosa nova" (new thing)
avant-garde movement in jazz.

"It was easy to predict that the blues and traditional forms
would endure," said Ellis, "but the remarkable thing is that so
many of Jimmy Giuffre's predictions for 1984 have already been
realized. As for Ellington's forecast—well, it's not 1984 yet; we'll
have to wait and see, but I'm dubious about the 'one great big
music' theory. My experiences in 1964-5, working under Lukas
Foss as a creative assistant at the University of New York in
Buffalo, convinced me that there is a bigger dichotomy between
jazz and classical minds than I had ever dreamed. The younger
symphony men are familiar with jazz, but it is not a familiarity

of love. It is as if they are slumming. In fact, Bill Russo's remarks in this chapter typify the attitude of many classical men when he says he is disillusioned with improvisation. It is very wrong to imply that writing is more important. Improvisation is exciting and indispensable; the two must work hand in hand.

"Classical musicians by and large feel that jazz is a popular art form, and that the only really serious, profound music is their own. Lukas Foss, who is a main figurehead in improvisation in classical music, once told me that the improvising group he had was valuable in as far as it gave him a lot of good ideas for his compositions. He wasn't really interested in exploring improvisation *per se*.

"The differences between jazz and classical music are mainly twofold. One is the matter of improvisation, but more important than that is the question of rhythm and time. This is really nonexistent in classical music. Someone may tell you that a Bach fugue will swing. It can indeed be made to swing by a jazz musician; but a classical musician, if he's playing it correctly, will not swing.

"It may be possible for a classical string section to swing, if they have to, but it will take years of practice. You simply cannot take a classical musician and say 'Okay, I want you to play this with a jazz feeling.'"

I asked Ellis whether he believes that by 1990 jazz will be accepted as a classic music in itself, with its own traditions, its own prestige and standing in society at large.

"No, not in the same sense as traditional classical music. This rhythmic element, which is absent from classical music of all kinds, is a very emotional, physical thing that makes jazz more acceptable as a popular music. There are two separate traditions and they are far apart. Jazz uses a different language rhythmically and tonally, and it doesn't use the tempered scale. A blue note is not 'in tune,' it's not part of the tempered system. Of course, classical music eventually may have to abandon the tempered system too."

"How do you think jazz musicians will be able to change,"

I asked, "in order to expand their own horizons?"

"I'd like to see a rhythmic revitalization. Jazz rhythms when they were first developed vitalized our entire popular culture. The African slaves saved American culture rhythmically from the sterility that you find in classical music. The next source of rhythmic stimulation may be Indian music, because this has the most intricate system.

"We have already explored just about all the vertical and horizontal organizations of tones; on that level we are at an impasse, so we have to figure out new ways of making the notes meaningful. The twelve-tone system is not the answer, because it is not aurally perceptible; it has to be seen on paper. But if we explore all kinds of new crossrhythms and polyrhythms, we can arrive at something significantly new and enlarge the framework of jazz immeasurably.

"Many people have not yet figured out exactly what music is. They don't realize that it is closely related to dancing—either popular or classical dancing; there is a relation between the bodily movements and the essence of a lot of music. Along with an expansion of the rhythmic facets of jazz, there should be a great broadening of the concepts of dancing in coördination with it.

"As for the so-called free-form music, it is hampered by the fact that a lot of the young musicians playing it are not bothering to learn anything about the legitimate technique of playing their instruments. Instead of learning about form, melody, harmony and organization, they just get up and express themselves. This is one way of achieving something new, but the results most of the time are just not interesting, not worthwhile or meaningful. This must be realized, because too many people are saying to themselves, 'This is something interesting, something important,' when in reality they are fooling themselves. They are really bored to death, and afraid to admit it; or perhaps they enjoy being bored, which is even more tragic."

"One final question. Do you believe that in 1990 jazz will survive as a distinct, unique and clearly identifiable musical form?"

"Definitely," said Ellis. "I think it would be a tragedy if it didn't."

Ellis is almost certainly right in his prediction, for the jazz musician of the 1960s tends to be far more advanced than his predecessors in technique, in academic knowledge of all branches of music, and in the vitally important sense of being part of a mobile art form. Jazz today, as always, is a young man's art. Though some of the major creative figures are men of middle or upper middle age, they are the exceptions. The main force of new ideation will always stem from musicians young in mind and body. Similarly, though a few of the performances committed to records by the founders of jazz four decades ago may have occasional intrinsic listening value for the present-day ear, most of what we hear in our retrospective surveys of the first days of jazz recording has failed to survive the passage of time. The early jazz, which can be examined by musicians only in terms of antiquity and nostalgic interest, is giving way inexorably to a music that has been maturing rapidly during the past decade. Today one can sense that the music now in the process of creation is far more likely to show durability and to render itself susceptible to subjective enjoyment a generation from now.

Chaucer summed up the nature of every art, of every field of learning, of the whole evolutionary process, with these lines:

For out of olde feldes, as men seith
Cometh al this newe corn fro yeer to yere
And out of olde bokes, in good feith
Cometh all this new science that men lere

And in the opening lines of *The Parlement of Foules* he synthesized the esthetic process:

The lyf so short, the craft so long to lerne,
Th' assay so hard, so sharp the conquering.

If we are trying to find our bearings, to establish a lasting scale of values, we should do well to bear these words in mind and to remember that, after all, the first century of jazz has still run only two-thirds of its course.

A specially produced LP on Verve records (MGV 8230), entitled *The Anatomy of Improvisation,* includes ten of the actual improvised solos reproduced and analysed in the chapter by the same title (Chapter 22). Also, Charlie Christian's solo, *Up On Teddy's Hill,* is available on Everest 5233; Benny Goodman's *Slipped Disc* on Columbia GL 500, Louis Armstrong's *Muggles* on Columbia ML 54385, John Coltrane's *Greensleeves* on Impulse 6, and Ornette Coleman's *Congeniality* on Atlantic 1317.

Decca DXF 140, a four-volume album (*The Encyclopedia of Jazz on Records*) featured the work of many of the important artists mentioned in Chapters 6 through 21. The four LPs are available separately as *Jazz of the Twenties* (Decca DL 8398), *Jazz of the Thirties* (DL 8399), *Jazz of the Forties* (DL 8400) and *Jazz of the Fifties* (DL 8401). A series entitled *Jazz of the Sixties* was released in 1965 on Vee-Jay Records: Vol. I (*Giants of the Saxophones*) on VJ 2501, Vol. II (*Blues Bag*) on VJ 2506, Vol. III (*Voices, Traditional and Modern*) on VJ 2511.

NOTES

CHAPTER 2

1. Marshall Stearns, *The Story of Jazz* (New York: Oxford Press, 1956), pp. 3, 4, 6.
2. Rudi Blesh & Harriet Janis, *They All Played Ragtime* (New York: Alfred A. Knopf, 1950), p. 149.
3. Barry Ulanov, *A History of Jazz in America* (New York: Viking Press, 1952), pp. 11, 12.
4. Ibid. p. 18.
5. Ibid. p. 19.
6. Interview on WABD-DuMont Television, New York City, between Mike Wallace and Mahalia Jackson on *Night Beat* show.
7. Blesh and Janis, op. cit. p. 24.
8. Ibid. p. 17.

CHAPTER 3

1. Rudi Blesh & Harriet Janis, *They All Played Ragtime* (New York: Alfred A. Knopf, 1950), pp. 190, 191.
2. Institute of Jazz Studies Seminar in Record Changer, July-August, 1953.

CHAPTER 4

1. Andre Hodeir, *Jazz, Its Evolution and Essence* (New York: The Grove Press, 1956), pp. 47, 48.
2. As quoted by Rex Harris in *Jazz* (Penguin Books).
3. William L. Grossman and Jack W. Farrell, *The Heart of Jazz* (New York: New York University Press, 1956), p. 254.
4. Rudi Blesh, *Shining Trumpets* (New York: Alfred A. Knopf, Inc., 1946), pp. 183, 186.
5. Andre Hodeir, op. cit. pp. 53, 55, 59.
6. Stephen Longstreet, *The Real Jazz Old and New* (Baton Rouge: Louisiana State University Press, 1956), p. 51.
7. William L. Grossman and Jack W. Farrell, op. cit. p. 180.
8. Ibid. p. 184.
9. Orrin Keepnews and Bill Grauer, *A Pictorial History of Jazz* (New York: Crown Publishers, Inc., 1955), p. 59.

10. Andre Hodeir, op. cit. p. 32.
11. Leonard Feather, *The Encyclopedia of Jazz* (New York: Horizon Press, Inc., 1955), p. 12.
12. Orrin Keepnews and Bill Grauer, op. cit. p. 59.

CHAPTER 7

1. Nat Shapiro and Nat Hentoff, *Hear Me Talkin' to Ya* (New York: Rinehart and Company, 1955), p. 403.

CHAPTER 8

1. Andre Hodeir, *Jazz, Its Evolution and Essence* (New York: The Grove Press, 1956), pp. 63-77.

CHAPTER 9

1. Andre Hodeir, *Jazz, Its Evolution and Essence* (New York: The Grove Press, 1956), pp. 147, 148, 152, 153.

CHAPTER 15

1. Marshall W. Stearns, *The Story of Jazz* (New York: Oxford Press, 1956), Chapter 1.
2. Gene Krupa, "School for Skins" (Chicago: Duke Magazine, June, 1957), p. 18.
3. Ibid.

CHAPTER 18

1. Leonard Bernstein, *What Is Jazz?* (New York: Columbia Records, CL 919).
2. Nat Shapiro and Nat Hentoff, *Hear Me Talkin' to Ya* (New York: Rinehart and Company, 1955), p. 243.
3. Ibid. p. 149.

CHAPTER 19

1. Orrin Keepnews and Bill Grauer, *A Pictorial History of Jazz* (New York: Crown Publishers, Inc., 1955), p. 63.

CHAPTER 20

1. Nat Shapiro and Nat Hentoff, *Hear Me Talkin' to Ya* (New York: Rinehart and Company, 1955), p. 205.

INDEX